The World Bank and the post-Washington Consensus in Vietnam and Indonesia

This book explores the history, structure and current operations of the World Bank, an organisation that has rarely received the critical attention its importance merits. The author provides an original analysis of the interaction between economic theory, political practice and the Bank's development praxis.
Engel starts with a detailed examination of the development theory and practice of the World Bank from its Keynesian origins to the current shift through the Washington Consensus to the so-called post-Washington Consensus. Drawing on the Project Appraisal Documents for some 113 loans, secondary literature and interviews with World Bank staff, government officials, academics and non-governmental organisations the author goes on to analyse the Bank's lending practices in two countries, Vietnam and Indonesia. The case studies enable the development of empirically based conclusions regarding the impact of Bank policies on the economic and social development of these nations, making possible an assessment of the extent to which the rhetoric of the post-Washington Consensus has been incorporated into the Bank's lending practices.

This book will be of interest to both advanced undergraduate and graduate students as well as specialist audiences in the fields of international political economy, development, international organisations and Southeast Asian Studies.

Susan Engel is a lecturer in the School of History and Politics at the University of Wollongong, Australia.

ASIA'S TRANSFORMATIONS

Edited by Mark Selden, Cornell University, USA

The books in this series explore the political, social, economic and cultural consequences of Asia's transformations in the twentieth and twenty-first centuries. The series emphasizes the tumultuous interplay of local, national, regional and global forces as Asia bids to become the hub of the world economy. While focusing on the contemporary, it also looks back to analyse the antecedents of Asia's contested rise.

This series comprises several strands:

Asia's Transformations aims to address the needs of students and teachers. Titles include:

Debating Human Rights
Critical essays from the United States and Asia
Edited by Peter Van Ness

Hong Kong's History
State and society under colonial rule
Edited by Tak-Wing Ngo

Japan's Comfort Women
Sexual slavery and prostitution during World War II and the US occupation
Yuki Tanaka

Opium, Empire and the Global Political Economy
Carl A. Trocki

Chinese Society
Change, conflict and resistance
Edited by Elizabeth J. Perry and Mark Selden

Mao's Children in the New China
Voices from the Red Guard generation
Yarong Jiang and David Ashley

Remaking the Chinese State
Strategies, society and security
Edited by Chien-min Chao and Bruce J. Dickson

Korean Society
Civil society, democracy and the state
Edited by Charles K. Armstrong

The Making of Modern Korea
Adrian Buzo

The Resurgence of East Asia
500, 150 and 50 year perspectives
Edited by Giovanni Arrighi, Takeshi Hamashita and Mark Selden

Chinese Society, second edition
Change, conflict and resistance
Edited by Elizabeth J. Perry and Mark Selden

Ethnicity in Asia
Edited by Colin Mackerras

The Battle for Asia
From decolonization to globalization
Mark T. Berger

State and Society in 21st Century China
Edited by Peter Hays Gries and Stanley Rosen

Japan's Quiet Transformation
Social change and civil society in the 21st century
Jeff Kingston

Confronting the Bush Doctrine
Critical views from the Asia-Pacific
Edited by Mel Gurtov and Peter Van Ness

China in War and Revolution, 1895–1949
Peter Zarrow

The Future of US–Korean Relations
The imbalance of power
Edited by John Feffer

Working in China
Ethnographies of labor and workplace transformations
Edited by Ching Kwan Lee

Korean Society, second edition
Civil society, democracy and the state
Edited by Charles K. Armstrong

Singapore
The State and the culture of excess
Souchou Yao

Pan-Asianism in Modern Japanese History
Colonialism, regionalism and borders
Edited by Sven Saaler and J. Victor Koschmann

The Making of Modern Korea, 2nd Edition
Adrian Buzo

Re-writing Culture in Taiwan
Edited by Fang-long Shih, Stuart Thompson, and Paul-François Tremlett

Asia's Great Cities
Each volume aims to capture the heartbeat of the contemporary city from multiple perspectives emblematic of the authors own deep familiarity with the distinctive faces of the city, its history, society, culture, politics and economics, and its evolving position in national, regional and global frameworks. While most volumes emphasize urban developments since the Second World War, some pay close attention to the legacy of the longue durée in shaping the contemporary. Thematic and comparative volumes address such themes as urbanization, economic and financial linkages, architecture and space, wealth

and power, gendered relationships, planning and anarchy, and ethnographies in national and regional perspective.
Titles include:

Bangkok
Place, practice and representation
Marc Askew

Hong Kong
Global city
Stephen Chiu and Tai-Lok Lui

Representing Calcutta
Modernity, nationalism and the colonial uncanny
Swati Chattopadhyay

Singapore
Wealth, power and the culture of control
Carl A. Trocki

The City in South Asia
James Heitzman

Global Shanghai, 1850–2010
A history in fragments
Jeffrey N. Wasserstrom

Asia.com is a series which focuses on the ways in which new information and communication technologies are influencing politics, society and culture in Asia.
Titles include:

Japanese Cybercultures
Edited by Mark McLelland and Nanette Gottlieb

Asia.com
Asia encounters the Internet
Edited by K. C. Ho, Randolph Kluver and Kenneth C. C. Yang

The Internet in Indonesia's New Democracy
David T. Hill and Krishna Sen

Chinese Cyberspaces
Technological changes and political effects
Edited by Jens Damm and Simona Thomas

Mobile Media in the Asia-Pacific
Gender and the art of being mobile
Larissa Hjorth

Literature and Society is a series that seeks to demonstrate the ways in which Asian Literature is influenced by the politics, society and culture in which it is produced. Titles include:

The Body in Postwar Japanese Fiction
Edited by Douglas N. Slaymaker

Chinese Women Writers and the Feminist Imagination, 1905–48
Haiping Yan

Routledge Studies in Asia's Transformations is a forum for innovative new research intended for a high-level specialist readership, and the titles will be available in hardback only. Titles include:

The American Occupation of Japan and Okinawa*
Literature and memory
Michael Molasky

Koreans in Japan*
Critical voices from the margin
Edited by Sonia Ryang

Internationalizing the Pacific
The United States, Japan and the Institute of Pacific Relations in war and peace, 1919–1945
Tomoko Akami

Imperialism in South East Asia
'A fleeting, passing phase'
Nicholas Tarling

Chinese Media, Global Contexts
Edited by Chin-Chuan Lee

Remaking Citizenship in Hong Kong*
Community, nation and the global city
Edited by Agnes S. Ku and Ngai Pun

Japanese Industrial Governance
Protectionism and the licensing state
Yul Sohn

Developmental Dilemmas
Land reform and institutional change in China
Edited by Peter Ho

Genders, Transgenders and Sexualities in Japan*
Edited by Mark McLelland and Romit Dasgupta

Fertility, Family Planning and Population Policy in China
Edited by Dudley L. Poston, Che-Fu Lee, Chiung-Fang Chang, Sherry L. McKibben and Carol S. Walther

Japanese Diasporas
Unsung pasts, conflicting presents and uncertain futures
Edited by Nobuko Adachi

How China Works
Perspectives on the twentieth-century industrial workplace
Edited by Jacob Eyferth

Remolding and Resistance among Writers of the Chinese Prison Camp
Disciplined and published
Edited by Philip F. Williams and Yenna Wu

Popular Culture, Globalization and Japan*
Edited by Matthew Allen and Rumi Sakamoto

medi@sia
Global media/tion in and out of context
Edited by Todd Joseph, Miles Holden and Timothy J. Scrase

Vientiane
Transformations of a Lao landscape
Marc Askew, William S. Logan and Colin Long

State Formation and Radical Democracy in India
Manali Desai

Democracy in Occupied Japan
The U.S. occupation and Japanese politics and society
Edited by Mark E. Caprio and Yoneyuki Sugita

Globalization, Culture and Society in Laos
Boike Rehbein

Transcultural Japan
At the borderlands of race, gender, and identity
Edited by David Blake Willis and Stephen Murphy-Shigematsu

Post-Conflict Heritage, Post-Colonial Tourism
Culture, politics and development at Angkor
Tim Winter

Education and Reform in China
Emily Hannum and Albert Park

Writing Okinawa: Narrative Acts of Identity and Resistance
Davinder L. Bhowmik

Maid In China
Media, mobility, and a new semiotic of power
Wanning Sun

Northern Territories, Asia-Pacific Regional Conflicts and the Åland Experience
Untying the Kurillian Knot
Edited by Kimie Hara and Geoffrey Jukes

Reconciling Indonesia
Grassroots agency for peace
Birgit Bräuchler

Singapore in the Malay World
Building and breaching regional bridges
Lily Zubaidah Rahim

Pirate Modernity
Delhi's media urbanism
Ravi Sundaram

The World Bank and the post-Washington Consensus in Vietnam and Indonesia
Inheritance of loss
Susan Engel

* Now available in paperback

Critical Asian Scholarship is a series intended to showcase the most important individual contributions to scholarship in Asian Studies. Each of the volumes presents a leading Asian scholar addressing themes that are central to his or her most significant and lasting contribution to Asian studies. The series is committed to the rich variety of research and writing on Asia, and is not restricted to any particular discipline, theoretical approach or geographical expertise.

Southeast Asia
A testament
George McT. Kahin

Women and the Family in Chinese History
Patricia Buckley Ebrey

China Unbound
Evolving perspectives on the Chinese past
Paul A. Cohen

China's Past, China's Future
Energy, food, environment
Vaclav Smil

The Chinese State in Ming Society
Timothy Brook

China, East Asia and the Global Economy
Regional and historical perspectives
Takeshi Hamashita
Edited by Mark Selden and Linda Grove

The Global and Regional in China's Nation-Formation
Prasenjit Duara

The World Bank and the post-Washington Consensus in Vietnam and Indonesia

Inheritance of loss

Susan Engel

Routledge
Taylor & Francis Group
LONDON AND NEW YORK

First published 2010
by Routledge
4 Park Square, Milton Park, Abingdon, Oxon OX14 4RN
605 Third Avenue, New York, NY 10017

Routledge is an imprint of the Taylor & Francis Group, an informa business

Typeset in Times New Roman by
Taylor & Francis Books

British Library Cataloguing in Publication Data
A catalogue record for this book is available from the British Library

Library of Congress Cataloging in Publication Data
Engel, Susan.
The World Bank and the post-Washington consensus in Vietnam and Indonesia : inheritance of loss / Susan Engel.
p. cm. – (Routledge studies in Asia's transformations)
1. World Bank–Vietnam. 2. World Bank–Indonesia. 3. World Bank. I. Title.
HG3881.5.W57E54 2009
332.1'53209597–dc22
2009004478

ISBN: 978-0-415-54743-7 (hbk)
ISBN: 978-0-20-387316-8 (ebk)

For my father, Walter and my boys, Mika and Till

Contents

Illustrations

Tables

Figures

Acknowledgements

Thanks go to the University of Wollongong, especially the Faculty of Arts and the Centre for Asia Pacific Social Transformations Studies (CAPSTRANS) for the financial support, which made the project possible. There were a number of people who gave me time and support while researching in Vietnam and Indonesia, these include in Vietnam: Philip D. Gray (World Bank), Duc Hai (Southern Institute of Social Sciences), David Payne (VUFO-NGO Resource Centre), Irene Nørlund, Pham Tra (WACO) and Carrie Turk (World Bank). In Indonesia: Scott Guggenheim (World Bank), Taufik Rinaldi (World Bank), Dr Sudarno Sumarto (SMERU), Andrew Steer (Country Director Indonesia, World Bank), Rudsi Tagaroa (GAPRI), Dr Mangara Tambunan (Center for Economic and Social Studies) and Fabby Tumiwa (Working Group on Power Sector Restructuring). Their insights made this a significantly more informed work, though of course I am solely responsible for the good and bad.

There have also been a number of friends and colleagues without whom this project would never have been completed, first and foremost thanks to Andrew Wells but also to Rob Castles, Ravi Palat and Mark Selden. Nichole Georgeou, Margaret Hanlon, Julia Martinez, Michael Wilson and Heather Yeatman commented on various drafts. Thanks also to the anonymous reviewers whose thoughtful comments improved the final version.

Abbreviations

ADB	Asian Development Bank
CAS	Country Assistance Strategy
CDF	Comprehensive Development Framework
CGAP	Consultative Group to Assist the Poorest
CGI	Consultative Group on Indonesia
CGV	Consultative Group for Vietnam
CPRGS	Comprehensive Poverty Reduction and Growth Strategy
DPD	Indonesian Regional Representative's Council
DPR	Indonesian House of People's Representatives
DPRD	Indonesian Regional People's Representative Assembly
ECOSOC	Economic and Social Council of the United Nations
EFF	Extended Fund Facility
EIRTP	Eastern Indonesia Regional Transport Project
EOI	Export-Oriented Industrialisation
FDI	foreign direct investment
GDP	gross domestic product
GNI	gross national income
GNP	gross national product
GoI	Government of Indonesia
GoV	Government of Vietnam
HCMC	Ho Chi Minh City
IBRD	International Bank for Reconstruction and Development
ICB	international competitive bidding
ICSID	International Centre for the Settlement of Investment Disputes
IDA	International Development Association
IDT	Program for Villages Left Behind
IFC	International Finance Corporation
IGGI	Inter-Governmental Group on Indonesia
IMF	International Monetary Fund
IPE	International Political Economy
IPP	Independent Power Producer
IR	International Relations
ISI	Import Substitution Industrialisation

JBIC	Japan Bank for International Cooperation
KDP	*Kecamatan* Development Project
KIP	*Kampung* Improvement Program
MIGA	Multilateral Investment Guarantee Agency
MIP	Market Improvement Program
MPR	Indonesian People's Consultative Assembly
MTEF	Medium-Term Expenditure Framework
NBER	National Bureau of Economic Research (US)
NCB	national competitive bidding
NGO	non-governmental organisation
NIE	New Institutional Economics
NPE	New Political Economy
ODA	Official Development Assistance
OECD	Organization for Economic Cooperation and Development
OP/BP	Operational Policy / Bank Procedures
OPEC	Organization of Petroleum Exporting Nations
PDI	Indonesian Democratic Party
PRSC	Poverty Reduction Support Credit
PRSL	Policy Reform Support Loan
PRSP	Poverty Reduction Strategy Paper
PWC	Post-Washington Consensus
R&D	Research and Development
RE	Rural Electrification
SAC	Structural Adjustment Credit
SAL	Structural Adjustment Loan
SBA	Stand-by Arrangement
SECAL	Sectoral Adjustment Loan
SMEs	Small to Medium Enterprises
SOE	state-owned enterprise
TEPCO	Tokyo Electric Power Company
UDC	Urban Drainage Company
UDP	Urban Development Project
UN	United Nations
UNDP	United Nations Development Program
UNCTAD	United Nations Conference on Trade, Aid and Development
UPP	Urban Poverty Project
US	United States of America
USAID	United States Agency for International Development
VBARD	Vietnam Bank for Agriculture and Rural Development
VIPs	Village Infrastructure Projects
WATSAL	Water Resources Sector Adjustment Loan
WDR	World Development Report
WSCs	Water Supply Companies
WSSLIC	Water Supply and Sanitation for Low Income Communities

Part I

The World Bank, its history, structure and operations

1 Introduction

This project attempts to analyse the extent and nature of the shift of the World Bank from the so-called Washington Consensus to the post-Washington Consensus (PWC). It does so by evaluating the shift in the Bank's underlying development discourse, as embodied in its statements, reports and operational guidelines from its origins through to recent events. It then goes a step further by examining actual lending practices in two case studies, Vietnam and Indonesia. These detailed studies, which conclude in 2004, make it possible to present empirically based conclusions about the extent to which the shift in rhetoric to the PWC has been incorporated into lending practices, thus providing insights into its lending discourse more generally. This is a particularly pertinent task given that the economic turmoil, which started in 2007, has prompted questioning of economic thought in general and neoliberalism in particular. Even Alan Greenspan, former chairman of the US Federal Reserve, has questioned his previous iron faith in markets: '[t]he whole intellectual edifice' he said 'collapsed in the summer of last year' (Anon 2008).

This kind of questioning *should* extend to the policies and practices of the World Bank. While the current World Bank President Robert Zoellick acknowledged that the global financial crisis is a 'manmade catastrophe', the Bank response to the crisis seems to involve little more than expanded financing. This was its response to the debt crisis, which broke out in 1982 – a response which only ultimately added to many developing countries debt problems. In line with the project's Gramscian inspiration, the analysis of the form and content of the Bank's modus operandi is undertaken with the aim of challenging mainstream development discourse and more broadly the dominant global financial hegemony, which the Bank both reflects and propagates.

This project sits at the intersection of Development Studies and International Political Economy (IPE) and is informed by a critical IPE approach that was pioneered in studying the World Bank by scholars such as Susan George, Walden Bello and Robert Wade. It is Robert Cox's work though, which introduced the work of the Italian Marxist Antonio Gramsci to IPE, that shapes the theoretical and political position of this book. Gramsci analysed the creation of specific forms of hegemony by dominant social forces and Cox applied this approach to the international sphere. My interpretation and reading of Gramsci is framed by critical IPE literature and its ambition to supersede positivist international relations scholarship. Gramsci's work has been the subject of many interpretive debates and it is beyond the scope of this book to engage fully in these or in a comprehensive account of his work. The purpose of clarifying Gramsci here is not to articulate a universal Gramscian framework; rather it is to explore concepts and ideas that are useful for understanding and analysing the forms and operations of IPE today (Morton 2003; Rupert 1998).

I will return to the neo-Gramscian approach and concept of hegemony a little later in the introduction. However, first let me briefly introduce the World Bank and examine why it is such an interesting and important organisation to study.

What is the World Bank?

What we now refer to as the World Bank Group, started with one small, conservative banking institution – the International Bank for Reconstruction and Development (IBRD), which was established through the Bretton Woods agreements of 1944. The World Bank became a group in 1956 with the formation of the International Finance Corporation (IFC) and was further expanded with the creation of the International Development Association (IDA) in 1960; the International Centre for the Settlement of Investment Disputes (ICSID) in 1966; and the Multilateral Investment Guarantee Agency (MIGA) in 1988.[1] However, as the World Bank Group itself states, the term 'World Bank' refers only to the IBRD and the IDA – the Bank's two development lending arms, which are the focus of this book.

The IBRD and IDA were each established with their own Articles of Agreement but they operate as a single entity – they share the same staff, headquarters and president, who is always an American. A country must be a member of IBRD to be a member of IDA, as it must be a member of the International Monetary Fund (IMF) to be a member of the IBRD. The Board of Governors and Executive Directors of the IBRD are *ex officio* those of the IDA, so long as the members of each are also members of the IDA. The 24 Executive Directors of the IBRD comprise five appointees from the countries with the five largest shareholdings and 19 Directors elected by the remaining Governors. This means that the largest shareholders in the IBRD automatically have Directors in the IDA, regardless of their level of subscription. In both organisations, voting is based on the number of shares or the level of subscription. In the case of appointed Directors, they are able to cast the number of votes held by the member who appointed them and, in the case of elected Directors, the number of votes that were cast for them in their election.

The Bank is a 'specialized agency' of the United Nations (UN), as per Articles 57 and 63 of the UN Charter. Article 63 of the Charter gives the Economic and Social Council (ECOSOC) primary responsibility for coordinating specialised agencies. However, even under the highly decentralised and 'somewhat vague co-ordinating authority' (Taylor 2000: 102) of ECOSOC, the Bretton Woods institutions are 'rather "special" specialized agencies' in that they function autonomously from the direction and control of UN officials (Mason and Asher 1973: 58). This relationship is discussed further in Chapter 2, which examines the establishment of the IBRD.

The principal difference between the IDA and IBRD is that IDA provides zero interest loans (called credits) to the poorest of countries, defined in 2007 as those with a per capita income of less than $1,025, whereas the IBRD provides loans to middle income and credit-worthy poorer countries at current market rates. IDA loans generally are over longer terms (now 20, 35 or 40 years), have a 10-year grace period, and attract a three-quarters of a per cent annual service charge. IBRD loans are shorter terms (generally a maximum of 25 years), have only a five- or seven-year grace period and attract market-based interest rates, calculated at a small premium over the London Interbank Offered Rate, which can range from half a per cent to over 10 per cent. The IBRD raises most of its funds from international financial markets, while the IDA requires regular replenishments from governments in developed countries as well as receiving profits transferred from the IBRD. In the 10 years to 2004, IBRD lending averaged 67 per cent of total new commitments, through the range varied from 55 to 75 per cent (World Bank 2004u: 29, 1999c).

Why the World Bank?

Since the 1980s, the Bank has been at the centre of a new neoliberal global intellectual hegemony in development theory and practice. As an international organisation, it had credibility and a veil of independence that made is useful for promoting the interests of international, particularly US capital, over a number of decades (Bello 1994: 32–34; Ritzen 2005: 99–101). US support for the Bank may also be seen as part of its attack on the agenda of such UN development agencies as the UN Development Program and the UN Population Fund, which had historically pursued a more radical development agenda (Gosovic 2000: 454). These UN agencies approached development as not merely catch up by developing economies but transformation of global economic and political structures, requiring some contribution from the West. By contrast, despite its dedication and rededication to poverty eradication on a number of occasions since the 1970s, the Bank has remained a conservative and mainstream lender whose theory and practices support the current world and especially US neoliberal hegemony.

The World Bank is the largest and most powerful global development agency. In 2007, it added its 185th member and had offices in over 100 countries. Its development-lending arms – the International Bank for Reconstruction and Development (IBRD) and the International Development Agency (IDA) – have cumulatively lent $590.2 billion to the end of the 2006 financial year (World Bank 2006b).[2] In the 2004 financial year, the last year of the case studies in this book – it committed $20.1 billion in new loans and it disbursed just over $17 billion in loans and $3.28 billion from trust funds (World Bank 2004u: i, 112). Co-financing of its loans by other bi- or multilateral development agencies further expands its influence. The Bank's $20.3 billion was equivalent to 7.3 per cent of foreign direct investment (FDI) flows to developing countries in 2004, which amounted to $275 billion (United Nations Conference on Trade and Development 2006: 300). However, over 46 per cent of FDI flows to so-called 'developing countries' went to just five recipients: China, Hong Kong, Mexico, Brazil and Singapore. If you deduct these flows, FDI to developing countries was $128.7 billion and Bank assistance equalled 15.6 per cent of their total value. Bank disbursements to its 47 African borrowers in 2004 were equivalent to 26.8 per cent of the value of FDI flows to these countries (United Nations Conference on Trade and Development 2006: 299–300; World Bank 2004u: 29).

The relative significance of the Bank's lending operations in purely financial terms has ebbed and flowed over the years but it remains at the forefront of investment decisions guiding the priorities of private investors. The *Doing Business* series of flagship publications, which started in 2004, have been 'most influential' and only added to the Bank's relevance to the private sector (Banerjee *et al.* 2006). This capacity to impact on private capital markets may be of greater consequence than the dollars the Bank lends. Moreover, the authoritativeness of the Bank's analysis and model of development have only increased over the last two decades. This is because as well as offering loans and grants, the Bank provides technical assistance and advice; mobilises economic survey missions; undertakes sectoral surveys; and organises consultative groups of major donors to review the progress of particular countries development programs and policies. As Graham Harrison (2004: 129) states its involvement in countries is 'more profound and intimate' than any component of its program indicates; it proactively shapes 'the methods by which government policy is made and executed; it funds administrative reform to build up new techniques of administration … [and] it aggressively shapes the discursive limits of the "politics of the possible"'.

The Bank is the largest development research organisation in the world and probably the largest development training organisation in the world. The Bank has a larger research and analytical capacity than many of the developing countries it lends to. Through the World Bank Institute, it trains around 47,000 financial and development specialists per year. The main targets of its training programmes are developing country government officials and its own staff, though in more recent years the Institute has broadened its reach to include staff from non-governmental organisations (NGOs), journalists, academics and other development specialists; they even train parliamentarians, secondary school teachers and children. In 1996, it set about intensifying its research strengths through the Knowledge Bank initiative, which includes a massive web presence. The Bank's research capacity is many times larger than any university research department, indeed it is far greater than the research capacities of many of the nations it services. According to Nicholas Stern and Francisco Ferreira (1997: 593), by the early 1990s it had several hundred people working full-time on research and many more who spend part of their time on research activities.[3] It is not only the main source of research for its own staff, but for other development agencies and multilateral banks and for the World Trade Organization, which initially had only limited research capacity.

The Bank uses its research selectively to promote a particular view of development. This was highlighted in a recent Bank-commissioned review of its research by a group of prominent economists (Banerjee *et al.* 2006). The review highlighted the way that the Bank promoted and extensively used research by David Dollar and Aart Kray on the relationship between growth, openness and poverty reduction, which essentially argues that countries (across time and space) that are open to trade and have 'sound' policy settings have achieved better poverty reduction. The review by prominent economists found that:

> much of this line of research appears to have such deep flaws that, at present, the results cannot be regarded as remotely reliable ... The problem is that in major policy speeches and publications, it [the Bank] proselytised the new work without appropriate caveats on its reliability ... Nor has it corrected itself to this day.
>
> (Banerjee *et al.* 2006: 53)

Nevertheless, the Bank remains very influential in development economics debate (Broad 2006: 395–96). Indeed Asunción St. Clair (2006: 86) argued that 'the methodological tools of development economics, and mathematical and statistical knowledge, have become over time a virtual monopoly of the Bank'. Moreover, she highlights how the Bank has become central to the process of legitimating development economics knowledge through its publication of key development economics journals, conferences, training programmes, web presence and funding of development research. While the Bank's influence in development economic knowledge production is not unchallengeable, through its various shifts in approach, its ideas have remained hegemonic.[4]

Understanding hegemony

Hegemony was used by Gramsci to describe 'a relation, not of domination by means of force, but of consent by means of political and ideological leadership. It is the organisation of consent' (Simon 1991: 22). Gramsci was predominantly interested in how the working classes can organise consent and thus hegemony within a country; however, he also analysed the nature and form of bourgeois hegemony. Anderson claimed that it was this later use of 'the concept of hegemony for *a differential analysis of the structure of bourgeois power in the West*' that 'was a new and decisive step' (Anderson 1976: 20). This later usage of hegemony is also where he conceptualised its unique combination of coercion and consent (Anderson 1976: 31).

Hegemony operates in society across both the economic structure and the superstructural levels of civil society and political society (Augelli and Murphy 1993: 128). According to Anderson and others, there are discrepancies in Gramsci's work between the formulation and inter-relations of these levels. He identified three different conceptions of economy, state, civil society: the first involves a distinct dichotomy between civil society and the state, with hegemony located in civil society and domination located in the state (Anderson 1976: 26). This conception is seen in the oft-quoted passage from Gramsci:

> [w]hat we can do, for the moment, is to fix two major superstructural 'levels': the one that can be called 'civil society', that is the ensemble of organisms commonly called 'private', and that of 'political society' or 'the State'. These two levels correspond on the one hand to the function of 'hegemony' that the dominant group exercises through society and on the other hand to that of 'direct domination' or command exercised through the State and 'juridical' government.
>
> (Gramsci 1996: 138)

The second conception is more of a balance between state and civil society with hegemony as a combination of coercion and consent operating in both spheres (Anderson 1976: 31). The third formulation, suggests a civil society–state nexus. Anderson (1976: 35) understood this formulation as the state encompassing political and civil society. He was suspicious of this blurring of the boundaries, suggesting that it inhibits the development of a 'scientific theory of the total articulation of capitalist social formations'. Randall Germain and Michael Kenny (1998: 13–14) argued it is most appropriate to acknowledge the presence of all positions – or the possibility of finding them – in Gramsci. However, my position is that it is precisely the rejection of dichotomous modes of analysis in this third formulation that is most reflective of Gramsci's historicist approach and thus, provides a more sophisticated understanding of state–civil society relations while maintaining a distinction between them.

For Gramsci, hegemony is organised through leadership, alliances and networks in a context of continuous ideological and political struggle. Consent can be obtained by combining the interests of various social forces around particular populist causes such as struggles for democracy, or it can be obtained through compromise and persuasion. As Gramsci said:

> [o]bviously, the fact of hegemony presupposes that the interests and tendencies of those groups over whom hegemony is exercised have been taken into account and that a certain equilibrium is established. It presupposes, in other words, that the hegemonic group should make sacrifices of an economic-corporate kind; these sacrifices, however, cannot touch the essential ... the decisive core of economic activity.
>
> (Gramsci 1996: 138)

Here we have also the idea that each hegemonic system is organised around a set of core ideas that cannot be challenged without overturning the hegemony, which, following Richard Howson (2006: 25), are termed here 'hegemonic principles'. The ideological and political struggles of hegemonic groups are designed to change the theoretical, social and also cultural framework of social forces to assure that they support their hegemony.

Ideology, the framing of knowledge, is one of the key terrains on which hegemonic struggles are fought. In a historically organic form, Gramsci argued that ideology organises human thought and action and it structures the practical and moral framework (Simon 1991: 59). Equally though, in Gramsci's thought, social organisation (especially work) frames ideology, producing a frequently reductionist 'common sense'. Ultimately, as Roger Simon (1991: 61) pointed out: 'Gramsci considers that an ideology is not to be judged by its truth or falsity but by its efficacy in binding together a bloc of diverse social elements, and in acting as cement or as an agent of social unification'. In liberal democratic societies ideological dominance is achieved via legitimation and validation and this involves a genuine engagement with non-hegemonic discourse, bounded by hegemonic principles such as the private ownership of property and the use of markets to generally manage the production and distribution of goods and services. In other words, ideology is never mere manipulation or brainwashing.

Ideology is a difficult terrain for counter-hegemonic struggles because of 'the tendency of public discourse to make some forms of experience readily available to consciousness while ignoring or suppressing others' (Lears 1985: 577). The working classes, in particular, tend towards passive submission to an inherited, 'uncritical and largely unconscious' common sense (Simon 1991: 64–65). Equally though, Gramsci pointed out that the constructed nature of common sense can make it a fertile ground for informing resistance to hegemony. There are tensions in the discussions of ideology in the *Prison Notebooks* that T. J. Jackson Lears (1985: 578–82) explained as remnants of the concept of false consciousness in Gramsci's work and which, he suggested, tend to obscure 'subjective' needs (family, community, religion, etc.) that are not underpinned by class. Thus, he argues a Gramscian approach can be reproached for ignoring the fact that 'most radical anti-capitalist protests have been rooted not in Marxist universalism but in local traditions undermined by industrialization'.

The efficacy of ideology is partly the product of specific agents, 'organic intellectuals', who enunciate, organise and reform its components. As Gramsci (1971: 4) put it, every social force 'creates one or more strata of intellectuals who give it homogeneity and an awareness of its own function not only in the economic but also in the political and social fields'. These intellectuals are the organisers of the superstructure:

> [t]he intellectuals are the dominant group's 'deputies' exercising the subaltern functions of social hegemony and political government. These comprise:

> 1. The 'spontaneous' consensus given by the great masses of the population to the general direction imposed on social life by the dominant fundamental group; this consent is 'historically' caused by the prestige (and consequent confidence) which the dominant group enjoys because of its position and function in the world of production. 2. The apparatus of State coercive power which 'legally' enforces discipline on those groups who do not 'consent' for the whole of society in anticipation of moments of crisis of command and direction when spontaneous consent has failed.
> (Gramsci 1971: 12)

Gramsci's belief in the power of organic intellectuals to transform the working class is somewhat difficult to understand in today's social and political circumstances, at the same time there is little doubt that intellectual production has played a significant role in the ascent of neoliberalism, which is a crucial element of the current international hegemony. Gramsci's discussion and analysis of ideology is a useful antidote to mainstream IPE, which generally remains silent on this issue.

If dominant forces are successful, meaning that they predominate for a long duration, Gramsci labelled this ensemble of interests as an 'historic bloc' (Simon 1991: 32–33). Historic blocs are not always hegemonic. The concept of historic blocs is important because it is linked to the economic base, through the decision-making framework, thus historic blocs craft the production and distribution of goods and services. Equally, the concept enables analyses to go beyond the traditional Marxist focus on class, promoting an analysis of social forces that is not limited to ownership of the means of production. Analysis can incorporate issues of culture, populism, religion, theory and ideology (Lears 1985: 571). For a critical IPE approach, historic blocs provide a concrete means to overcome mainstream closure on the content of the state by adding analysis of economic, social and cultural relations to structural realist assumptions about the basis of international relations. Viewing states as historically contingent and constructed historic blocs involving economic, political, social and cultural influences produces a very different understanding of global processes.

Historic blocs are not static – social forces are constantly shifting, influenced by counter-hegemonic movements as well as shifting groupings within the dominant social forces. Gramsci highlighted two types of change in his analysis, one is short-term and non-structural, whereas the other is significant, structural and often long lasting. Structural change generally results in reshaping all elements of the historic bloc – institutions, alliances and ideology (Simon 1991: 39). Gramsci (1971: 222) did not dismiss either form of change because 'a social form "always" has a marginal possibility for further development and organisational improvement'. However, he had a particular interest in the response of dominant social forces to significant changes in socioeconomic systems and concluded that they normally employ a strategy of 'passive revolution' or 'revolution from above'. Passive revolution is a way that dominant social groups manage social change to ensure their dominance is maintained and, at the same time, the possibility of oppositional change is minimised or, indeed, excluded (Sassoon 2001: 8). The primary form of this strategy is utilisation of the institutions of the state to achieve structural changes in the economy to shape a new historic bloc (Simon 1991: 50). This analysis is very relevant to understanding the role of an international institution like the World Bank.

Gramsci saw that the advance to socialism required labour and other emancipatory movements to combine to build counter-hegemony. This requires a prolonged strategy of moral and ideological reform, which Gramsci labelled 'war of position' to distinguish it from the 'war of movement' of the Russian Revolution where power was seized through a frontal attack on the state. This latter strategy, he suggested, was not suitable for liberal capitalist societies with complex state–civil society formations, which can easily overcome direct attacks. War of position is, however, a difficult strategy as there is a constant danger that acceptance of incremental gains within the existing hegemony will capture a movement and negate its long-term revolutionary potential.

Hegemony, for Gramsci (1996: 187), is not just an organising concept, it also has epistemological value. While noting the debates around his epistemological (ontological and methodological) position, this work is informed by an understanding of Gramsci as a historicist. As Adam Morton (1999: 4) contended, this demanded research: 'based on critical reflection which involved acknowledging the role played by existing forms of thought and their relation to the actual world which produced them and in which they were received'. This project then, takes practical inspiration from Gramsci – while engaging with the significance of theoretical and philosophical debates around hegemony, it uses them to undertake a detailed and concrete analysis of the day-to-day operations of the World Bank, the aim of which is to contribute to the political struggle against the operations of the Bank and other international institutions whose existence, in the final analysis, does little to improve the lives of millions in the developing world. However, this approach does not reduce all development efforts to a capitalist conspiracy or claim that organisations like the World Bank always operate consistently. Rather, it paints a complex picture of ideologies, social formations and relations of production that generate compromise, conflict and change.

Hegemony and world order

There remains, however, a problem in the theoretical approach for this project; hegemony, for Gramsci, is organised and analysed at the national level – understanding the specific social, historical and cultural organisation within a country is seen as essential to an emancipatory project (Simon 1991: 35). Indeed, Gramsci wrote at a time when nation-states dominated Europe and North America but in other parts of the globe colonial relations intersected with local traditions and structures in diverse ways. That is, it was not yet certain that the international system would, to a large extent, be structured by nation-states. However, Gramsci was aware that social forces were driving the creation of nation-states and regional and international levels of action. In one of his key notes, 'Analysis of Situations. Relations of Force' he stated that 'international relations intertwine with these internal relations of nation-states, creating new, unique and historically concrete combinations' (Gramsci 1971: 182). The acknowledgement in Gramsci's work of the existence of an international or global level of action extends to the possibility of 'combinations of States in hegemonic systems' (Gramsci 1971: 176). The 'Analysis of Situations' note asks the question: 'Do international relations precede or follow (logically) fundamental social relations?' The answer: 'There can be no doubt that they follow … However, international relations react both passively and actively on political relations' (Gramsci 1971: 176). In his notes on economic trends and developments (1995: 221), Gramsci noted that 'the world is a unit, whether we like it or not'. This world is made up of states, which are structurally differentiated – there are 'hegemonic states' and 'subaltern states' and the history of the latter needs to be understood at least partly in relation to the history of the former. Moreover, in a discussion on international trade and tariff barriers, he pointed out that states have made 'various attempts at organising the world market and establishing the most favourable position in it' (Gramsci 1995: 232). Here too, is the idea that domestic hegemonic social forces can exert their influence internationally.

From Gramsci's somewhat sketchy comments on the international realm, Cox (1986) attempted to construct an explicit Gramscian analysis of hegemony at the international level or, as Cox called it, the level of world orders. He has done this in an age where the world is more interconnected than ever through a whole series of international institutions. Cox's schema involved analysis of hegemonic and non-hegemonic forces in three inter-related spheres of historically current activity, namely social forces, states and world orders. Relations of production fundamentally shape social forces and this, for him, was the starting point for analysing hegemony (Cox 1986: 220–25). His focus on production has led to critiques from Gramsci-inspired scholars and others, of an overemphasis on economic relations at the expense of ideology, culture, etc. While the critique does have some substance, Cox noted that for him production is a holistic concept incorporating the production and reproduction of goods, knowledge, ideas and institutions (see Bieler and Morton 2004: 89). Understanding the social relations of production, which are not restricted to the boundaries of states, facilitates analysis of dominant groups both across states and world orders.

In contrast to much mainstream IPE theory, Cox does not accept the unity of the state as a given. Forms of state need to be explained via the analysis of state and civil society (social forces) connections (Cox 1986: 223; Augelli and Murphy 1993: 129–30). They can be influenced by the structure of the world order and can influence the structure. Cox utilised the Gramscian idea of an historic bloc to analyse the development of forms of states and their underlying dominant social forces as well as their movements towards hegemony. And following Gramsci too, the purpose of this was always a practical one – only through such mediations can an understanding of the potentials for resistance and transformation be developed (Cox 1986: 230).

In the final sphere of world orders, Cox retained (as in Gramsci) the national sphere as the foundation of the hegemonic historic blocs. Cox (1996: 137) proposed that a 'world hegemony is thus in it beginnings an outward expansion of the internal (national) hegemony established by a dominant social class'. However, a national hegemony can form the basis of a world order if the hegemony is universalist and the national state can ensure its development and protection. As Andreas Bieler and Morton (2004: 93) explained: '[h]egemony can therefore operate at two levels: by constructing an historical bloc and establishing social cohesion *within* a form of state as well as by expanding a mode of production *internationally* and projecting hegemony through the level of world order'. As important as the internationalisation of production is the internationalisation of the state. Cox perceived the current hegemony as an outwards expansion of the dominant American historic bloc and he labels this: *pax americana.* The legitimating ideology of *pax americana* is neoliberalism. Reconciliation of the world economy and domestic pressures under it involves practices of policy harmonisation, varied roles for key state agencies and active international institutions (Cox 1986: 230–32). Cox also identified a range of ways in which hegemony is expressed by international organisations as both the products of the hegemonic world order and institutions that facilitate the expansion of the rules of that order, in this case neoliberalism. Institutions function to legitimate rules, engage social forces in developing countries in an order and they serve to 'absorb counter-hegemonic ideas' (Cox 1996: 138). This legitimating role is one the World Bank is playing during the current global financial crisis despite the challenges being made to neoliberalism. To Cox's schema highlighting international order, I would add that hegemony can have regional dimensions and that regional structures and relations can mediate the impact of national and international historic blocs.

Randall Germain and Michael Kenny (1998) questioned the accuracy of Cox's (and other critical IPE scholars') reading of Gramsci. But, as Morton (2003: 120) argued, this critique represents a kind of 'austere historicism,' which suggests that the ideas of writers in the past are not relevant to analysis today. Further, as Morton demonstrated, austere historicism is not consistent with Gramsci's theoretical or political project, which was a transformative one (Morton 2003: 120; Rupert 1998). Thus the purpose of understanding Gramsci in critical IPE is not to articulate a universal Gramscian framework, rather it is to explore concepts and ideas that are useful for understanding and analysing the forms and operations of IPE today.

The historical sociologist Giovanni Arrighi (1993) explained world hegemony somewhat differently from Cox, as 'the power of a state to exercise governmental functions over a system of sovereign states'. However, his analysis of the shift from the previous period of hegemony, which he called 'Free-Trade Imperialism' to the current period of US hegemony, also highlights the importance of institutions, rules and norms. Arrighi (1993: 182) argued that in:

> comparison with Free-Trade Imperialism, the institutions of US hegemony have considerably restricted the rights and powers of sovereign states. The principles, norms, and rules to which states must submit have increased in number and have become tighter, while a growing number of supranational organisations have acquired autonomous power to overrule the interstate system.

The strength of this system is demonstrated by the fact that it is very difficult to operate outside of the network of institutions, norms and transnational corporations, except at enormous cost (Arrighi 1993: 182). With the increasing incorporation of the former Soviet Union, China and other former communist states into the global economy, this argument is more salient today than when it was written over a decade ago.

While taking the work of Cox as my starting point, I hope through this case study of the World Bank in Vietnam and Indonesia to more effectively incorporate Gramsci's framework and example by building a deeper understanding of the relationship between *pax americana* and the World Bank. Thus, this interrogation considers that the Bank should be studied as an institution that serves the interests of the dominant hegemony, *pax americana*, by promoting its dominant ideology – neoliberalism even in the midst of a global financial crisis which has questioned that ideology at least at the margins. It is important to make the proviso that hegemony is both historically contingent and never complete – there are always challenges, complexities and counter-hegemonies. This study of the Bank explores not just how and where the Bank has successfully legitimised rules or supported particular social forces and ideologies but also where it has not been successful, that is where the gaps or tensions have surfaced.[5]

Chapter outline

The theoretical assumptions used here suggest that an analysis of the World Bank should start by examining it as part of the larger hegemonic struggle of the post-Second World War period. This is essential background for any project attempting to deconstruct the Bank's current practice. Further, as Gramsci (1995: 11) suggested it is important to examine how organisations and ideas 'adjust to different historical epochs and different countries', thus the book starts with a history of the Bank. Chapter 2 explores the origins of the Bank, that is the postwar economic planning culminating in the Bretton Woods conference in 1944. In line with the Gramscian approach, the foundations of the Bank are explained with reference to two major changes of the era: first, the major shift in power that took place in the first half of the twentieth century, which resulted in the decline of British hegemony and the rise of *pax americana*. Second, the 'revolution' in economic theory influenced by the economist John Maynard Keynes that led to changed ideas about the role of the state in the economy and civil society which changed the ideological terrain of the post-Second World War period. In this light, the Bank's Articles of Agreement developed at Bretton Woods are analysed as not simply the product of debates between the British and Americans, rather, and more profoundly, as reflections of the postwar compromise between classical/neoclassical commitments to free trade and markets and the Keynesian commitments to planning and welfare. Ben Fine (2001b: 133) has labelled the outcome of this compromise: the Keynesian welfare, modernisation model of development.

Chapter 3 explores the evolution of the World Bank from the first meeting of its Executive Directors at Savannah in 1946 through to the introduction of structural adjustment lending at the end of the reign of long-term Bank President Robert Strange McNamara in 1981. The Bank started out as a small, hard-nosed and conservative lender to only a handful of mostly medium income countries. It simply ignored the welfare component of the 'Keynesian, welfare, modernisation model' and focused largely on infrastructure. Its growth in the 1950s and 1960s was hampered by the ambivalent attitude of the then US administrations; nevertheless, the Bank's size and development agenda gradually expanded. Just after McNamara took over as Bank president, the Nixon Administration set out to reorganise US hegemony by restructuring the international monetary and financial system to ensure that the US dollar and US private capital remained at its centre (Gowan 1999: 19–23). This plan provided a boost to the World Bank, as expanding its lending was a way of encouraging private US banks in the same direction. This shot in the arm, combined with McNamara's obsession with size and expansion, made the Bank by the end of the 1970s, *the* leading international development agency. McNamara's term ended as neoliberalism swept the West, thus the chapter explores the theoretical development of neoliberalism and its first impact on the Bank – structural adjustment lending.

Chapter 4 explores how the Bank's commitment to a set of core principles known as the Washington Consensus was consolidated. The Washington Consensus centres on commitment to macroeconomic stability, outward orientation and domestic liberalisation. In the 1980s, Washington Consensus policies were implemented fairly simplistically and often with high social costs to the poor in developing countries. This made the policies unpopular and too difficult to implement. Even the Reagan Administration realised that the Bank's efforts were frequently counter-productive and in 1986 they replaced the strict neoliberal Alden W. Clausen with the more politically astute Barber B. Conable. However, the supremacy of the Washington Consensus in the Bank was not really challenged until the early 1990s. In fact, the Bank's shift away from it is most strongly associated with Clinton Administration appointee, James D. Wolfensohn. The Bank's post-Washington Consensus is the political product of the slightly more state-friendly international atmosphere with a 'liberal' government in power in the USA. Theoretically, it reflects the increasing prominence of New Institutional Economics as a challenge to some components of neoclassicism. It also reflects the incorporation of aspects of the critique of the World Bank's development model from NGOs, in particular regarding the Bank's weak focus on poverty reduction and a lack of local participation in framing development agendas. The chapter identifies the key differences between the Washington Consensus and the PWC that are more fully explored in the case studies.

Part II of the study commences with explanation for selection of the case study countries – Vietnam and Indonesia – and the methodology used in examining Bank lending practices. The periods selected for the case studies are 1993–7 to examine Washington Consensus lending and 2000–4 to examine post-Washington Consensus lending.

The case studies follow a similar structure starting with an overview of political, social and economic developments in each country focusing on the post-1990 period as an essential context for the analysis of Bank lending. They then explore the history of provision of development assistance to each country and the specific role of the World Bank within them. The Bank's key planning documents for each country are analysed to identify change between and within the case study periods. Then an analysis of Bank lending to each country in each case study period is undertaken. The analysis is organised using the Bank's sectors of lending, for example water supply and sanitation or agriculture, forestry and fishing. The conclusion provides the opportunity to contrast the experiences in each case study using the key differences between the Washington Consensus and post-Washington Consensus outlined in Chapter 4.

2 Creating a World Bank

Most histories of the World Bank focus on the relative contributions (and power) of the United States and Great Britain at the Bretton Woods Conference and/or their two principal negotiators, John Maynard Keynes and Harry Dexter White (George and Sabelli 1994; Kapur *et al.* 1997; Mason and Asher 1973; Oliver 1971). This chapter analyses the Bretton Woods negotiations in the context of the broader social, political, economic and theoretical developments of the Second World War era. In Gramscian terms, it explores the shift from British to American hegemony through analysis of their associated historic blocs. The Articles of Agreement of both the International Bank for Reconstruction and Development (IBRD) and the International Monetary Fund (IMF), finalised at Bretton Woods, New Hampshire, in July 1944, are revealed as the product of the change in global hegemony and the shift in thinking about international economic management. This latter shift in response to a range of challenges including the Great Depression, the seeming success of Russian economic planning, the New Deal and the 'revolution' in liberal economic thought known as Keynesianism.

The changing international order from the First World War

Both communism and the Great Depression were central to the changing view of the role of the state that led to new ideas and practices in economic planning at an international level. Giovanni Arrighi (1994: 269; 1993: 175–77), using a Marxist model of capital accumulation, traces the origins of the rise of the United States and the decline of Great Britain to the mid-nineteenth century, linked by the rise of the German state. The First World War subsequently sealed the fate of the British Empire and fundamentally reordered the debtor/creditor relationship between Great Britain and the United States – the two key players in the establishment of the Bretton Woods institutions. The First World War also saw the 'birth' of Russian and international communism and the war's settlement initiated the Great Depression, both of which were central to the changing view of the state that produced new ideas and practices in economic planning at an international level. The liberation movements in the former colonial dependencies are also part of the overall global shifts central to the argument of the book.

The First World War disrupted Britain's hegemonic position in the international economy (Arrighi 1994: 270). During this war, Britain's imports increased at an unprecedented rate – mainly armaments and basic goods, primarily from the United States, which reduced the large US foreign debt owed to Britain and reduced Britain's foreign investments by one-quarter. Britain's losses were compounded by the Russian revolution followed by its abrogation of war debts, many of which were owed to British investors. Britain and other European industrial countries lost traditional export markets, including those centred on colonial empires as most of the colonies became increasingly self-sufficient during the war (Crouzet 2001: 177). Finally and importantly, Britain lost its capacity to organise the international monetary system in its own interests. On the positive side, at the end of the war Britain still had significant (though reduced) gold reserves and claims on foreign incomes, German war reparations and an extensive and profitable colonial empire, which the war in fact expanded.

By the end of the First World War, the United States had purchased many British owned assets in the United States and had accumulated large war credits. It had increased its invisible earnings, becoming a net creditor and developed a large trading surplus leading to a significant net current account surplus (Arrighi 1994: 271; Ikenberry 1992: 306). From this point, the United States integrated itself into the world economy and assumed an unprecedented dominance. One upshot of this was that the US dollar became a major international reserve currency. Russia suffered enormous losses during the First World War, and economic and social chaos continued during and after the revolution through to 1921. Thereafter, economic growth rapidly took off, in part because the chaos destroyed much production and growth started from such a low base (Kennedy 1989: 323).

The interwar years saw the re-establishment of the gold standard and a fixed exchange rates system, which, by the mid- to late 1920s, included the United States and most European countries. European efforts at creating an international financial system were rebutted by the US government, which was not yet hegemonic and thus did not have the institutional capability or the interest to organise it (Arrighi 1994: 271–72; Peet 2003: 30–32). The fixed exchange rate system made adjustments to shocks difficult. The tendency to overvalue exchange rates and deflationary monetary policy resulted in frequent balance of payments crises (Crouzet 2001: 176). Even during the years of relative prosperity, 1925–9, the whole system was reliant on large capital flows from the United States, especially to Germany, which used these flows for reparation payments and investment. In the 1920s, US productivity grew significantly faster than in debtor countries, making it very difficult for them to service, let alone repay, their debts. Dependence on the US dollar increased and the United States acquired foreign assets at an unparalleled rate. When the flow of US dollars slowed in 1928 and further in 1929, the effects across the entire West were extensive and severe.

With the drying-up of short-term capital flows, most governments put in place a range of protectionist measures to stabilise their currencies (Arrighi 1994:

274; Hobsbawm 1999: 98–99). They turned inwards looking for solutions, leading to a structural collapse in world trade and finance. The scale of the disaster was extraordinary: in Europe from 1929 to 1932/3 industrial output fell by 27 per cent, in the United States it fell by 45 per cent (Crouzet 2001: 179). Unemployment was on 'an unimagined and unprecedented scale', in 1932–3 unemployment in the United States was around 27 per cent, in Britain it was 22–23 per cent and in most of Europe it exceeded 24 per cent, reaching a staggering 44 per cent in Germany (Hobsbawm 1999: 92). There were two important outcomes of the Depression, first it persuaded policy-makers that the unprecedented rate of unemployment could produce social and political chaos or indeed revolution. The growth in organised labour in the West and the Russian Revolution were further proof of this possibility. Second, it provided concrete evidence of the inadequacies of 'free markets' in achieving optimal economic and social outcomes, let alone maintaining political stability.

Commitment to planning was strengthened by the example of Russian communism from the late 1920s – workers and policy-makers looking to Russia saw an economy unaffected by the Depression. Rapid industrialisation took place under the Five Year Plans, industrial production tripled between 1929 and 1940 and there was no unemployment, though the social and personal costs of Stalinism were immense. The economic achievements 'impressed foreign observers of all ideologies' (Hobsbawm 1999: 96; Kennedy 1989: 321–25). Equally, Nazi Germany utilised strong state planning models to eliminate unemployment by the end of the 1930s. Thus, as Eric Hobsbawm (1999: 96) notes, '"Plan" and "Planning" became buzz-words in politics'.

Politicians, intellectuals, policy-makers and citizens in the United States and other Western liberal capitalist countries had overwhelming evidence that 'free markets' did not necessarily achieve full employment and that state planning could work (Ikenberry 1992: 292). The case for government planning (utilising the knowledge of experts) and an expanded role for the state solidified when economic theory caught up with practice via 'Keynesianism', which developed from John Maynard Keynes's *General Theory* (1936).[1] There was a profound change in the approach of liberal capitalist states to the role of government intervention in the economy – there was a new openness to the idea of economic planning and of state participation in the economy. This receptiveness to national economic planning at a state level also influenced thinking about the possibilities for economic cooperation at an international level – a development that eventually resulted in the establishment of the World Bank. Keynesianism thus underpinned the Bank's development theory and practice for decades.

The Great Depression was also a 'landmark in the history of anti-imperialism and Third World liberation movements' (Hobsbawm 1999: 204). Although Britain had been dealing with independence movements in some of its colonies, especially those with large expatriate populations, it was really only with the large-scale economic dislocation of the Depression that these movements became widespread. The effects of the Depression were even more profound in many of the dependent economies than in the Western liberal states, because their terms of trade deteriorated dramatically (Hobsbawm 1999: 213). Some industrialisation did take place in settler colonies during the First World War and again during the protectionist era of the Depression; nevertheless, most colonies remained, or were reduced to, overwhelmingly agrarian and rural societies. The severe impacts radicalised many local elites, who had previously supported and had been implicated in colonial rule. The independence movements already under way in Egypt and India expanded, and, by the mid-1930s, there were powerful movements organising in French North Africa and Indochina and in Dutch-controlled Indonesia.

In the United States, the commitment to planning was taken up in the mid-1930s with the New Deal policies of the Roosevelt administration. However, these policies were only partially implemented and 'were insufficient to stimulate the economy and take advantage of this underutilized productive capacity' (Kennedy 1989: 331). In 1937, when the United States finally seemed to be undergoing a slow recovery from the Depression, Department of Treasury economists (the 'men of sound judgement' as John Kenneth Galbraith (1977: 218) ironically labelled them) successfully convinced the Roosevelt administration to follow classical economic prescriptions: spending was cut and taxes increased in order to bring the Federal budget into balance. This led to a new slump and a renewed increase in unemployment. The 1937 recession made Keynesianism respectable in Washington. However, as Galbraith (1977: 221) argues, policy actions continued to be 'half-hearted' and in 1939 unemployment was still at 17 per cent, until '[t]he war then brought the Keynesian remedy with a rush'.

The shift in hegemony that was heralded by the First World War was solidified by the Second. The Keynesian 'rush' provided by the Second World War unleashed a massive expansion in US productive capacity:

> [i]ts standard of living was higher than any other country's, but so was its per capita productivity. Among the Great Powers, the United States was the only country which became richer – in fact, much richer – rather than poorer because of the war.
>
> (Kennedy 1989: 358)

US gold reserves at the end of the war were around two-thirds of the world's total. It had half of the world's manufacturing production and a third of all production; it was also the world's greatest exporter. For the first time, the United States had a net current account surplus that was significantly larger than its trade surplus. It had near complete control over international liquidity and world financial power became centralised in the city of New York (Arrighi 1994: 275).

In addition to aiding the United States' drive to becoming hegemonic economically, the Second World War changed its internal political alliances (as Gramsci would say, its historic bloc) by the blow it dealt to the isolationist element in the US Congress. It was clear that US security was no longer inviolable. As Arrighi (1994: 276) puts it: 'US political isolationism had reached the point of diminishing returns'. Many policy-makers felt that the failure of the United States to take a leadership role in the interwar period had encouraged the turn to protectionism that they identified as the prime cause of the war. Further, they considered that the level of mal-distribution of income across the (liberal capitalist) globe would hurt US foreign trade and investment. The Roosevelt administration's foreign policy was fundamentally an extension of New Deal philosophy, which saw government spending as the key to social advancement. In foreign policy, aid was seen as the equivalent to domestic social welfare; it would provide security, deter communism and draw states into a liberal market system (Arrighi 1994: 277).

Before considering the debates in the US Administration and Congress during postwar planning and the ratification of the Bretton Woods agreements, the chapter explores the ideological terrain of the period, especially the shift in economic thinking that took place prior to, and during, the Second World War. It explains the origins of the Keynesian, welfare, modernisation model that was the dominant approach in nation-state development for three decade after the Second World War (Fine 2001b: 133).

Changing economic theory: neoclassical economics and Keynesianism

Economics was well established as a discipline by the interwar period. Neoclassical economics largely superseded classical economics in the 1870s and had developed a set of central assumptions, concepts and theories (Roll 1973: 369, 455). Many of its underlying assumptions and commitments still derived from classicism, in particular the commitment to private property, individual freedom and limited government intervention and the assumptions about labour and capital mobility and objective individual wants (Roll 1973: 427). However, neoclassical economics was clearly a break from classicism, with a more individualistic approach to society, which emphasised consumption, demand and utility (of conglomerations of individuals), over production, supply and costs.

The operational form of the new individualism was a psychological and subjective approach to value, 'utility', which replaced the classical Labour Theory of Value. The utility approach posited that value is determined by a subjective estimate of utility tied to quantity. The focus on utility went hand-in-hand with the so-called 'marginal revolution', which focused economics on measuring small changes in economic quantities. The research agenda was formed by Gossen's Law on diminishing returns and the theory of marginal utility, which provides a measure of the 'alteration in the subjective conditions which would be occasioned by either the disappearance or the addition of some object' (Roll 1973: 426). The focus became deriving optimal utility by examining marginal increases in consumption.

The other main element of the neoclassical research agenda was its focus on equilibrium, at the level of individual and markets and at the aggregate social level. General equilibrium was simply the sum of individual equilibriums. The key question for economists was: is there theoretically a price configuration for commodities at which supply equals demand? And if 'there is such a theoretical price configuration, can general equilibrium be obtained … and would the general equilibrium state be stable?' (Gee 1991: 83). One of the first neoclassical economists to deal with this issue was Léon Walras (1834–1910). Walras's solution built on the work of Jean-Baptiste Say, in particular, Say's Law, which posits that supply creates its own demand, and therefore there is no oversupply or undersupply of commodities. Examining general equilibrium, Walras theorises that every demand, or desire to purchase something at a particular price, involves giving up money in order to do so; thus when consumers realise demand they supply someone with money of equal value. Every realised demand is also, effectively, a supply. At the aggregate level, the aggregate of all demand equals the aggregate of all supply at the general equilibrium price. This is the point of general equilibrium (Gee 1991: 84–85). Walras demonstrated that a general equilibrium price theoretically exists; however, the problem of demonstrating whether general equilibrium can be attained in the real world remained (Gee 1991: 85). General equilibrium models rely on the following assumptions: individuals are price takers, implying perfectly competitive commodity markets; all firms make the same 'normal' rate of profits, implying perfectly competitive factor markets; and there is freedom of entry. An understanding of the key neoclassical ideas is required for both the Keynesian critique of general equilibrium and the work of later neoclassical economists who became powerful voices in development economics and practice.

As James Meade (1975: 82) pointed out, the 'Keynesian revolution' needs to be seen as a two headed animal – 'first, the theoretical revolution in economic analysis; and, second, the practical revolution in governmental policies'. In terms of economic analysis, Keynes's *magnum opus* was *The General Theory.* It provided both an extensive critique of neoclassical economics and developed an alternative framework for analysing liberal capitalist economic relations (Love 1991: 147). Keynes's critique of classical macroeconomics was based on assumptions he deduced from its microeconomics, he started with an analysis of the labour market and determinants of output that produce a supposed natural tendency towards full employment (and the associated level of full-employment output). In relation to the operation of markets, Keynes agreed with the neoclassical proposition that increases in aggregate demand would lead to price rises relative to money wages, but charged that workers with increasing job opportunities would not resist an associated fall in real wages. However, he disagreed that labour is focused on the acquisition of commodities and not subject to the 'money illusion', and suggested that workers do not necessarily withdraw their labour when the price of wage-goods increased and they could not establish real wages through their money wage agreements.

On Say's Law, Keynes argued that it is not necessarily the case that incomes from production are spent at rates that result in market clearing and that various agents in the economy have differing and incompatible interests (Love 1991: 151). Next, he demonstrated that the interest rate does not, in fact, provide a simple connection between the decisions of savers and investors, as they have differing interests. As James Love (1991: 151) pointed out:

> [t]he importance of Keynes's comments on the classical theory is that once the nexus between savings and investment is broken, Say's Law no longer serves to avoid the possibilities of 'overproduction' and the possibility is admitted of having unemployment due to a deficiency of effective aggregate demand.

Keynes and other Cambridge economists had challenged the quantity theory of money, that money is exogenous to the economy, by demonstrating that cash holdings fluctuate with people's confidence in the economy (Love 1991: 152). In *The General Theory*, Keynes added a further dimension via an analysis of speculation driven by the profit motive. The main determinants of the amount of speculative liquidity held are the actual interest rate, the degree of uncertainty about future interest rates and the extent to which expectations parallel actual interest rates (Love 1991: 153). From this, Keynes concluded that money and monetary policy does impact on the rate of interest and the level of aggregate demand in the economy.

Building on this critique, Keynes developed an alternative framework whose key concept was effective demand – this is defined as the point at which aggregate demand and aggregate supply intersect and, as such, represents the point at which entrepreneurs' expectations of profits are maximised at an equilibrium rate of employment (Roll 1973: 486). The aggregate supply function is determined by firms' short-term expectations plus input costs, which produces a derived demand for labour. Aggregate demand is a function of employment derived from its relationship to expenditure and income. The key outcome of this formulation is that the level of employment, particularly in the short-term, is dependent on the level of aggregate demand and given that 'decisions on spending and on employment and production level are taken by different groups with different motivations, the level of employment resulting from the interaction of the aggregate demand and supply functions is not automatically a position of full employment' (Love 1991: 156).

Aggregate demand was at the centre of Keynes's framework in *The General Theory*; therefore, it examined three key factors influencing consumption and investment spending. First, the propensity to consume – for Keynes, real income was the main influence on consumption. Short-term consumption was presented as largely a stable, increasing function of real income with the proviso that people do not spend all of any increase in real income, instead they save an increasingly greater portion (Love 1991: 157–58). This is Keynes's famous Multiplier Theory, which in J. R. Hicks's statistical formulation became very influential in the teaching of economics. Second, consumption and investment spending were influenced by the marginal efficiency of capital.

This was a function of expectations and confidence, investment and the fact that information on the likely yields and the marginal efficiency of assets does not determine interest rates. The new development here was the key role that business confidence plays in determining the level of aggregate demand. The third influence was interest rates. Keynes's theory was built around the relationship between the preference for liquidity and nominal cash holdings; this made money a factor influencing output and employment (Love 1991: 160). His Liquidity Preference Theory held that people choose to hold liquid assets in preference to capital assets as they are safer or when they believe the current price of capital assets is too high (Meade 1975). The preference for holding cash, combined with the argument that it is difficult to lower interest rates beyond a certain point, meant if people saved more interest rates might not decline and investment increase. It could be that total demand would fall, which would flow through to reduced investment, employment and eventually savings. The outcome would be an equilibrium at a level of less than full employment (Galbraith 1975: 134).

The General Theory functioned as a theoretical tool to understand economic and social problems with great contemporary resonance (see Roll 1973: 455–58). It remained broadly within the liberal capitalist tradition and maintained the neoclassical and classical commitment to markets and private property. Keynes's critique was written with the purpose of saving liberal capitalism (and economics as a discipline) and making it function more effectively by not replacing it (Hunt 2002: 404; Robinson 1978: 65). Keynesianism has a capacity for diverse theoretical and policy-oriented interpretations that range from relatively conservative market-oriented to interventionist and welfare-statist positions. The World Bank's Articles of Agreement favoured a more conservative market-oriented approach.

Keynesianism and the later growth of development economics helped consolidate the nation-state as *the* way to organise society, and it gave the state a central role in development (Berger 2004). It both coincided with, and contributed to, changes in civil and political debates in most capitalist societies regarding the appropriate role and reach of the state. This was the revolution in practical governmental policy that Meade (1975: 87) and others argued was 'of much greater importance and significance for the welfare of mankind' than the revolution in macroeconomics.

Concurrently with Keynes's contribution, major advances in the statistical sophistication of national income accounting measures occurred. Pioneering work started in the 1920s; however, the theoretical developments of Keynesianism provided a significant stimulus to statistical methods. Time series data were developed using a Keynesian scheme of income/consumption and savings/investment. By the mid-1940s, general agreement had been reached that the purpose of statistics was to measure goods and services available for national consumption or wealth creation and development of social accounts for use in 'both diagnosis and prescription in economic policy' (Roll 1973: 508). The World Bank later utilised these agreed techniques and purposes and became a key disseminator of them across the developing world. Indeed, statistical representations of economic concepts remain their primary instrument for assessing the life quality of people in developing countries.

Early postwar economic planning

(Non-communist) Postwar political and economic planning was dominated by the administrations in the United States and Great Britain and by the compromises they made to organise an international system to meet their interests. US global production and military hegemony, on the whole, set the agenda for economic planning, the US even provided drafts plans to which Great Britain and the other allies responded. Later, it hosted the key international conferences that created the postwar international structure. Dumbarton Oaks (August 1944) established 'the basic principles that would underlie and infuse the future United Nations Charter', and the San Francisco Conference (April 1945) developed the UN Charter in a mere two months (Groom 2000: 14). However, the first conference on postwar planning, Bretton Woods (July 1944), was concerned with the international economic order and shaped the character and nature of the institutions subsequently created.

Despite US prewar isolationism, the US Administration, in particular the State Department, began economic and political planning as early as the autumn of 1939, prior to becoming directly involved in the Second World War (Gardner 1980: 5). Peter Gowan (2003: 25; Peet 2003: 33) explained this phenomena as the product of a US project 'to penetrate existing capitalist states and reorganize their internal arrangements to suit US purposes'. However, a Gramscian approach suggests that hegemony requires more than coercion, which may be why the focus of postwar economic negotiations in the United States shifted from the State Department to the Treasury. In contrast to the State Department's sometimes aggressive tactics to push a controversial trade agenda, the Treasury shared a growing consensus with the British and others regarding the need for organisation of a postwar monetary system (Ikenberry 1992: 295–98).

The State Department and other parts of US political and civil society remained dominated by a laissez-faire philosophy that opposed government action and thought that the (supposedly) efficient allocation of world resources should be left to the international economic 'market' (Gardner 1980: 2–3). The laissez-faire approach was reinforced by the US political structure, which tended to subordinate international considerations to domestic ones. Fred Block (1977: 38–42) labels this group as 'business internationalists' and notes their key representatives in the State Department were Cordell Hull, Dean Acheson and William Clayton. In contrast, the Treasury Department and other sections of political/civil society were influenced by the inter-war 'lessons' and the Depression and as a result were committed to early, detailed planning for the postwar world, US involvement in postwar international institutions and adequate planning for postwar economic management (Gardner 1980: 4). Block (1977: 35) called this group national economic planners; they were represented in the Treasury Department by Henry Morgenthau and Harry Dexter White.

The Treasury view predominated during the later war years, partly because of its capacity to cooperate with the British. But the Bretton Woods institutions were significantly shaped by the trade-offs made in negotiating approval from a Congress dominated by those committed to laissez-faire (Gardner 1980: 77; Scammell 1983: 13). Nevertheless, the degree of autonomy given the US (and British) technical experts to develop plans and negotiate was remarkable (Ikenberry 1992: 297). It was Harry Dexter White from the US Treasury who drafted the 'Suggested Plan for a United and Associated National Stabilization Fund and a Bank for Reconstruction and Development of the United and Associated Nations in 1941'. By 1943, White had:

> abandoned the ambitious design of the international bank … and the fund became the major focus of his attention. When the plan for the fund was published in mid-1943 it was without a design for the bank. When the bank proposal was finally made public it had been stripped of the trappings of an international central bank, for the bank had been reduced to a more traditional international lending agency.
>
> (Block 1977: 46)

The British only really commenced detailed postwar planning in 1943. Keynes's plan for an International Clearing Union, produced largely as a response to the White plans, allowed expansion to add a body for postwar relief, rehabilitation and reconstruction (equivalent to the Bank), if it was not provided for elsewhere (see Block 1977; Gardner 1980; Mason and Asher 1973; Oliver 1971). However, no specific plans were drafted. White's plan became the basis for negotiations, but it was strongly Keynesian even if it was significantly less expansionary than Keynes's plan. During the course of these negotiations the Bank came to be known as the International Bank for Reconstruction and Development (IBRD).

Key features of the IBRD's articles of agreement

Purposes

The purposes of the Bank are listed below.

(i) To assist in the reconstruction and development of territories of members by *facilitating the investment of capital for productive purposes*, including the restoration of economies destroyed or disrupted by war … and the encouragement of the development of productive facilities and resources in less developed countries.

(ii) To *promote private foreign investment* by means of guarantees or participations in loans and other investments made by private investors; and when private capital is not available on reasonable terms, to *supplement private investment* ... .

(iii) To promote the *long-range balanced growth of international trade and the maintenance of equilibrium in balances of payments* by encouraging international investment for the development of the productive resources of members, thereby assisting in raising productivity, the standard of living and conditions of labor in their territories.

(iv) To arrange the loans ... so that the more useful and urgent projects, large and small alike, will be dealt with first.

(v) To conduct its operations with due regard to the effect of international investment on business conditions in the territories of members ...

(www.worldbank.org)

It is clear from the Purposes that the Bank was an institution designed to operate within, and indeed support, the expansion of a liberal capitalist international order and one clearly structured around nation-states. Three themes in the Purposes stand out: the relative commitment to reconstruction versus development; the emphasis placed on private investment and private markets for capital; and the Keynesian commitments to planning and labour conditions.

From White's early drafts to the discussions at Bretton Woods, reconstruction rather than development was at the forefront of the planners' minds. White's April 1942 draft identified the main objective of the Bank as, 'to provide capital for relief and reconstruction and otherwise facilitate a smooth post-war transition' (Oliver 1971: 27). Victor Urquidi (1996: 39), a member of the Mexican delegation to the Bretton Woods conference, confirmed that in the April 1942 draft, '"development" of the less developed nations was not to be one of the primary purposes of the Bank as outlined by White, though some recognition was give to the role of private direct investment'. Urquidi argued that the Mexican delegation was responsible for furthering the interests of economic development at Bretton Woods, highlighting the amendment the Mexican delegation submitted to Article III, Section 1(a) on Use of Resources. The amendment added to the clause that Bank resources were 'exclusively for benefit of members', the statement 'with equitable consideration to projects for development and projects for reconstruction alike' (Urquidi 1996: 40–42). However, the following Section, 1(b), gives 'special regard' to the costs of reconstruction and thus, to an extent, negates the focus on development.

The priority given to reconstruction was also evident in the way US bureaucrats used it to 'sell' the Bank to Congress. They indicated to Congress that the alternative to support for the Bank would be a loan to the British (Gardner 1980: 139). Further, as Edward Mason and Robert Asher (1973: 23) in the Bank's first official history, pointed out, the members with the most shares were largely concerned about issues of reconstruction and that was reflected in the early loans of the Bank. While the creation of the Bank can be seen as a remarkable step in international cooperation, it is clear that the Western liberal states at the core of its establishment were concerned with furthering their interests rather than with broad-scale international 'development'.

Clause (ii) of the Purposes on promoting private foreign investment is not simply neoclassical theory and practice, as it points to the system's hegemonic principles – markets and private investment. This clause focused the Bank on guaranteeing private investments rather than loans, a notable shift from White's 1942 draft, which placed equal emphasis on the Bank making loans out of its own capital (Oliver 1971: 28). The increased emphasis on guaranteeing private loans was one of the major contributions of the Europeans – the British and Dutch in particular. Mason and Asher (1973: 26) confirmed that it 'was all but the universal expectation of the founders of the Bank that its primary function would be to guarantee private investments'. In reality, direct lending has been the major focus of the Bank. This clause on private investment also highlights the 'appeal to economics rather than ethics' palpable in the Bretton Woods negotiations. As the Bank's second official history by Devesh Kapur, John Lewis and Richard Webb (1997: 70) pointed out, this pragmatism 'has colored the Bank's development efforts' ever since.

It is plausible that without the innovations proposed by Keynes and his colleagues in economic theory and practice, White's proposals for international bodies to regulate international economic relations would not have been conceived.[2] The connection to Keynesianism is visible in the Bank's underlying premise that the (liberal capitalist) international economy would not, left to its own devices, provide the capital required for reconstruction and development at a level that achieves near full employment. This was precisely what *The General Theory* argued theoretically and what the Great Depression had so potently demonstrated. Clause (iii) of the Purposes promoting 'the long-range balanced growth of international trade and the maintenance of equilibrium in balances of payments' potently combines classical commitments to free trade with Keynesian concerns of growth and adjustment.[3] The belief in the capacity of government planning and management by experts demonstrated in the Purposes also reflects Keynesian influence. The (limited) commitment to counter-cyclical investment on both a country and world scale in clause (v) is clearly a Keynesian remedy; however, this is an area where, perhaps unfortunately, the Bank has never dared to subsequently tread.

Bank membership and capitalisation

Membership of the Bank is only open to countries that are members of the IMF. The final size and structure of capitalisation, as outlined in Article II, largely followed the model in the White plan. The initial capital stock of the Bank was $10 billion, made up of 100,000 shares worth $100,000 each. Increases in the capital stock must be agreed to by 75 per cent of the IBRD's total voting power. As of 30 June 2002, it had 1,570,895 shares and a total capital stock of $189,505 million.

The British were successful in influencing the amount of subscribed capital that was paid in to the Bank. White's 1942 draft specified 50 per cent be paid in initially, whereas the final agreement was only 20 per cent with the remaining 80 per cent only called in to meet losses (Mason and Asher 1973: 20). Richard Gardner (1980: 118) posited that the conservative British position was because they themselves neither expected to use the Bank to obtain a loan, nor to be able to make a large contribution for lending to others, thus giving them limited influence. Of the 20 per cent paid-in subscription, only 2 per cent must be paid in gold or US dollars and the remaining 18 per cent in the member's currency. Given that, during the early years of Bank operations, the US dollar was the only convertible currency, the Bank's early loanable funds were in effect limited to the US contribution plus the contribution of other members in US dollars or gold (Mason and Asher 1973: 23–24). The small initial capital stock and even smaller paid-in component made the Bank reliant on financial markets for capital, which profoundly shaped its subsequent operations.

Lending capacity and conditions

White's early plan for the Bank included provisions for issuing its own international banknotes, which he assumed would be 'as good as gold'. This would have made its lending capacity many times the paid-in capital (Oliver 1971: 32). However, despite White's protests and the initial support of the US delegation, the Bank emerged from the Bretton Woods negotiations with a conservative lending capacity – as per Article III, Section 3 the Bank can only lend or guarantee amounts equal to a maximum of 100 per cent of its capital subscriptions, reserves and surpluses. Given Bank reliance on borrowed funds (which initially meant the New York capital market), this may have been a necessary strategy to gain investment support during an unstable period; however, it has significantly constrained the Bank ever since. The conservative debt-to-lending ratio reinforced the idea of a 'businesslike Bank' that came out of Bretton Woods (Kapur *et al.* 1997: 70).

White considered that the Bank's below-market interest rates would result in a high demand for its funds, and thus his 1942 draft included a number of tools to ensure that Bank loans be productively employed and repaid (Oliver 1971: 39). Many of these are in the Bank's Articles. Article III, Section 4, on conditions requires, among other things, that: (i) member governments guarantee loan repayments; (ii) loan funds must not be able to be borrowed on the market in the prevailing conditions; (iii) a 'competent committee' (i.e. experts) study each proposal and submit a written report of recommendation; (iv) the Bank should, using a prudent assessment (that is, examination of national accounts), be confident of the capacity of the borrower to repay the funds; and (v) 'Loans made or guaranteed by the Bank shall, except in special circumstances, be for the purpose of specific projects of reconstruction and development'. The overall impression is of a cautious lending programme, centred on market strictures and 'disciplined' by (Western) experts.

Interestingly, Section 5 of Article III specifies that loans are to be untied; in other words, they can be spent in the territory of any Bank member. Since 1951, this commitment has been linked to requirements in loan agreements for international competitive bidding where possible (Mason and Asher 1973: 26). Recently, the establishment of Trust Funds under the Bank's auspices has given donor countries a way around this clause. This section also contains anti-corruption measures, specifying that loans must be used 'only for the purposes for which the loan was granted' with due regard to 'economy and efficiency and without regard to political or other non-economic influences or considerations'.

Operations

Article IV returns to the issue of the source and types of Bank lending. At Bretton Woods there was a shift in 'the emphasis of Bank operations away from lending its own paid-in subscriptions and toward the lending of borrowed funds or the guaranteeing of private loans' (Oliver 1971: 49). This not only reflected the British influence to limit paid-in amounts but also anchored the Bank to Western capitalist financial markets. Section 3, Article IV, specifies that Bank loans are generally denominated in the currencies of members, 'other than the member in whose territories the project is located' and only in 'exceptional circumstances' cover the local currency components of loans. Exceptional circumstances has been the subject of differing interpretations by the Bank over the years – the interpretation has become increasingly liberal and the tendency to allow funding for local currency components of projects has grown. Section 4 gives the Bank 'complete discretion' over the terms and conditions of loans and guarantees (Mason and Asher 1973: 27). Combined with the requirements under Article III, Section 4, the Bank is given extraordinary capacity to set conditions on loan agreements.

Section 10 of Article IV says the Bank shall:

> [n]ot interfere in the political affairs of any member; nor shall they be influenced in their decisions by the political character of the member or members concerned. Only economic considerations shall be relevant to their decisions, and these considerations shall be weighed impartially in order to achieve the purpose stated in Article I.

It is clear that the distinction made between politics and economics is an artificial and theoretical one and the Bank over its history has made decisions that show how blurred this line frequently becomes. For example, for most of its history, the Bank did not make loans to public enterprises engaged in the manufacturing sector, arguing that such enterprises were not likely to be efficiently managed – is this an economic or a political judgement?

Organisation and management

Little time was spent at Bretton Woods on the Bank's organisational structure – Article V is 'nearly an exact copy of the Fund's Articles XII and XIII'

(Mason and Asher 1973: 29). The Article covers the issues of voting rights, management structure and office location. The agreement on voting rights points to the 'realist' heart at the centre of what has, at times, been portrayed as a somewhat 'idealist' attempt to create international organisations to manage postwar international economic relations at Bretton Woods. Voting rights are linked to the amount of shares held – each member has 250 votes plus one additional vote for each share of stock held. The largest shareholders – the countries that provide the main guarantee behind the Bank's bond issues and loans on money markets – are Organization for Economic Cooperation and Development (OECD) countries. Indeed, there is little incentive for developing countries to have large subscriptions to the Bank because subscriptions are independent of borrowing rights, in contrast to the Fund, where subscriptions are linked to drawing rights (Mason and Asher 1973: 30).

The voting formula, derived from White's 1942 draft for the Bank, was completed with only minor changes. White initially proposed each member only receive 50 votes plus one additional vote for each share of stock held (Oliver 1971: 27). The increase to 250 basic votes was a compromise to ideals of equal representation over the power-based formula. However, as capital increases have occurred there has been no matching increase in the basic votes; thus the value of these has significantly declined (Leech and Leech 2006: 33).

White also proposed that no one country should have more that 25 per cent of the total votes. This derived from his belief that subscriptions should be linked to national incomes and assessment that the American Congress could only be induced to a subscription of around $2.5 billion. If, as he assumed, the US subscription was to be 25 per cent, this gave a figure for total capitalisation of $10 billion. The 25 per cent was important as it gave the US an effective veto on most key decisions, as these would, in his draft, require a four-fifths majority vote. The final voting formula for Bank decisions (other than amendment of the Articles, see below) was 50 per cent of the votes cast, thus reducing direct US influence. However, with the Soviet Union's refusal to ratify the Bretton Woods agreement, the United States initially had 35.07 per cent of votes and the United States and European countries combined controlled 74 per cent of votes (Mason and Asher 1973: 800–02). Despite the influx of new members in the 1960s, by June 1971 the United States and the Europeans still held 61 per cent of the vote. As of March 2007, the United States controlled 16.84 per cent of the votes and the combined voting power of Western Europe, North America, Japan, Australia and New Zealand was over 56 per cent (World Bank Group Website).

A Board of Governors, consisting of representatives appointed from each member country, oversees the Bank. The Board's responsibilities include: admitting or suspending members; increasing or decreasing the capital stock; and adjudicating appeals on interpretations of the Articles made by the Executive Directors. Nominally, most of the formal power in decision-making lies with the Executive Directors who are responsible for the 'conduct of the general operations of the Bank'. In reality the President and senior management have substantial control. Directors are elected for two-year terms and are paid by the Bank, not by member governments. The original 12 Executive Directors was expanded to 24 through a series of increases, the last in 1995 (Kapur *et al.* 1997: 1205). Five Executive Directors are appointed directly by those member countries with the largest number of shares (United States, Japan, Germany, UK, France) and the remainder are elected by the Board of Governors. Smaller states generally pool their votes in relatively stable groups, with the job of Executive Director often passed around members of a group.

Directors are able to cast the same number of votes at meetings that they received at their election. These groups have often resulted from historical or colonial relationships or from geographic factors. There are a number of groups with one member (generally a developed country) who dominates the group.[4] At Bretton Woods, the British and the United States disagreed about the role of the Executive Directors. Keynes and the British felt that the Directors should see themselves as international civil servants. The United States wanted and achieved 'close governmental control' of their representative (Mason and Asher 1973: 30). But this is not the case for group-elected Directors, who can be voted in by a group comprising more than 20 states, yet there are no rules about whose interest they are there to represent (Leech and Leech 2006: 40–41; Woods 2006: 190–92). Theoretically, the Executive Directors select the President of the Bank; however, an informal agreement between the United States and the Europeans means the United States selects the head of the Bank and the Europeans the head of the IMF (see following chapter for details). The President is the chief of operating staff of the Bank and controls its ordinary business 'under the direction of the Executive Directors'.

Article VIII specifies the requirements for amendments to the Articles – most amendments require three-fifths of the members with 85 per cent of the voting power. This was increased from 80 per cent in 1989, leaving the United States (16.41 per cent of voting power) with an ongoing veto on amendments. One hundred per cent of members are required for amendments that modify the right to withdraw from the Bank; rights to subscribe to increases in the authorised capital stock; and limitations on liability.

The British compromised on the location of the principal offices of the Bank (and Fund), which, as stated in the Articles of Agreement, were to 'be located in the territory of the member holding the greatest number of shares'. Undoubtedly the Bank's location in the United States has had a profound influence on the Bretton Woods twins. The controversy surrounding their precise location continued at the first meeting of the Bank and Fund in Savannah.

Selling the Bretton Woods agreements to Congress

President Roosevelt did not forward the Articles of Agreement of the Bank and Fund to Congress until January 1945. Beforehand, there was a major publicity campaign to gain support for the institutions and the formation of an opposition, which, although not broadly based, created some difficulties for the US Administration (Gardner 1980: 129; Block 1977: 53–55). The opposition was largely focused on the operations of the Fund; however, contrary to the commonly held position that the Bank 'escaped practically unscathed', the debate had a significant impact on the Bank (Mason and Asher 1973: 33–34). There was an attack on the (supposed) relative lack of control by the United States, particularly in relation to the Fund's provision of liquidity. This resulted in the administration tightening its national control over the Fund and Bank by subordinating American Executive Directors to a National Advisory Council and increasing the commitment to conditionality (Gardner 1980: 135–5). These issues were further played out in Savannah.

The US Administration claimed that the Bank and Fund could deal with postwar transition and reconstruction problems. They argued that if the institutions were not ratified, special reconstruction aid for Britain would be imperative. As Gardner (1980: 140) noted, the enthusiastic atmosphere of the time also contributed to the tendency 'to claim all good things for the Bank and Fund'. At the end of the day, the ideas behind the Bretton Woods agreement played enough of a politically integrating role to ensure their passage through the US Congress as well as garnering broader international support. John Ikenberry (1992: 316) noted that the Bretton Woods Agreements 'allowed political leaders and social groups across the political spectrum to envisage a post-war economic order in which multiple and previously competing objectives could be met simultaneously'. It was, in Gramscian terms, a change in the intellectual terrain that helped shape changing historic national blocs and, in a time of crisis and hope, facilitated a change to the underpinnings of international (but US led) capitalist hegemony.

The Soviet Union did not take part in the ceremony in Washington to deposit the ratifications for the Bretton Woods twins on 27 December 1945. Documents released from the Russian foreign ministry in the mid-1990s show that, until shortly before this ceremony, Soviet officials were in fact preparing to join the institutions (James and James 1994: 616–17). It seems that the Soviet Union postponed its decision, in part, to improve its leverage on the United States for greater postwar financial assistance. However, growing Cold War tensions resulted in an end to discussions about US loans.

The death of Roosevelt in April 1945 had already tipped the scales of power in Washington. Even as the Bretton Woods Agreements were passed, the State Department was reasserting its control over US foreign policy. The State Department, dominated by business internationalists, opposed the Bretton Woods agreements and pursued an alternative strategy based on the Key Currency Plan of John Williams, which meant a major loan for Britain in return for their cooperation in moving towards a liberal world economy. The resurgent nationalism, the 'tense and critical atmosphere' of the loan negotiations with the British, where the United States tended to coercive tactics and the developing Cold War tensions, provided the backdrop to the meeting at Savannah (Gardner 1980: 207).

Conclusion

This chapter has covered ideological, theoretical and political territory in explaining the origins of the IBRD. It has explored the transfer of international hegemony from the British to the United States, which originated from a structural crisis linked to the Depression and war. It was equally associated with the development and implementation of new ideas about the international organisation and management of capitalism. Nevertheless, the establishment of the Bretton Woods institutions was dependent on a small window of opportunity for change that was quickly closed by shifts in the US historic blocs and by rising Cold War tension.

Through consideration of the roles of White and Keynes, this chapter has placed the Bretton Woods negotiations in the context of the broader hegemonic developments of the Second World War era. In particular, it has examined the increasing acceptability of government planning provoked by the Depression and the impact of Russian communism, which was given theoretical expression in Keynesian economic theory. In practice this became the Keynesian, welfare, modernisation model, which provided the intellectual and practical backdrop for the founding of the World Bank at Bretton Woods. This contextualisation allows for a different interpretation of the Bank's Articles of Agreement, highlighting its ongoing classical/ neoclassical commitment to free trade overlaid with Keynesian commitments to state investment and planning. It positions White and Keynes as fundamentally committed to the Keynesian, welfare, modernisation project and their differences as the product of commitments to the perceived needs of their respective countries and governments.

Analysing the Articles and the debates between Keynes and White highlight the hegemonic principles underlying the system. For example, White's voting system linked to countries' capital subscriptions to the Bank was designed to give the United States a dominant role and it was approved at Bretton Woods with only minor modification. Analysis of the Keynes/White debates also gives an insight into the tensions within this hegemony; for example, Keynes wanted the Bank to have a more international focus that he believed would be friendlier to British capitalism. He attempted unsuccessfully to achieve this in his challenges over the role of Executive Directors and location of Bank offices. Thus the changing structures of global economic, financial and military power coincided with a theoretical and institutional realignment. The Bank's origins and purpose reflect these major transformations.

3 From Savannah to structural adjustment

This chapter reviews the Bank's growth from a small, relatively conservative lender, which had difficulty finding a president, to the leading international development agency. As President throughout the 1950s, Eugene R. Black oversaw the slow growth of a hard-nosed banking organisation that lent to a handful of mostly medium-income countries. It was a bank focused on infrastructure projects, in particular power and transportation. The 1960s was a decade of two halves for the Bank, the first half saw a notable expansion not just of the organisation but of its mission through the creation of the International Development Association (IDA) in 1961. George D. Woods' presidency (1963–8) saw further expansion in the Bank's mission. Despite this expansion, the second half of the 1960s was a difficult time for the Bank both fiscally and politically as the problems of the US economy limited its budget and as US foreign policy turned inward and became more conservative, slowing the Bank's expansion. Nevertheless, Woods' expansionary vision set the tone for the subsequent presidency of Robert Strange McNamara; Woods even lobbied for McNamara's selection.

McNamara's term had two distinct phases: 1968–73 and 1974–81. During the first phase, the key development was the rapid growth in the Bank's lending portfolio. The second phase was marked by McNamara and the Bank's 'discovery' of poverty and a strategy to address it – integrated rural and later urban development programmes. McNamara's tenure ended as neoliberalism became the intellectual force behind *pax americana*. In the Bank, neoliberalism made its appearance through the introduction of structural adjustment lending. While the Black and Woods' presidencies established much of the Bank's organisational and operational structure, it was McNamara's reign that transformed the Bank from a reflection of *pax americana* to an institution that was a key force in establishing and reproducing that hegemony.

The inaugural meeting of Bank and Fund at Savannah

The inaugural meeting of the Board of Governors of the International Monetary Fund (IMF) and World Bank took place from 8 March 1946, in Savannah, Georgia. Keynes, leading the British delegation, wanted to ensure the organisations were internationalist and expansionary. However, the atmosphere in

Washington had changed: US political views were less internationalist and they employed coercive tactics to achieve national interests. The US delegation, led by the relatively conservative Fred Vinson, Secretary of the Treasury, wanted the Bretton Woods twins subject to relatively close (i.e. US) government control. They opposed Keynes' lobbying to appoint White as the first managing director of the Fund. Vinson did not have a good relationship with White and, one month prior to Savannah, had been given an FBI report by President Truman naming White as a probable Soviet spy (Van Dormael 1978: 287).[1] To block White, the US delegation argued it was necessary for the Bank to be headed by an American in order to gain the confidence of Wall Street and that as it would be unseemly for an American to be head of both the Bank and Fund, a European should head the Fund (Block 1977: 74–75; Mason and Asher 1973: 39–40). This led to informal agreement that the United States selects the head of the Bank and the Europeans the Fund. The agreement continues to this day.

To ensure the internationalism of the institutions, Keynes – having agreed at Bretton Woods that they be located in the United States – wanted them in New York near the UN rather than in Washington, where they would be directly subject to pressures from the US Administration (Block 1977).[2] Vinson stepped in again and had the US President instruct the delegation that no compromise on location was acceptable. As Gardner (1980: 259) highlights, this 'decision was an important victory for the idea of close [US] national control of the Bretton Woods institutions. It was to have a profound effect on their future development'. With a view to insulation from the US Administration, Keynes wanted the Executive Directors to be part-time positions paid at medium levels. The United States insisted on full-time Executive Directors with high salaries by contemporary international standards. The US view of close control prevailed at all levels at Savannah, this ensured that the Bank and Fund were part of the US historic bloc, part of *pax americana* (Block 1977: 74; Mason and Asher 1973: 38–40).

The first meeting of Executive Directors of the IMF and World Bank took place in Washington on 7 May 1946. There was no president. The US had difficulty finding a suitable candidate prepared to assume the role (Caufield 1998: 50). They needed someone with high-level experience, contacts and standing – preferably in the banking sector as the Bank would be reliant on finance markets (Wall Street in particular). However, the US finance industry was suspicious of international schemes, given the experience of the Great Depression, and of the International Bank for Reconstruction and Development (IBRD) proposal. They persuaded Eugene Meyer to take the role (previously editor and publisher of *The Washington Post*) and on 4 June he became President. The Bank formally opened for business on 25 June 1946.

Early Bank operations: 1946–9

There was relatively little lending activity from 1946 to the end of 1948 and that which did occur was primarily for postwar reconstruction projects. The

Bank started developing its business-oriented, technocratic model for lending. This model had its origins in the Bank's Purposes but was reinforced by new appointments to the Bank (mostly bankers and technical experts) and its difficulty in raising capital. These factors and the priority given to infrastructure projects shaped the Bank's 'character' for over a decade.

Without having raised capital or committed any loan funds, Meyer resigned as President after just six months on the job. His resignation is generally attributed to frustrations with the Bank structure, which gave the Executive Directors a large degree of formal control and the President responsibility without authority (Mason and Asher 1973: 47). The US Administration had difficulties finding a replacement; John J. McCloy was asked twice and was only convinced to take up the position after a commitment that the Executive Directors would interfere less with day-to-day operations (Mason and Asher 1973: 49–50; Sommers 1984: 31). This pushed the Bank towards a hierarchical structure with strong central control by a single individual – a model that continues. This structure also reinforced US influence over the Bank with an American President, selected by the current US Administration in the context of the Bank being close to the United States physically.

McCloy started work in March 1947 bringing Robert L. Garner as Vice President and Eugene R. Black as US Executive Director. These appointments started another tradition in the Bank – a preference for senior management with commercial backgrounds. McCloy was a Wall Street lawyer who, as was common at the time, had had administration experience as Assistant Secretary of War (1941–5). Garner had been a banker and vice president of the General Foods Corporation. Black had been a vice president of the Chase National Bank of New York. It is not surprising that the 'faith of the new trio in private investment as a panacea for the economic ills of the world was almost boundless' (Mason and Asher 1973: 51). None of the senior management of the Bank had development backgrounds, another tradition that continues. This is not surprising for the Bank's establishment period: early Bank staff member, Davidson Sommers explained 'when the Bank started, people in the West didn't know much about the developing world except as colonies. They didn't know much about development lending, didn't know much about development economics' (cited in Kapur *et al.* 1997: 82–83).

Another factor shaping Bank operations was the initial difficulty it had in raising capital. The Great Depression led to significant suspicion among Americans about international bonds. Many individual US states still had bans on the sale of foreign bonds, and some actually 'imposed new bans specifically aimed at the World Bank' (Caufield 1998: 50). However, at the end of the Second World War, the United States was the only country with surplus funds to purchase bonds. The subsequent difficulty in raising capital contributed to the Bank's early cautiousness with loans and its close scrutiny of proposals to ensure they were sound, and appeared to be so to Wall Street.

In April 1947, the first of the Bank's early reconstruction loans was finalised. The loan to France was followed by three further reconstruction loans to

Western European countries – the Netherlands, Denmark and Luxembourg. However, the IBRD was simply not large enough to meet Europe's financial need (Scammell 1983: 29). In early June 1947, George Marshall, Secretary of the State Department, made a speech at Harvard University acknowledging the scale of the transition problem. Shortly thereafter a massive US balance of payments support programme for Europe was launched – the Marshall Plan ran from 1948 to 1952 and disbursed over $12.7 billion in three years, contrasting to the Bank's paltry commitment of just $497 million of loans by late 1948 (Kapur *et al.* 1997: 74). The Marshall Plan was not just 'magnificent philanthropy' it was also 'the price to the United States of building a ring of containment to Soviet territorial ambition' (Scammell 1983: 31). Equally, it was the price of building an economic sphere that was sympathetic to US needs; it was in a number of ways the price of *pax americana*.

The IBRD continued to lend to developed countries, but reconstruction lending essentially ended with the loan to Luxembourg in August 1947. McCloy understood that once the Marshall Plan was operational, IBRD reconstruction aid would be redundant (Kapur *et al.* 1997: 74). As William Ascher (1990: 117) points out, the Plan may have ended much of the flow of funds to Europe but it did not change the Bank's underlying rationale of facilitating, predominately US, private capital investment to the world. Indeed, the growing Cold War gave a new urgency to that mission. It was now a question of where to lend, and the search for a new target took some time. With its only loan during 1948, a development loan to Chile, the Bank started out in its new market – developing countries (Mason and Asher 1973: 53).

In January 1949, President Truman's famous four points speech underlined the growing Cold War threat and gave legitimacy to the Bank's focus on developing countries through its hastily added final point, which '*inaugurated the "development age*"' (Rist 1997: 71). It is worth quoting from the speech because not only was it part of the inspiration for the formation of the IDA (Peet 2003: 116), but the similarities with what was to become the Bank's development model are striking.

> Fourth, we must embark on a bold new program for making the benefits of our scientific advances and industrial progress available for the improvement and growth of the underdeveloped areas. …
>
> The United States is pre-eminent among nations in the development of industrial and scientific techniques. The material resources which we can afford to use for assistance of other peoples is limited. But our imponderable resources in technical knowledge are constantly growing and are inexhaustible.
>
> I believe that we should make available to peace-loving peoples the benefits of our store of technical knowledge …
>
> And, in cooperation with other nations, we should foster capital investment in areas needing development.

> The old imperialism – exploitation for foreign profit – has no place in our plans. What we envisage is *a program of development* based on the concepts of democratic fair dealing.
>
> (cited in Rist 1997: 71, emphasis added)

The Bank commenced research to determine what its 'productive purposes' were and which types of key investments would not receive financing from private sources as stipulated in the Articles of Agreement. The Bank's senior managers considered that light manufacturing and export industries in developing countries should be funded from private sources, so they were excluded from consideration. Further, McCloy, Garner and Black were ideologically opposed to investment in state-run enterprises other than utilities. A consensus that dominated Bank lending for over a decade was reached fairly quickly, namely that public utilities, especially electricity, transport and communications, were the key prerequisites for achieving economic growth via private investment (Mason and Asher 1973: 150–51 and 458–61). Despite being designed by practitioners, the impact of the 'Keynesian, welfare, modernisation consensus' is visible, although the welfare component, the most controversial element for business internationalists, was simply dropped. The Bank's consensus extended to avoiding public investment in welfare-related areas such as sanitation, education and health care as their contribution to economic growth was 'less measurable and direct than that of power plants' (Mason and Asher 1973: 151).

In determining which public utilities to fund, Urquidi, an early Bank staffer, notes the 'Bank's "bottom line" in judging a project was the "times earned column" on a spreadsheet' (Urquidi 1996: 48). This is an example of the privileged status of newly available economic data and national accounting. The Bank's public focus on individual projects could be misleading – it was just as interested in a lender's overall creditworthiness and thus in its overall economic policy priorities and settings (Kapur *et al.* 1997: 125).

By 1949, Bank assessment of loans had turned into a programme involving the Bank managing the development of loans proposals and providing technical assistance to that end. Here is the Keynesian, modernisation model's emphasis on (Western) 'experts'. The Bank's assessments covered development, assessment and supervision of projects and the planning and management of economies utilising data on monetary, fiscal and balance of payments positions to determine policy. The model of the 'fly-in, fly-out' Western expert became the norm. The economist, Albert Hirschman (cited in Rich 1994: 74), described how, to assist planning in Columbia, the Bank expected him to formulate within a few weeks:

> some ambitious economic development plan that would spell out investment, domestic savings, growth and foreign aid targets for the Columbian economy over the next few years. All of this was alleged to be quite simple for experts mastering the new programming techniques: apparently there now existed adequate knowledge, even without close study of local

> surroundings, of the likely range of savings and capital-output ratios, and those estimates, joined to the country's latest national income and balance of payments accounts, would yield all the figures needed.

The level of confidence in economic data and the methods of econometric analysis are quite remarkable. Although data on government revenue, expenditure and national trade had been collected for a long time and attempts to estimate national income were made in the 1860s, it was not until the Second World War that the first attempts were made in the West to produce reliable national accounts (Cairncross 1988: 17–19). The quality of data collection in many developing countries was questionable to say the least, and the decisions made about the composition of national accounts impacted on economists' understanding. In particular, the decision not to include household production in national accounts discounted its importance in the economy and its role in balancing activity during economic downturns (Ironmonger 1988: 41–42).[3] This skews comparisons against economies with significant peasant or subsistence economies. The new programming models in which the Bank expressed so much faith were also in their early stages of construction and tended to (and still do) stress parsimony (Boumans 2005: 180). Faith in numbers remains a feature of the Bank's lending and analytical activities.

Along with providing experts, the Bank assisted developing countries to build local autonomous planning agencies (Rich 1994: 75). Staff in such agencies were trained by the Bank and had close intellectual relationships with Bank staff. They were often central to organising and managing Bank-funded projects and they promoted Bank-favoured macro- and microeconomic policies and influenced components of domestic historic blocs.

The Bank took its role in loan supervision to greater depths than mainstream banks (partly in order to win the trust of finance markets). The loan to Chile incorporated most of the key conditions that *still* characterise Bank lending, including 'close scrutiny and discussion of proposals; conditionality related to monetary, fiscal, and balance of payments policies that would bear on a country's capacity to repay; supervision of these funds; and a negative pledge' (Kapur *et al.* 1997: 81).[4] The principal condition on the loan to Chile was settlement with owners of prewar bonds on which the government had defaulted. Settlement of outstanding debt is a hegemonic capitalist principle that remains a core condition for access to Bank funds.

In 1948, the Bank commenced research for producing and publishing estimates of incomes in various countries (Kapur *et al.* 1997: 83). From these humble beginnings, the Bank became the largest development research organisation in the world. By the end of the 1940s, despite limited lending activity, most of the elements that dominated the Bank's management of lending through the 1950s and beyond were in place: a strong centralised bureaucratic structure; a conservative approach to lending that resulted in strong loan conditionality; a strong focus on infrastructure; and a belief in technocratic expertise to provide solutions to development problems. These techniques were in themselves scaffolds for a capitalist *pax americana* and they enabled Bank programmes that supported its various components of *pax americana*.

The 1950s

Lending got going after January 1949 and grew steadily during the presidency of Eugene Black from 1 July 1949. Ultimately though, it remained at rather modest levels throughout the 1950s: from 1949 until April 1961 (when the IDA was founded) the Bank made 280 loans in 56 countries, to the value of $5.1 billion (Kapur *et al.* 1997: 85). Up until 1957 annual commitments averaged only $307 million per annum; though they jumped to $600–700 million per annum in 1958–60, due primarily to increased assistance to India as it confronted a balance of payments crisis (Kapur *et al.* 1997: 90–92). World Bank lending remained dwarfed by US bilateral assistance, which averaged more than $1.8 billion per annum in the early 1950s. The focus remained on financing public utilities and infrastructure: power and transport accounted for over half of lending in the 1950s and over 78 per cent of loans to developing countries (Gwin 1997: 86). Dams were a major activity; they are included under various Bank sector classifications but made up a quarter of lending during Black's tenure (Caufield 1998: 73). Some 43 per cent of Bank loans in this period went to countries with already high levels of income and 10 per cent went to loans for colonial development – for projects largely designed to meet the raw material needs of Europe (Kapur *et al.* 1997: 93–99).

During the 1950s, the strength of the influence of US foreign policy concerns and priorities on the Bank became discernible. Anti-communism was more than a little visible in the Bank. President McCloy publicly and repeatedly stated that the Bank would 'create markets for U.S. trade ... [and] stop Communism' (cited in Caufield 1998: 53). Loans to encourage anti-communism were made to India (from 1949), Ethiopia and Nicaragua (from 1951) to cite just a couple of examples. Kapur *et al.* (1997: 102–3) argue that US political priorities clearly influenced Bank lending; this was a 'meeting of minds ... helped along by routine meetings with State Department officials, in which the Bank was often urged by State to "support" specific countries'. There are a few instances where the Bank has supported left-wing regimes (Tanzania and Romania for example), just as there are a few instances where the Bank has made loans despite the objections of its largest donors (e.g. 1978 to the Socialist Republic of Vietnam). They are notable as exceptions, made to demonstrate the Bank's notional independence, which even the US government has acknowledged is necessary for a Bank promoting capitalism sympathetic to *pax americana*.

The Bank's development model firmed during this period. As it expanded and sought to expand influence over lenders, a more sophisticated and academic approach to development was needed. One consequences of this was the establishment of a training institute and 'think tank' in 1956, the Economic Development Institute. Three features stand out about the Bank's development model during this time: it was never systematically described in Bank documentation (Mason and Asher 1973: 467); it selected elements from academic discourse to fit its ideas; and its model was quite different from that of UN development agencies and bilateral donors who focused more on basic needs. While it may have been a small player among UN agencies in its early years, it became the organisation with enough resources to implement its development agenda (Caufield 1998: 62).

How did the Bank's development model fit with the blossoming field of development economics during the 1950s? One of the most significant academic propositions put forward in the 1950s was the Prebisch–Singer thesis. This was derived from work published separately by Raúl Prebisch and Hans Singer on first–third world trade in 1950, which reached similar conclusions. Their work challenged the neoclassical theory of comparative advantage, which implied that countries should specialise in products in which they have relatively abundant factor endowments (Todaro 1977: 279–80). The Prebisch–Singer thesis said that, over time, the terms of trade for primary commodities declined because capital concentration and higher profit margins from industrialisation did not occur as much in competitive primary product markets as in manufacturing sectors (Rapley 2002: 13). Declining terms of trade for primary commodities would exacerbate the propensity of prices in industrialised countries to rise more quickly those than in less industrialised countries. This trend would be strengthened by differences in the income elasticity of demand, in other words by the consumer's tendency to increase demand for manufactured goods as their incomes rise.

The Prebisch–Singer thesis concluded that, over the long-term, developing countries would have to export ever-increasing quantities of primary commodities just to maintain their levels of imports from the industrialised world. To increase their imports, developing countries would have to increase exports even further. As John Rapley (2002: 14) notes, the consequence was that developing countries needed to 'alter the structure of the economy's production otherwise they would sink deeper into poverty'. Further, the implication was that trade between industrialised nations and those dependent on primary products – generally developing nations – involved unequal exchange (Rist 1997: 115).

The Prebisch–Singer thesis was a key impetus in the development of Dependency Theory, which set out to explain the empirical failure of 'trickle down' growth in Latin America (Rist 1997: 116). Dependency Theory went beyond the Prebisch–Singer thesis and posited that the world trading system, in concert with a section of the indigenous bourgeoisie, acted to shift wealth from traditional to the modern sectors. This occurs both within a developing society (the periphery) and between it and an already industrialised (core) one, contributing to a process of underdevelopment. Wealth, via exploitation, moves from the underdeveloped periphery to the developed core and, importantly, the core is *responsible* for the process of creating underdevelopment and impoverishment of the periphery.

The Prebisch–Singer thesis and Dependency Theory were quite influential in many developing countries. In practice, the resultant policy proposals were promotion of state-led development and import substitution industrialisation (ISI). State-led development produced policy proposals ranging from promotion of autarky to the more common proposition that the state had a key role in the distribution of investment and mediation of inequality (Rist 1997: 115). ISI is a way of promoting industrialisation by restricting imports of manufactured goods using tariff or non-tariff barriers as protection for local industries. State-led development and ISI became the developmental doctrine in much of Latin America, India, parts of Africa and in East Asia. Its outcomes were not always as planned. Where it was one part of an overall development programme and used strategically (e.g. East Asia) it showed promise, but in many countries it became associated with inefficiency and corruption (for an overview see Rapley 2002: 25–46).

Many mainstream economists believed the Prebisch–Singer thesis would not occur under free market conditions. Alternatively they argued, as per Paul Rosenstein-Rodan, that a 'big push' in infrastructure investment and careful development planning would combat declining terms of trade (Rapley 2002: 14). The World Bank's evolving development paradigm drew significantly on this idea, but it was equally informed by Modernization Theory, which was more in line with its founding fathers' ideas regarding development. Evolving from the behaviouralist turn in mostly US social science, Modernization Theory aimed to duplicate the conditions that had promoted development in the industrialised world in developing countries. As Mark Berger (2004: 47) notes, it had 'an emphasis on Fordist pay and production arrangements, Taylorist forms of labor organization, and a "paternalistic and protective", but modernizing state'. Its main conclusions about the reasons for underdevelopment were a shortage of capital (thus the prescription to increase savings) and an inappropriate value system (prescription: education in capitalist values). Modernization Theorists saw that underdevelopment was an initial phase and that developing countries would 'catch up' with some assistance from the West, which was assumed to be relatively benign (Rapley 2002: 15). It complemented the Bank's ideas about the necessity of 'trickle down' growth, with industrialisation starting in specific sectors and, thanks to comparative advantage, spreading across the economy (Kapur *et al.* 1997: 115). In the Bank's version, light industry was the key to 'take off' and borrowing governments were encouraged to promote this sector, rather than heavy industry, which was promoted by UN bodies, some academic analysis and, of course, many developing country governments. The Bank's would provide the infrastructure necessary for 'take off'. Social welfare would be dealt with in due course, as a result of development and need not form a specific part of lending. For Berger (2004: 61–62), Modernization Theory like much subsequent development economics:

> conflated capitalist development with national development and turned nation-states that flowed from complex and contested histories into unproblematic units to be developed and modernized, equating the governments of

> those nations with the nations themselves. This is directly linked to the way in which development economics and the idea of national development rested on an elitist and technocratic approach that conceived of development as a technical problem outside of history and politics.

The Bank's paradigm was not inconsistent with aspects of the work of development economists of the period from different sides of the fence and this contributed to its legitimacy. For example, the structuralist work of Prebisch emphasised the need for large-scale industrialisation, although apart from infrastructure the Bank saw that this should be achieved through the market (Kapur *et al.* 1997: 119). The classically shaped work of W. Arthur Lewis was also influential. Lewis saw that the rural sector was inefficient and that labour would have to be transferred to more productive industrial uses to achieve development (Todaro 1977: 188–91; Toye 1993: 52). Lewis' recasting of poverty as an employment problem facilitated debate among classically trained economists on addressing poverty and influenced the Bank's understanding of development during the McNamara years (Kapur *et al.* 1997: 226–27). Yet its approach remained at odds with many bilateral donors, in particular the United States, whose aid programme had a strong focus on winning the 'hearts and minds' of Third World peasants and thus funded social programmes in health, water supply and education.

The main change to the Bank's development thinking during the 1950s was on the absorptive capacity of developing countries. Initially, the Bank management firmly believed that absorptive capacity was very limited and that developing countries should raise the local currency requirements for projects domestically (Mason and Asher 1973: 480). By the mid-1950s, it saw much higher needs in developing countries. By the end of the 1950s, the Bank faced the problem of net negative transfers in some countries; that is, where borrowers pay more money back to it (typically in interest) than it disburses in new loans (Rich 1994: 79). It became clear to some at the Bank that, given a limited number of borrowers, continued lending may create a debt crisis: it would need to close its door once it had lent a certain amount or to continue to lend at a higher level. It was not coincidental that the Bank's revised understanding of absorptive capacity fitted with the reality of its need to continually increase lending to maintain fund flows and to avoid being dwarfed by large, predominately bilateral, capital flows.

The IBRD's lending jumped in the late 1950s and its sectors of lending expanded too: education, industry and agriculture were the main beneficiaries. Despite this, the outlook for the IBRD by the end of the 1950s was not great – its developed country borrowers were becoming too 'developed' to meet the criteria in the Bank's Articles of Agreement that countries should not be able to access commercial credit. Further, many of the big borrowers were already facing problems with their levels of debt according to the Bank's existing debt-servicing ratios and the least-developed countries were not considered creditworthy enough to access IBRD funds (Mason and Asher 1973:

380). The establishment of the IDA in 1960, which expanded the Bank's lending capacity, was a godsend to the Bank, yet one with a sting in the tail – the IDA's need for regular replenishments by its big donors gave those donors new capacity to influence the Bank, and the United States remained the major donor (Woods 2006: 27–28).

The IDA and the 1960s

Bank President Eugene Black welcomed the IDA's establishment despite reservations about its potential impact on the IBRD's standing in financial markets. Black acknowledged that the IDA was in part the product of Cold War politics increasingly being played out in developing countries (Kapur *et al.* 1997: 136). The IDA was a multilateral channel for soft loans to promote anti-communism but also part of a second wave of building development institutions that occurred between 1958 and 1962. Developing countries had called for a new large development fund under UN control (called the Special United Nations Fund for Economic Development). A World Bank-controlled fund was, for the Eisenhower administration, preferable to a UN agency, because the Bank's weighted voting structure gives significant control to the United States and the West, whereas UN agencies (the Security Council aside) have a one country one vote system and, by the end of the 1950s, the UN was numerically dominated by developing countries. The United States also preferred the Bank's business-like approach to development compared to the operations of other agencies (Kapur *et al.* 1997: 137). Moreover, the United States initially envisioned the IDA as a way to deal with its excess holdings of non-convertible currencies, although at the end of the day this did not occur (Mason and Asher 1973: 386–93).

The IDA was created under separate Articles of Agreement rather than by amendment of the IBRD Articles. This was due to Black's concerns to protect the IBRD's standing in financial markets but it also prevented attempts to revise the IBRD's Articles (Mason and Asher 1973: 389–90). The IDA's Articles are largely a duplication of the IBRD's, with three exceptions: first, they specify which countries are developed (Part I) and which are developing (Part II) and link contributions to this status. This division was a way of rationing access to IDA resources, which were likely to be oversubscribed.[5] Second, the voting structure is marginally more favourable to developing countries – in March 2007, Part I countries controlled 62.77 per cent of the IBRD's votes while they controlled only 58.44 per cent of the IDA's votes (World Bank Group Website). Third, despite misgivings of the Bank's senior management, the Articles allow the financing of social projects. This was not only the product of the demands of developing country members, the United States and other developed countries saw social expenditures as essential to combating communism. The focus remained on project financing; however, the definition of a 'specific project' was enlarged to include sectoral efforts. In this way, the IDA paved the way for greater programme lending (Kapur *et al.*

1997: 168; Mason and Asher 1973: 391–94). IDA funds are called credits to distinguish them from IBRD loans.

The Bank's expansion into social areas proceeded slowly in the 1960s. It was constrained by the initial IDA capitalisation of only $1 billion (of which only around $750 million was in useable funds). Generating enough quality proposals was always a problem for the IBRD, whereas IDA resources, given their concessional nature, were and continue to be oversubscribed. Their allocation is an ongoing issue of Board and public debate.[6] In 1962, new Bank lending commitments jumped to over $1 billion per annum for the first time, and they exceeded this level for the rest of the decade with two exceptions (Mason and Asher 1973: 192). This was the product of increased Bank membership – it jumped from 68 in 1961 to 110 in 1969 – as well as a combination of new IDA resources and a gradual expansion in IBRD loans (Kapur *et al.* 1997: 187). Lending to developed countries from the IBRD slowly declined throughout the 1960s; however, the last loan to a developed country was not until 1979.

Much of the expansion during the 1960s was due to George D. Woods, who became President in January 1963. Another ex-banker, Woods was familiar with the Bank as he had been on a number of missions in the decade or so prior to his appointment (Kapur *et al.* 1997: 175–76). He came into the role with the Bank in a unique situation of increased resources from the IDA and significant retained earnings from IBRD loans yet limited investment opportunities for IBRD resources. His first major job as President was to recommend to the Board how to deal with excess IBRD reserves, and he did not recommend cutting lending or interest charges or increasing reserves. Rather, his plan was 'to create investment opportunities through new types of lending and new clients. Wood's agenda implied riskier lending, a larger staff, more hands-on development assistance, and in general, a relative increase in the Bank's nonfinancial role' (Kapur *et al.* 1997: 197).

This expanded agenda was not focused on poverty alleviation but allowed lending in what had previously been regarded as 'soft' sectors, such as water supply, agriculture, health and education. The case for lending in these sectors was a business one, they were now seen as profitable investments, a case which was assisted by developments in calculating economic rates of return in these areas. The expanded loan agenda did not impact until the late 1960s – agriculture went from two per cent of lending in the 1950s to 11 per cent across the 1960s, but water, education and health expenditures remained minimal (Kapur *et al.* 1997: 140–41).

Despite notable resistance from a number of Board members, Woods did see some of his agenda implemented. His success was most visible in the growth of the organisation (Kapur *et al.* 1997: 187). Indeed, professional staff and the administrative budget both grew at a higher rate than during the McNamara reign, with which Bank growth is most closely associated. However, lending grew more rapidly under McNamara. Many of the new professional staff were economists, who Wood's saw as 'agents of change'. Yet they were not as interested in expanding the Bank's approach as he had hoped. The increase in the number of economists relative to the number of technical specialists significantly contributed to greater overall intervention in borrowing countries' general economic policy settings (Caufield 1998: 91; Kapur *et al.* 1997: 212). They increased the Bank's research output too – of particular note, a 14-volume attack on the Indian approach to economic development (in particular, ISI) published in the mid-1960s (Broad 2006: 390–91).

Wood's expansionary plans were slowed dramatically by the middle of the decade. The US balance of payments difficulties, which began in 1960 but became serious by 1965, led the Treasury to deny the Bank access to US markets in 1966. This limited IBRD loan funding in 1967–8. US foreign policy once again became more conservative and inward looking; a general negativity regarding the outcomes of aid prevailed. This atmosphere, combined with bad relations between Woods and the then US Secretary of Treasury, contributed to a lengthy negotiation for the second IDA replenishment. It did not take place until 1968, constraining IDA disbursements. By mid-decade, debt problems were clearly visible in many of the Bank's borrowers, although this did not greatly impact on the Bank's lending. As Catherine Caufield (1998: 93) explained, on debt restructuring: 'the Bank felt that this was a task for other lenders not itself, and it should be achieved not by cutting back on lending, but by rescheduling existing loans'.[7]

Woods' final legacy was his choice of Robert McNamara as a successor and his attempt to influence his directions, in particular focusing him on poverty alleviation. Woods' concern about poverty was apparent in the diversification and expansion of Bank projects, most notably agriculture. However, Bank staff were more focused on increasing output than on poverty alleviation (Kapur *et al.* 1997: 198–99).

The McNamara years: 1968–81

Much has been written about the McNamara years at the Bank, both supporters and critics see him as having a missionary zeal, as the man who introduced a poverty focus to the Bank and as the real founder of the modern Bank. McNamara did talk about issues of poverty from the start of his presidency, although for most of what can be regarded as its first phase, 1968–73, there was little action to address poverty other than increases in lending volume. In the second phase, 1974–81 McNamara 'found' integrated rural development and to a lesser extent urban development schemes as a way to transfer rhetoric into action. Ultimately, his increase in the size of the organisation contributed most to putting the Bank at the forefront of international development and thus expanding its role in the reproduction of *pax americana*.

With hindsight, it is possible to be a little more dispassionate about McNamara's role in the Bank's growth into a hegemonic development institution. It was Woods who played the pivotal role in the Bank shift towards social issues and in broadening its lending agenda. McNamara was as much a reflection of the trends and beliefs of his generation as the iconic figure he became. Kapur *et al.* (1997: 219) claimed that the 'sudden upgrading of poverty alleviation under McNamara was an exceptionally personal decision'. Yet this downplays Woods' influence on the direction of the Bank and on McNamara regarding the importance of poverty reduction. It has also been convincingly argued that McNamara's concern for poverty and meeting people's basic needs grew, at least initially, from his concern about the spread of communism (Bello *et al.* 1982: 24–25; George and Sabelli 1994: 47–52). Further, McNamara was raised in a generation in which welfare was an accepted part of social compromise (even in its limited US form) and he entered government as a member of the Kennedy team promising a Great Society. In this sense, McNamara was simply reinserting welfare into the 'Keynesian, welfare, modernisation model' that existed at the Bank's origins. The focus on McNamara also ignores the growing international concern regarding poverty which resulted in the formation of the IDA; the new academic interest in poverty; popular worries about poverty; and the focus on basic needs in the American aid programme from the 1950s. This focus operated during the campaign in Vietnam (even if it was more concerned with winning the 'hearts and minds' of peasants than with their wellbeing), which of course McNamara had directed as Secretary of Defence.

McNamara was obsessed with statistics, measurement, size and scientific management and he was a pioneer in this field (Caufield 1998: 97–99; George and Sabelli 1994: 41–44). He was part of the first generation trained at the Harvard Business School in control accounting, and he implemented these techniques in the US Air Force during the war and at Ford Motor Company after it (Shapley 1993). Coming to the Bank from the Department of Defense, McNamara's reliance on managerialism and data in his leadership of the Bank was probably reinforced by the reality that he 'was notably uninformed about the developing world' (Kapur *et al.* 1997: 217).[8] Much of his focus on data came down to an interest in scale and from his earliest days in the Bank, McNamara was determined to increase the size of the Bank. Deborah Shapley (1993: 471), McNamara's biographer notes, 'McNamara knew he wanted a big Bank before he knew for certain what to do with it'.

After 1969, the Bank was encouraged to expand lending by the Nixon Administration. According to Gowan (1999: 22), the Administration saw that increasing World Bank lending would encourage private US banks to follow – enlarging the role of private American financial operators was central to its strategy to maintain *pax americana* through centralising the role of the United States and the US dollar in the international financial system. This strategy was operationalised with the abrogation of the Bretton Woods agreements in 1971/73, which made the US dollar *the* international currency through removing the discipline and alternative of the gold standard (Gowan 1999: 19–23). It also made the United States the only country in the world that could change the relative value of its currency without great domestic cost; could direct international interest rates via its domestic policy; and faced only a limited balance of payments constraint. Gowan (1999: 4) concludes that the post-1971 international financial arrangements more effectively promoted *pax americana* than the Bretton Woods arrangements did.

It is not surprising that the most significant outcome of McNamara's presidency was the expansion of lending. In the first phase of McNamara's presidency, there was a 131 per cent increase in new loan commitments; they averaged over $2.8 billion per annum (Kapur *et al.* 1997: 217). During the second phase, lending averaged over $9.9 billion per annum (Kapur *et al.* 1997: 234). Sometimes pressures to lend mitigated policy influence, but size increased the Bank's influence in developing countries and extended it into new areas of government action, particularly social areas.

The number of Bank staff continued to grow, more than 1000 new staff were appointed in McNamara's first three years. This growth transformed the Bank more and more into a large bureaucracy (George and Sabelli 1994: 118). The vast majority of the new professional staff had an economics or finance background, so the Bank often had more and better trained professional economists working for it than developing countries – size matters. Moreover, McNamara 'truly grasped the overall importance of broader economic research for the bank' (Broad 2006: 392). During his tenure, research became one of the Bank's vice presidencies and the research that was carried out was increasingly neoclassical and neoliberal. This research became the basis of the policy conditionality in the Bank's structural adjustment lending.

McNamara believed that the way projects are administered matters; he gave much attention to administrative reform in the first phase of his presidency. Country Program Papers were introduced in 1968, which, as Rich pointed out, represent an extraordinary 'vision of global central planning' based on belief in Bank technocrats (Rich 1994: 85).[9] In 1970, McNamara added the Operations Evaluation Unit, which would for the first time evaluate the outcomes of Bank projects. This focus increased the Bank's level of intervention in developing countries, although the pressure to lend generally outweighed administrative concerns. The 'rush to meet targets reached a point of near absurdity toward the end of the Bank's fiscal year ... During McNamara's tenure, 40 percent of all IBRD loans were pushed through in the last two months of the fiscal year' (Caufield 1998: 102). Staff members 'often complained that the pressure to lend resulted in poorly prepared and poorly executed projects' (Caufield 1998: 101). Yet, as George and Sabelli (1994: 44) noted, equally interesting was that it was *Bank staffers* designing *all* aspects of projects. Despite populist calls for greater participation and an enhanced role for civil society, these disappeared from the Bank during the McNamara years.

The second phase of the McNamara presidency began with a speech at a World Bank/IMF conference in Nairobi in 1973. Here, McNamara introduced a focus on integrated rural development. This was not McNamara's first idea on how to focus the Bank on poverty; over the years, McNamara gave speeches about a range of other issues: population, unemployment, environment, land reform, public health, the environment and even income distribution. But for the most, 'rhetoric outran implementation' and they did not translate into projects (Kapur *et al.* 1997: 217). Agricultural lending had increased in importance during McNamara's first phase and jumped from 20 per cent of overall IBRD/IDA new lending approvals in 1969–73 to 29 per cent in 1974–82. The education, water supply and sanitation sectors remained at around 5 per cent of new approvals in both periods, and health and population, and nutrition were tiny (Kapur *et al.* 1997: 234–35). McNamara's broad interests did have more influence in the Bank's 'vastly expanded' research programmes (Kapur *et al.* 1997: 222).

McNamara's basic needs approach at first gained little popularity outside the Bank. Developing countries were focused on the creation of a New International Economic Order (NIEO). However, developed countries would not accept the idea of non-interference in domestic policies that NIEO promoted, whereas the basic needs approach justified intervention on the basis of solidarity with the poor (Rist 1997: 163–64). Basic needs eventually also received approval from many developing country governments and also from the Third World Forum (an independent international association of intellectuals from the Third World) and the International Labour Organization. So the basic needs approach not only increased intervention in developing countries it improved the Bank's legitimacy as a development agency and its relations with non-governmental organisations (NGOs) (Rist 1997: 165); it was a classic hegemony strategy combining coercion and consent.

Despite his concern with poverty, McNamara did not contest the Bank's disdain regarding social welfare approaches to poverty. Economic productivity and growth was still the priority (Caufield 1998: 100). Integrated rural development was the first area that McNamara hit upon that offered the possibility of both direct growth in the productivity and in the income of the poorest and that fulfilled the Bank's project model. It was also potentially replicable on a grand scale (Kapur *et al.* 1997: 249, 309). Rural development projects also provided some political solution to rural volatility: they aimed to de-link smallholder farmers from tenant farmers and the landless and link them instead to national markets, giving them a stake in the system (Bello *et al.* 1982: 70–71, 25). Yet the Bank was not overly successful in its focus on smallholders, because, even at the end of McNamara's term when agriculture accounted for one-third of new approvals, most Bank projects still targeted richer farmers and employed capital-intensive models and cash cropping. Moreover, the overall outcomes of both traditional agriculture projects and the smallholder-focused integrated rural development projects were less than a roaring success, even on the Bank's own terms (Bello *et al.* 1982; Caufield 1998: 108–14). It is difficult not to agree with Caufield's (1998: 108) conclusion that the Bank may have chosen to highlight its activities with the poor but it actually 'acted consciously, out of a conviction that the best way to create new wealth is to invest in the wealthy, not the poor'.

On debt, McNamara was more liberal than his predecessor and was even more determined than Woods not to have the Bank engaged in debt rescheduling

(Kapur *et al.* 1997: 1003–09). He believed that developing countries needed additional capital in order to improve productivity and growth and in this way improve their capacity to meet loan repayments in the long term (Caufield 1998: 126; Toussaint 1999: 128). McNamara thought that the World Bank needed to lend *more* to make up for what he saw as developing countries' inadequate access to finance, and he took it upon himself to encourage commercial banks to increase lending. Of course, debt levels in some developing countries were already problematically high by 1973 (due in part to Eurodollar loans). After 1973, balance of payment problems for non-oil exporting nations were severe and the subsequent petrodollar phenomenon significantly contributed to the build up of debt in developing countries. McNamara's response was not to curb lending but to argue that loan funds should be used to fund exports, which would enable debt servicing (Toussaint 1999: 128).

McNamara stepped down before 1982, when the debt crisis really became public, but the increased lending and attitudes of the Bank during his reign must be acknowledged as a contributing factor. During McNamara's presidency, in the context of an international system that lacked a way to prevent instability, the Bank's response to debt was to 'bail out' developing countries in crisis (Gowan 1999: 35), which fitted with *pax americana*'s project of financialising the global economic system to its benefit. The growth in private lending and the oil crisis reduced Bank influence in some countries but for the more numerous losers during the oil crisis, leverage increased. The crisis also served to sharpen the Bank's focus – publicly social objectives were relegated to second place behind economic stabilisation, prior to neoliberal hegemony demanding it (Kapur *et al.* 1997: 321). In the medium-term, debt problems enhanced the Bank's capacity to impose conditionality because of the amounts owed to it and its role as a lender of last resort.

It is not possible to finish with the McNamara presidency without noting that it was he who formally introduced structural adjustment loans (SALs) to the Bank in 1980, in what George and Sabelli (1994: 55) called his 'parting gift' to the Bank. It seems that the idea of conditional structural adjustment lending belonged to Ernest Stern, the then Vice President Operations. In May 1979, he wrote McNamara a memorandum proposing conditional loans for middle-income countries to support macroeconomic reform. Apparently Stern was cautious in his advocacy because of the likely political profile of SALs (Kapur *et al.* 1997: 507). For McNamara, SALs were a way to get quick disbursing loans out to lenders – which he considered an even more urgent task since the second oil crisis. McNamara was ensuring that the Bank played its new US-designated role of 'bailing out' states – SALs offered a more efficient way of doing this. A proposal was presented to the World Bank Board in February 1980 and they approved it a couple of months later, after assuring themselves there would be proper coordination with the IMF.

Whether or not McNamara and Ernst recognised it, SALs reflected the new politico-economic climate that was spreading across the West and that came to prominence in the Margaret Thatcher and Ronald Reagan administrations in the UK and United States respectively, followed a couple of years later by Helmut Kohl in Germany. Underpinning this new neoliberal hegemony was the intellectual work of a group of neoclassically trained, neoliberal economists, led by Friedrich von Hayek and Milton Friedman, who rejected Keynesianism and developed a new diagnosis of the developed and developing world's problems.[10] This chapter concludes with an exploration of neoliberal analysis and how it came to be the dominant approach to economic analysis by the mid-1980s.

Neoliberal economic theory

Neoliberalism was a reassertion of a particular form of classical liberalism emphasising private property, minimal state intervention, individual rationality and utility maximisation. To achieve a productive economy, individuals must be allowed freedom to choose and to be fully rewarded for their labours (Rapley 2002: 52). Friedman added to neoclassical economics a focus on demand, consumption, utility and a preference for monetary policy (in particular control of the money supply and interest rates) to address economic cycles over fiscal policy (Keynes' preferred mechanism). This fondness for monetary policy had the added benefit of minimising state intervention in the economy. Rational expectations theory, which models how people forecast future events, expanded the neoclassical case against the state with the argument that people could increasingly foresee the direction of government policies and would adjust their behaviour, thus undermining government attempts to change policy (Rapley 2002: 54).

The neoliberal diagnosis of the developing countries' problems began in the 1940s with the work of P. T. Bauer, whose empirical work supposedly demonstrated that the rational actor assumption held true for developing countries (Rapley 2002: 55). He was concerned to show that smallholders do respond 'rationally' to local incentive structures as opposed to the view that their actions were the product of (natural) conservatism and/or local cultural and social practices. T. W. Schultz, building on Bauer's work, argued that smallholders do not make capital improvements on their land because of government policies that distort prices and take too much of their profit in order to fund industrial development. By the mid-1960s there was a rash of literature from neoliberal economists on the negative impact of many countries' incentive and price structures and on the way that state protectionism or overvaluation of the exchange rate negatively impacts the overall 'welfare' of the economy (Rapley 2002: 55–56).

In the 1970s neoliberalism became mainstream among development specialists. A study by Ian Little, Tibor Scitovsky and Maurice Scott (1970) was central to this. It examined the experience of seven developing countries in the post-war period and concluded that ISI was overall negative, predominately because it did not follow countries' 'natural' comparative advantage but also because of limited bureaucratic capacity to effectively direct ISI (Rapley 2002: 56). ISI supposedly increased income inequality; states were advised to follow export-oriented industrialisation (EOI). Further reports followed and while the initial report was relatively cautious in its conclusions, '[s]tronger – some might say dogmatic – expressions of neoclassical thought were to follow, as critics gained in confidence and grew convinced that their findings had thoroughly discredited the old statist development schools' (Rapley 2002: 57).

The critiques came together in a 1983 trade study by the National Bureau of Economic Research (NBER) that set up a simplistic dichotomy between ISI and EOI, the latter of which was supposedly practised fully by the successful East Asian tigers. In countries following ISI, the NBER study said that government interventions in markets for capital and labour distorted the relative prices of each, making capital relatively cheap and labour more expensive, leading to the elimination of many traditional labour intensive industries but creating few jobs (Rapley 2002: 58). The proposed solution to the problems was, not surprisingly, reduced government intervention across the whole gamut of the economy. The report also totally rejected Prebisch–Singer-type arguments and reformulated the benefits of trade based on comparative advantage to make it again attractive. The NBER analysis, along with most neoliberal-influenced studies, essentially ignored the role of the state in the development of the East Asian tigers. Nevertheless, this problematic neoliberal reading of East Asian development became central to the case for the adoption of Washington Consensus policies in developing countries and it did so in a way that 'naturalised' the existence of nation-states and liberal capitalism (Berger 2004: 156–59).

In the 1970s, a further string was added to the neoliberal bow through New Political Economy (NPE). It was pioneered by Anne Krueger (1974), who applied the rational utility maximisation thesis to politics via a study of the effect of quotas on firms (Rapley 2002: 59). Quotas create economic rents so, Krueger argued, plant managers will augment their access to these rents by increasing the capacity of a plant, regardless of current idle capacity. They do so to make windfall profits via on-selling of goods purchased under the quota system rather than through growth in production. Krueger's posited that this would result in a decrease in plant productivity because of increased overheads and that the quota system would expand corruption in industry and government. The Indian economist, Jagdish Bhagwati (1982) came to similar conclusions about the impact of what he labelled 'directly unproductive profit-seeking activities'. These studies resonated with fellow neoliberals because they supposedly demonstrated that efficiency losses from trade protection were higher than empirical studies had to that point indicated: it made the rather weak neoclassical argument in favour of trade liberalisation stronger (Toye 1993: 140).

Robert Bates (1981) published an influential study that built on the neoliberal analysis of urban bias in developing countries' government policy using the NPE framework (Rapley 2002: 60–61). This bias supposedly resulted in an inequitable price structure for rural production. Bates explained the bias by the disproportionate influence of urban industrialists allied with the urban working class on government policy in developing countries. Given the neoliberal faith in comparative advantage, Bates regarded this as counter-productive for development. As Rapley (2002: 61) pointed out, Bates' work was very influential in the World Bank and soon after it was published '"getting the prices right" became a guiding concern for the World Bank in Africa'.

NPE significantly contributes to 'a profoundly cynical view of the state in developing countries' (Toye 1993: 135). The proposition that individuals are only motivated by self-interest is an assumption 'breathtaking in its scope and pretension', which feeds into pessimism regarding the capacity of states in developing countries to implement 'sound' policies (Toye 1993: 136–37). This bias contributes to NPE's inability to undertake historically grounded socio-political analysis of state–market–civil society relations despites its pretensions as 'political' economy.

In summary, the neoliberal analysis of the problems in developing countries comprised three inter-related ideas or hegemonic principles: the public sector was overextended; there had been too much emphasis on physical capital formation, often at the expense of human capital formation; and the third world had developed too many market-distorting economic controls (Toye 1993: 70). Why did this analysis become so widely accepted? Similar to the link between the Depression and Keynesianism, the rise of neoliberal economics coincided with the economic crises of the 1970s for which it purportedly had an explanation *and* a solution. There was 'widespread doubt and anxiety about the wisdom of government activity in many developing countries' and 'some truth' in the neoliberal analysis (Toye 1993: 70). In contrast to the spread of Keynesianism, well-funded think tanks, World Bank researchers and many in the press set out to disseminate neoliberal views.[11] More than anything though, it was the election of the Reagan Administration in the United States that legitimated neoliberal economics. The Administration used neoliberal prescriptions to reshape the US historic bloc and a *pax americana* again engaged in reshaping the international scene to its requirements. Of course, not all developing countries had to be pushed; neoliberal regimes came to dominate the historic bloc in many developing countries, although not all of them by democratic means.

Conclusion

This chapter has demonstrated how the Keynesian, modernisation, welfare model that prevailed in the postwar years provided the impetus for the Bank's creation and the logic for its operation. During the 1950s, the Bank grew slowly; it largely lent for infrastructure projects to the more creditworthy developing countries. The establishment of the IDA in 1961 turned the Bank into a development agency and its lending volume and agenda expanded, although still relatively slowly. During McNamara's presidency the Bank grew more quickly and late in his term, the Bank size and standing gave it the capacity to help support *pax americana*. It was now a useful and growing force in the global neoliberal reconfiguration that was *pax americana* (Toye 1993: 77–78).

With neoliberal economics sweeping the world and governments espousing neoliberalism in power in the United States and the UK, the long-term presidency of Robert McNamara came to a close. McNamara had left a mixed legacy; he had on the one hand maintained the Bank's postwar development tradition based on the priority of economic growth but emphasising ideas from the 'overlapping combination of Keynesianism, welfarism, and modernisation' that dominated development (Fine 2001b: 133). In line with this, he expanded the Bank's agenda and operations and introduced a focus on poverty reduction. On the other hand, he left a now hegemonic Bank dominated by neoclassically trained economists, committed to parsimonious economic modelling and management using economic data. And he left them with a new tool, SALs, which strengthened the Bank's leverage and proved particularly powerful in promoting neoliberal policies in developing countries.

4 From Washington to post-Washington Consensus

This chapter takes up the story of the rise of neoliberalism in the Bank from 1981. It examines how neoliberalism becomes a set of hegemonic economic principles shared between the Bank, the International Monetary Fund (IMF) and the US government. John Williamson labelled these commitments and policies the 'Washington Consensus' in 1990 and they centre on commitment to macroeconomic stability, outward orientation and domestic liberalisation (Fine 2001b: 132). So, the term Washington Consensus indicates the way neoliberalism translated to the policies and programmes of the Bank and distinguishes this from the broader theoretical and political movement of neoliberalism outlined in the previous chapter.

Washington Consensus prescriptions dominated Bank lending and rhetoric remarkably quickly and were uncontested until the early 1990s. By the mid-1990s, the move away from the Washington Consensus was more pronounced as the Bank promoted its 'human face' under the new president, James Wolfensohn. Over time, the Bank's new rhetoric formed an identifiable approach to development, which has been labelled the post-Washington Consensus (PWC) to indicate both its continuities and discontinuities with the Washington Consensus. To date, the components of the PWC have not been outlined systematically. This chapter attempts to do precisely this and to identify the elements that distinguish the PWC from the Washington Consensus.

The Washington Consensus in full swing

The Reagan Administration appointed A. W. Clausen as Bank President in mid-1981; this represented a return to the Bank's traditional embrace of ex-bankers but he was also 'a representative of renewed capitalist doctrine concerning the limits of government and the virtues of flexible, self-adjusting markets' (Kapur *et al.* 1997: 511). He was influenced by neoclassical economics and New Political Economy (NPE), which increasingly dominated development theory and policy. His presidency was the death knell for the Bank focus on poverty, although its commitment was already on the wane prior to his arrival (Kapur *et al.* 1997: 333).

Clausen made major changes to the Bank's research department by replacing McNamara confidants with economists focused on a new research agenda centred on unquestioned faith in 'free markets' (Stiglitz 2002: 13). Krueger, a NPE pioneer, was appointed as the Bank's Chief Economist. However, as staff changes were not sweeping, the speed at which the new doctrines permeated the Bank suggests that the foundations for a shift were already in place; some are identifiable. Of the hundreds of economists hired during the McNamara reign most were neoclassically trained. A 1991 survey of staff in the Bank's Policy, Research and External Affairs branch showed 55 per cent of staff had higher degrees in economics or finance and 80 per cent of staff were trained in a handful of British and US institutions, where the training tends to be 'uniform' and, it should be added, neoclassical (Stern and Ferreira 1997: 586–88).[1]

Another factor in the quick adoption of Washington Consensus principles was that they suited the operational departments for whom poverty lending had been administratively complex and often not overly successful (Kapur *et al.* 1997: 334). Ngaire Woods (2006: 63) makes a similar point about institutional factors – the Washington Consensus provided staff in the IMF and World Bank with a template and this is a necessity for a hierarchical organisation with staff working all over the globe. Working to the template guarantees institutional backing. Management did also apply coercive techniques in ensuring Washington Consensus prescriptions were adopted and promoted. For example, Bank 'editing' of reports became much tighter; Krueger's Economic Research Staff did not analyse poverty; and its research programme was exclusively centred on showing economic liberalisation was good policy (Caufield 1998: 144–45; Kapur *et al.* 1997: 339). By the mid-1980s, the Bank and its research economists were 'seen to be leading the charge of the neoclassical resurgence' (Stern and Ferreira 1997: 539).

So what were the policy prescriptions of the Washington Consensus? They certainly did not utilise all the ideas of neoliberal economics because, as Woods (2006: 63) argued, the IMF and Bank have tended to ignore 'economic theories or policy prescriptions which would require greater resources or a different expertise'. Michel Chossudovsky (1997: 55–67) has provided a useful summary of the key policies of the Washington Consensus, which were carried out in two phases: first, short-term macroeconomic stabilisation carried out quickly via 'big bang' reforms; and second, long-term structural change via a range of detailed microeconomic reforms.[2] A brief outline of these policies follows.

Washington Consensus Policies phase one: economic stabilisation

This phase of short-term macroeconomic stabilisation is designed to control balance of payments and budgetary deficits. Implemented predominately by the IMF, key policies prescriptions include the following.

(1) Budgetary austerity to control deficits – this demands dramatic cuts in recurrent expenditure, in particular through cuts to public sector employment, social sector programmes and often investment programmes as well.

(2) Currency devaluation, often an end to currency controls or, at minimum, multiple exchange rate policies. Interestingly, the Bank tended to promote devaluation more than the IMF as it did not share the Fund's level of concern regarding inflation (Kapur *et al.* 1997: 514).
(3) Price liberalisation– often referred to as 'getting prices right', meaning ending subsidies and price controls. This generally affects areas such as staple foods and their production, while at the same time prices for energy, petroleum and other public utilities are set at or higher than world market prices. This is the so-called 'dollarisation' of domestic prices.

Washington Consensus phase two policies: structural reform

The IMF and World Bank implement microeconomic reform policies jointly. Key aspects are the following.

(1) Trade liberalisation – reduction and elimination of tariffs and quotas and encouragement of an export focus.
(2) Privatisation of state-owned enterprises and utilities, often linked to a programme of microeconomic reform in various sectors (e.g. power, water supply and sanitation, mining, health and education).
(3) Tax reform – promoted the introduction of value-added taxes that increase the tax burden on lower and middle classes and tax breaks for targeted investment.
(4) Land 'reform' – a misnomer as this essentially referred to ensuring the security and stability of private land ownership.
(5) Banking deregulation – this involved detailed changes to legislation, privatisation of state-owned banks and the setting up of independent central banks. The package of changes ultimately reduced central bank control over interest rates in favour of international markets.
(6) Liberalisation of capital movements, that is the removal of foreign exchange controls.
(7) A focus on poverty alleviation and social safety nets was added in the late 1980s. This actually involved cutting overall social expenditure and selectively 'servicing' the poorest (a supposedly low cost, efficient approach).
(8) Good governance – in the 1980s, this essentially meant the holding of multiparty elections but, in the post-Washington consensus era, it has taken on a life of its own.

Implementing the Washington Consensus

The debt crisis provided the Bank (and Fund) with greater capacity to impose Washington Consensus policies on cash-strapped developing countries.[3] The debt problem had been building for a number of years, but it took the Mexican default of August 1982 and the others that followed for the Bank and Fund to publicly acknowledge the extent of indebtedness and crisis. The Washington

Consensus policies applied to address the debt crisis acted to reinforce *pax americana*. Promoting currency devaluation, outward orientation and financial liberalisation provided a range of benefits to the United States – industry could access cheap inputs and its financiers were able to pay their debts, buy overseas privatised assets cheaply and play stock markets across the globe (Gowan 1999: 42, 56–57).

The main mechanism for promoting Washington Consensus policies was conditionality on structural adjustment loans (SALs). From the middle of the 1980s, the new sectoral adjustment loans (SECALs) also became popular in the Bank. Their narrower (sectoral) focus made them more effective in facilitating the Washington Consensus's second phase microeconomic reforms than SALs. These reforms were the Bank's responsibility in the division of labour between it and the IMF.[4] SALs and SECALs received significant critical attention, yet Bank investment loans remained the dominant form of lending and were as important a vehicle in pursuing the Washington Consensus agenda. For example, privatisation of utilities was generally pursued through investment loans.

SALs and SECALS disburse quickly and can be used for balance of payments difficulties or for meeting debt repayments (an area that had previously been the domain of the IMF). For those countries willing to accept adjustment loans (or with few other options), the Bank's influence was significantly expanded and deepened (Bello 1994: 27). In 1981, SALs were around six per cent of Bank lending, by 1987–90 adjustment lending (SALs and SECALs) accounted for almost 30 per cent of lending. In 1991–3, it dropped to 20 per cent of Bank lending (Kapur *et al.* 1997: 517–21). The number of conditions on adjustment lending increased from an average of 34 in 1980–82 to 56 in 1987–90. At the same time as adjustment lending was increasing, overall Bank lending increased. Average annual Bank commitments grew from $5.3 billion in the period 1970–9 to $15.69 billion in 1980–9 (Kapur *et al.* 1997: 6). This reinforced Bank leverage over borrowing countries.

The Reagan Administration's relationship with the Bank was turbulent. Although ideologically antagonistic to it, they had appointed Clausen, whose strong neoliberal views they applauded. A 1982 report they commissioned from the US Treasury on the Bank concluded that the Bank had been 'most effective in furthering our [US] global economic and financial objectives, and thereby also serving our long-term political/strategic objectives' (cited in Bello *et al.* 1982: 33). Nevertheless, in 1984, they cut their International Development Association (IDA) replenishment for 1985–7 by 35 per cent. The Reagan Administration felt this cut would 'encourage' the Bank to change the eligibility for restricted IDA funding from a basis of need to one of rewarding those progressing economic restructuring. Despite this hardline approach, they replaced Clausen when his five-year term expired because his dogmatic neoliberal approach provoked such strong criticism from both non-governmental organisations (NGOs) and borrowers that the Bank's capacity to play a role in promoting *pax americana* was reduced (Gowan 1999: 32). Among NGOs, environmental campaigners were particularly vocal, and their capacity to document Bank projects doing significant environmental harm proved quite damaging to the Bank.

Clausen was replaced in July 1986 with veteran Republican Congressman Barber B. Conable. His agenda was largely set by the Reagan Administration, who followed their IDA funding cut with a vote against the Bank's 1987 budget, arguing that the Bank's bureaucracy was bloated and needed a change of direction. Clausen formed a committee to oversee a Bank reorganisation. It reported back that:

> [f]irst, effective macroeconomic management and a sound policy environment have come to be, and will remain, at the heart of the development challenge ... Second, successful economic development increasingly depends on being able to deal with the interdependence of problems and on the effective integration of macroeconomic and sectoral issues.
>
> (Cited in George and Sabelli 1994: 126)

The first point reaffirms the centrality of structural adjustment and the second states that structural adjustment needs to occur in all sectors (George and Sabelli 1994: 126). In order that all of the Bank's projects line up with adjustment programmes, the report recommended reorganisation of the Bank around country programmes and abandonment of some of the old cross-sectoral departments such as water or energy. The report also repeatedly emphasised regaining and retaining 'intellectual leadership', concluding that there were not enough economists in the Bank. The reorganisation resulted in a 10 per cent reduction in staff numbers, although the reduction was short-lived. Further, new staff selection procedures were top down, which 'fostered a rampant cronyism in the Bank' (Caufield 1998: 179–80). This was a coercive project to shift the Bank's intellectual terrain and operations towards the Washington Consensus.

Despite the strictures put on Conable's presidency, he rededicated the Bank to the fight against poverty in 1987, increased the engagement with NGOs and allowed some shift back to lending in social sectors. However, the reasons for social sector engagement were new:

> [b]y engaging in social sector projects, the Bank found that, instead of simply pressing for blanket spending cuts, it was in a position to discuss with and persuade sector officials of the importance of finding alternative ways to finance, allocate, and deliver those services. Social projects thus became a friendlier and more constructive way to lead borrowers by the hand towards austerity.
>
> (Kapur *et al.* 1997: 348)

Moreover, expanding the social agenda allowed the Bank to respond to growing public pressure and critique without actually changing doctrine (Kapur *et al.* 1997: 369).

During Conable's tenure the debt crisis, which was a catalyst for implementing Washington Consensus policies, worsened – Third World debt rose from $785 billion in 1982 to $1.3 trillion in 1992. The composition also changed, with a larger portion owed to international financial institutions than private sources (Bello 1994: 69). This change in composition was partly due to an initiative on debt from US Treasury Secretary James Baker III in 1985. The Baker Plan did not involve debt relief, rather it pushed the IMF, the World Bank and private banks to provide additional resources to debtor countries and combined this with a requirement for enhanced structural adjustment measures (Bogdanowicz-Bindert 1986; Woods 2006: 49–50). Using coercive tactics, it was a continuation of the Nixon Administration's plan to ensure that US private financial operators dominated the international market (Gowan 1999: 19–23).

The 1989 Brady Plan also enhanced the Bank's role in debt relief. This plan, proposed by Baker's replacement Nicholas Brady, involved some debt forgiveness. Under it, the United States issued new bonds (called Brady Bonds) to be purchased by debtor countries using a combination of resources from the IMF, the World Bank, private banks and domestic resources. The Brady bonds were issued either with a discount to the original value of the loan or with a discount on the interest rates. Participation in the Plan was conditional on further structural adjustment measures (Woods 2006: 52). In the end, only 12 countries participated in the first round of the scheme because an interest rate reduction eased the pressure on many indebted countries. In a less coercively based approach to shoring up the Bank's role in *pax americana*, the Brady Plan reinforced the Bank's role in adjustment and enhanced its ongoing role in debt management (George and Sabelli 1994: 22) at the same time as it expanded the Bank's links and reliance on the US Treasury and improved US support (Gwin 1997).

A strong neoliberal World Bank provided the United States with an alternative to the UN. It helped facilitate its multipronged attack on the UN system, which involved weakening the overall UN system by pressure, budgetary constraints and mandate changes. In UN development agencies, it pushed to change the development agenda and refocus agencies on issues of traditional concern to the North; it even pressured agencies such as the United Nations Conference on Trade, Aid and Development (UNCTAD) to wind up having 'outlived their purpose' or others such as the United Nations Development Program (UNDP) to conform to the World Bank model (Gosovic 2000: 453–54). This programme was successful in removing sources of intellectual and policy challenge to the North-controlled hegemonic institutions and agenda, leaving the World Bank, by the time of the Asian Financial Crisis, the 'last man standing' (Gosovic 2000: 448).

Lewis T. Preston took over the Bank in late 1991, he was another ex-banker and was more committed to the core Washington Consensus agenda than Conable had been (Kapur *et al.* 1997: 371). Soon after his arrival, controversy around the Bank exploded. In December 1991, a memo from Lawrence H.

Summers, Chief Economist and Vice-President for Development, was leaked. It argued that the Bank should encourage more 'dirty' industries in developing countries (see George and Sabelli 1994: 98–100). Summers, despite being nominally a Democrat, clearly held very neoclassical and rigid views on economics. In a speech on 10 November 1991 in Bangkok, he asked:

> [w]hat can the West do to drive this process of reform [in Russia] forward? Number one: it can spread the truth. The laws of economics, it's often forgotten, are like the laws of engineering. *There's only one set of laws and they work everywhere.* One of the things I've learned in my short time at the World Bank is that whenever anybody says, 'But economics works differently here', they're about to say something dumb.
>
> (Cited in George and Sabelli 1994: 106, emphasis added)

One of Preston's first initiatives was to ask Willi Wapenhans, a Bank Vice President close to retirement, to report on the overall outcomes of the Bank's lending. The Wapenhans Report released in 1992 (and leaked in draft form) painted a fairly bleak picture of Bank operations. It concluded that the percentage of Bank projects that suffered from major implementation problems (seen in the Bank's own terms) increased from 11 per cent in the early 1980s to 37.5 per cent of projects completed in 1991 (George and Sabelli 1994: 224). Projects in the sectors of water supply and sanitation and agriculture performed worst. Surprisingly those projects that Bank staffers took longest to prepare were the least successful, probably indicating a lack of borrower ownership and input into the projects (George and Sabelli 1994: 224). The report was also one of the first to publicly acknowledge the problem of corruption in Bank projects; stating 'the evidence of gross non-compliance is overwhelming' (George and Sabelli 1994: 224). The Wapenhans Report was a fairly damning indictment of the Bank's implementation of Washington Consensus policies; nevertheless, in 1993 the Bank was still declaring structural adjustment a success (Bello 1994: 32).

Country and policy variations did increase in the late 1980s and early 1990s. Thus in 1997, Gustav Ranis (1997: 76) argued that the Consensus is 'more subtle and differentiated today than many critics have asserted'; however, he conceded that:

> the kernel of truth remains: the Bank is inhabited by a large number of highly talented professionals, largely economists, who have shown little willingness to dissent or deviate from what the in-house conventional wisdom is seen to be at any point in time; and analyses of government failure continue to have a much easier time than analyses of market failure.

Structural adjustment did not improve economic outcomes in most developing countries; indeed, the 1980s were labelled the 'lost decade'. Many suffered from zero or even negative economic growth, the number of people living in absolute poverty increased in a number of regions and the income disparity both within developing countries and between the developing and developed 'worlds' had widened. There were exceptions of course – the East Asian 'tigers' stand out precisely because they had not followed the Bank's development paradigm. The Bank would not acknowledge this. Indeed, from 1983 the Bank's research department funded a series of studies to strengthen the neoclassical interpretation of East Asian growth started by Little (Islam and Chowdhury 2000: 8). The high costs of Washington Consensus policies meant that despite its partial success in transforming domestic historic blocs in developing countries, the overall social costs of its policies were too high and the changes it achieved in economic policy were 'piecemeal' (Gowan 1999: 84). In a number of cases policy changes were reversed after short periods.

By the early 1990s, there was a growing body of work demonstrating the empirical and qualitative failures of the Washington Consensus approach.[5] Further, NGO voices were being heard – both those focused on critique and those who had, since the late 1980s, engaged with the Bank. These latter NGOs had some small victories in changing the Bank's approach in three areas: first, regarding the negative effects of structural adjustment, NGOs helped design temporary welfare programmes for those negatively affected; second, there was some increase in participation in projects; and third the Bank adopted environmentally impact assessments (Nelson 1995: 176–83). Overall the growing public critique of the Bank combined with the decision of the Clinton Administration to 'radicalise the programmes of various multilateral organisations in order to commit them to the radical opening of national economies' to encourage a slow process of policy change (Gowan 1999: 84). These are the foundations of the PWC.

The post-Washington Consensus

Similar to the link between the Bank's Washington Consensus and the rise of neoliberalism and the NPE from the 1970s, the PWC is linked theoretically to the development of New Institutional Economics (NIE) and politically to the decline of hardline neoliberal regimes in the West and the increasing voice of NGOs in the development debate. NIE expanded economists' views of what constitutes market failures – to problems of externalities, increasing returns to scale and monopolies it added issues of information failures and transaction costs.[6] The inclusion of these new dimensions led to a picture of markets with extensive imperfections as opposed to the neoliberal view of perfectly working markets (Fine 2001b: 4–5, 2005: 10–11). As Douglass North (1998: 17) stated, NIE:

> is an attempt to incorporate a theory of institutions into economics. However, in contrast to the many earlier attempts to overturn or replace neoclassical theory, the new institutional economics builds on, modifies and extends neoclassical theory to permit it to come to grips and deal with an entire range of issues heretofore beyond its ken.

NIE does not question neoclassical economics' methodological individualism or the utility maximisation assumption; however, it does reject its conception of instrumental rationality in favour of bounded rationality, that is the idea that human rationality is constrained by factors such as 'emotional affect, limited cognitive ability and imperfect information' (Kaufman 2007: 18). This creates space to explain the existence of social structures and institutions by individuals who create these 'within and between market and non-market forms of organisation', and it allows institutions and non-market (i.e. social) factors a key role in mitigating market failure and thus improving the efficient functioning of markets (Fine 2001b: 9).

As Fine pointed out, the shift of the World Bank towards NIE was not simply the result of the weight of theoretical critique against the Washington Consensus, nor the analytical or theoretical superiority of the new 'paradigm'. It was connected to the Bank's relations with the IMF, in particular the need for differentiation after the convergence of policy prescriptions and lending instruments in the 1980s. It also reflected the need to justify the extension of conditionality beyond economic policy into issues of governance, which, one should add, provided the Bank with a new *raison d'être* for lending and thus for its very existence. The PWC was marketed as a response to calls for local 'ownership' of development programmes while at the same time facilitating compliance with the broadened agenda. The PWC also reflected the growing influence of Japan – an influential Washington Consensus sceptic – as a donor (Fine 2001b: 10–13). The Bank's level of engagement with NIE is also reflected in the limited impact it seems to have had on the Bank's own research operations, which remain dominated by Washington Consensus concerns (Broad 2006; Wade 1996, 2001a, 2002).

In tracing the shift to the PWC in the Bank, a key question is how far from the Washington Consensus does NIE and associated Bank reforms take the Bank? Before addressing this question, it is necessary to explore whether the developments in the Bank from the mid-1990s represent a genuine engagement with NIE and the NGO critique of Bank operations or whether they are better understood as a co-option of their language and concerns in order to continue the project of the Washington consensus.

It is not easy to identify when the shift to the PWC took place, it was not a radical shift but the culmination of incremental changes over a decade. There were some earlier signs of the shift but the Bank report, The East Asian Miracle (1993a), is a key marker of change. Produced at the behest of the Japanese government, it 'concedes for the first time in a major Bank publication the *fact* of extensive government intervention in most of East Asia' (Wade 1996: 23). The report only acknowledged the role of the state in promoting development through direct redistribution measures (in particular, primary and secondary education) and deliberate distortions of the incentive structures to promote exports (Burgess 1995; Wade 1996: 23–27). It ignored issues such as the political systems in these countries, including the relations between business and government, historical factors (such as land reform or the Cold War and its effect on foreign aid and foreign direct investment) and the role of the state manipulating price structures (not just for exports). Primacy is given in the report to the role of macroeconomic fundamentals in achieving growth, thus Wade (1996: 5) concluded 'the Bank emerges with its traditional paradigm unscathed'. Nevertheless, the theory and practice of the East Asian 'developmental state' was one of the most significant threats to the Bank's neoliberal orthodoxy as it challenged the Bank's beliefs about 'getting the prices right' (Masina 2006: 26).

Following the demise of the Soviet Union, the claims of the 'victory' of democracy and capitalism shored up the neoliberal project. In the Bank, the challenges posed by the 25 new members that joined the Bank between 1990 and 1994 hindered the shift away from the Washington Consensus. Most were ex-communist states and their addition as borrowers undoubtedly affected the budget and focus of the Bank. A new geographical region (Europe and Central Asia – ECA) was created and these countries did not want to be seen as developing countries – they were transition economies, whose need was 'restructuring rather than development' (Kapur *et al.* 1997: 373). This view also served *pax americana* because it justified the implementation of Washington Consensus policies in these countries (Gowan 1999: 42). So their arrival pushed the Bank's focus toward its middle-income clientele for whom the case for structural adjustment seemed clearer. In 1994, the Bank even changed its purpose from 'alleviating poverty' to 'helping borrowers reduce poverty and raise living standards' (Kapur *et al.* 1997: 373).

There is little doubt that the shift to the PWC is most closely associated with, and took place under, President James D. Wolfensohn. The nexus between theory and political events again came to the fore, as it was the Clinton Administration in the United States who appointed Wolfensohn.[7] The argument here is not that the Clinton Administration represented a dramatic break with US foreign and economic policy, rather that it had more belief than the previous Republican administrations in the 'centrality of state-political action in economic affairs' (Gowan 1999: 79). But the role of the state in this new formulation was little changed – it was a pro-capitalist state that wanted US goods, services and capital to have access to the globe. The belief in state action extended to a commitment to multilateral institutions: the aim was still to further US interests but through some allegiance to global rule-based governance. Wolfensohn, with his somewhat unconventional background and broad range of interests, fitted the Administration's vision for the Bank.

During his presidency, 1995–2005, Wolfensohn was central to a range of reforms and programmes, including the Highly Indebted Poor Country (HIPC) initiative (1996), Knowledge Bank (1996) and the Strategic Compact (April 1997) (Wodsak 2002: 63–71). A key marker of the Bank's 'reinvention of liberalism' was The State in a Changing World: World Development Report 1997 (WDR 1997) (Berger and Beeson 1998: 499). The Report maintained the neoclassical commitments to markets but, in line with developments in political economy, recognised the importance of state intervention 'in defining the structure of market-mediated economic relations' (Berger and Beeson 1998: 499). Gordon Crawford (2006) and Paul Cammack (2003: 5) have both pointed out that this new 'active and pro-capitalist state' is about reproducing private sector profits and capitalism and is in line with the Bank's neoliberal Washington Consensus project. Cammack's argument highlights the Marxist view of the role of the state as core to the reproduction of social relations. In the Gramscian formulation, each historic bloc is the product of complex economic and social forces, but the control by a dominant group of the apparatus of the state gives it the capacity to construct the historic bloc in particular ways. It is core to constructing hegemony.

How did this change in the role of the state impact on the Bank's operations? It initially refocused the Bank on policy or adjustment operations; this lending 'more than tripled from below \$5 billion in 1997 to \$15.3 billion in 1999' and 'institution building and governance' became the 'dominant themes' (Wodsak 2002: 74).[8] However, between 2000 and 2005, policy-based or adjustment lending returned to average levels of just over 30 per cent of new Bank commitments (\$5–6 billion per annum) but governance remained a dominant theme in lending (World Bank 2003r, 2006b). Whether through adjustment lending or governance programmes, the World Bank's renewed engagement with the state ultimately increased its capacity to promote or undermine specific elements of a state's historic bloc.

The Asian Financial Crisis followed publication of the WDR 1997 and gave added substance to the critique of the Washington Consensus. However, the international financial institutions and some neoliberal economists tried to present the Crisis as evidence of the failure of the East Asian 'developmental state' models – Asia was now the home of 'crony capitalism' (Masina 2006: 26). But their mishandling of the Crisis limited the impact of their reading of it. The brunt of criticism at the response of the international financial institutions to the Crisis was directed at the IMF; however, the Bank also received its share of critical attention, in particular its 'one size fits all' development prescriptions. Wolfensohn renewed his public relations offensive for the Bank, going as far as critically commenting on the social dislocation resulting from IMF adjustment. He also allowed the recently appointed Chief Economist, Joseph Stiglitz (2002) to speak critically about the IMF's approach to financial liberalisation, in particular capital account liberalisation in countries without mature regulatory systems. This NIE-based critique has gained currency among mainstream economics commentators (Broad 2004: 138–39).

The Bank's reform process continued in 1998 with a report entitled Assessing Aid: What Works, What Doesn't, and Why (World Bank 1998c). The report was based on an empirical analysis that utilises a general equilibrium growth model, the preferred methodology of neoliberal economics, not NIE. It focused on the debate about the link between aid and economic growth, maintaining neoliberal assumptions about the relationship between economic growth and poverty reduction. Its key conclusion was that aid only helps to increase growth in countries utilising 'sound' economic policies and good governance. Given the failures of conditionality in achieving 'sound' macroeconomic management in recipient countries, the report proposed 'selectivity' in aid contributions, meaning assessing current economic policies and institutional performance and developing targets around these themes to determine eligibility for aid. This process was meant to counter problems of limited local ownership of reform programmes, which was seen as a key reason for the failure of conditionality. Niels Hermes and Robert Lensink (2001: 5) demonstrated that the report's criteria for selecting good management are ill-defined and primarily refer to indicators of macroeconomic stability associated with the Washington Consensus. Ironically, a number of the report's proposals, such as reduction in government expenditures, may inhibit good governance by limiting development of a strong public sector.

In 1999, the Bank launched the Comprehensive Development Framework (CDF) and later in the year, the associated Poverty Reduction Strategy Paper (PRSP) process. The CDF is designed to improve poverty focus, country ownership and donor harmonisation. It relies heavily conceptually and practically on the PRSP process, which is where the concrete strategies and plans are developed through participating countries planning to reduce poverty. The WDR 1999/2000, produced by Stiglitz appointee Ravi Kanbur, claimed that the CDF goes beyond the Bank's traditional focus on economic growth to include social goals (World Bank 2000b: 21). The CDF, the Bank claims, emphasises:

> the interdependence of all elements of development – social, structural, human, governance, environmental, economic, and financial. It advocates: a holistic long-term strategy; the country in the lead, both 'owning' and directing the development agenda, with the Bank and other partners each defining their support in their respective business plans; stronger partnerships among governments, donors, civil society, the private sector, and other development stakeholders in implementing the country strategy; and a transparent focus on development results to ensure better practical success in reducing poverty.
>
> (World Bank Group Website)

The CDF is sold as a tool in contrast to a 'blueprint' approach. Yet there is a Sourcebook for the connected PRSP process – here is the Keynesian commitment to planning that produced the Bank, reorganised for the neoliberal age. The Sourcebook states the key requirements of a PRSP are that the country prepares it and that it focuses 'on *faster and broad-based economic growth*, which *requires* macroeconomic stability' (World Bank Group Website 2009, emphasis added). The ongoing commitment to the macroeconomic prescriptions of the Washington Consensus, including commitment to international integration, is one of the biggest blind spots of the process.

Doug Porter and David Craig (2004: 390) see PRSPs as the 'high water mark' of the PWC, or what they call 'inclusive' liberalism whose purpose is to embed, legitimate and secure neoliberal reform. At their best, PRSPs can be effective in identifying local needs and problems and utilising liberal values to promote 'positive freedoms'. But 'more commonly this convergence works in more conservative ways, within constrained, almost phoney forms of the social, propagating juridical rules and programmes of security and safety, while merely talking up participation and community' (Porter and Craig 2004: 392). PRSPs also effectively move conditions to being prerequisites for accessing assistance from the international financial institutions (Porter and Craig 2004: 394).

Country PRSPs are reviewed jointly by Bank and IMF staff against set guidelines to determine whether they provide 'a sound basis on which to proceed with assistance and debt relief' (World Bank 2003a: 38). Until 2005, PRSPs required approval from the Bank Board, which, as even the Bank's Operation Evaluation Department acknowledged, undermined country ownership (cited in World Development Movement 2005: 8). It is still the case that the Bank's Country Assistance Strategy (CAS) is not necessarily in line with a country's PRSP as the CAS is 'specifically to account to' the Bank's shareholders (World Bank 2003a). Looked at in this way, the CDF does seem more like a blueprint than a mere tool. As Cammack (2003: 11–12) stated the CDF is

> a blueprint for a complete set of social and governmental relations and institutions ... it is actually a means of shaping social and structural policies so that they reinforce and extend macroeconomic discipline, and subordinating them to imperatives of capitalist accumulation.

The CDF has a strong focus on wide participation in the planning, design and implementation of projects. Participants are meant to include various multilateral and bilateral agencies, all levels of government within a country, civil society and the private sector. Indeed, the strong language on participation in the CDF highlights the extent to which the Bank incorporated participation as a core component of the PWC as a response to the NGO critique of the Bank in this area. Responding to this critique was undoubtedly a part of the Bank's public relations push, which was relatively successful, at least until the departure of Wolfensohn.

There has been a broad range of experiences in operationalising participation, but, in practice, the Bank tended to focus on improving relations with other donors and has not integrated participation into 'mainstream practice' especially in project implementation (Wodsak 2002: 93–95). Participation in projects remains a privilege rather than a right. Cammack (2003: 12) argued that participation rhetoric needs to be understood as a deliberate strategy 'to induce people to experience tightly controlled and carefully delimited forms of market-supporting activity as empowerment'. Actually, as Ilan Kapoor (2005: 1214) pointed out, participation performs several functions: it is a disciplinary mechanism for both states and civil society and it is a way of co-opting their support for structural adjustment.

Where participation is part of loan projects it is often connected to a renewed interest in decentralisation – from 1993 to 1997, 12 per cent of Bank projects involved decentralisation (Hadiz 2004: 706). Theoretically, decentralisation is part of the PWC agenda of reordering social and political relations in addition to the Washington Consensus project of reordering economies. However, in practice, in the hands of Bank staff, it tends to become a 'technical problem' and works to exclude the political nature of policy-making. As Vedi Hadiz (2004: 698) explained, the emphasis, in particular, on the political insulation of technocrats is particularly ironic given the supposition that decentralization leads to good governance practices involving wider public participation in democracy. In fact, the general thrust of neo-institutionalist theory embraces democracy only insofar as technocrats (or technopols) can preside over politics unimpeded by the intervention of democratic or more radical agendas. Further, the act of implementing decentralisation projects immerses the Bank in supportive relations with locally entrenched elites and it tends to restrict the Bank's capacity to transform them. In its practical implementation, decentralisation tends to be entwined with the Washington Consensus goal of privatisation because decentralised and unbundled government enterprises are easier to corporatise and privatise. The tensions Hadiz identifies disappear, however, if the reordered social relations promoted by democratisation are understood as neoliberal relations not democratic ones. Moreover, these new relations minimise the role of the state and posit civil society as a distinct conceptual sphere to that of the state.

In 2000, the Bank finally publicly admitted, in a limited fashion, the negative impact of the Washington Consensus. A report by Bank economist William Easterly (2001) noted that growth in developing countries between 1980 and 1998 was 0.0 per cent. The WDR 2000/2001 also implicitly acknowledged the failure of Bank policies during this period.

The WDR 2000/2001 (World Bank 2000a) is the next logical place to examine the PWC as it demonstrates the impact of NIE. However, World Development Reports are not actual Bank policy and, although they reflect Bank thinking, WDR 2000/2001 was somewhat of an exception. According to Wade (2001a,b; 2002), the WDR drafted by Kanbur took NIE and the NGO agenda too seriously. The US Treasury and the Bank's neoliberal economists could not accept the strong focus on income inequality and empowerment of the poor, or the NIE-influenced view on the failures in capital markets and the recommendation to create social safety nets prior to structural adjustment (Wade 2001a: 1436–38). Kanbur resigned as the report was being finalised in the hope of preventing the Bank from disassociating itself from the (already revised and rewritten) report. However, his resignation did not prevent a number of further substantive changes to the text, in particular to the most widely-read sections, the introduction and conclusion (Wade 2001b: 134–35).

This episode indicated the end of 'the brief "springtime" at the Bank in the second half of the 1990s' (IDEAs 2004: 16). Other indications of the end of openness were Stiglitz's forced resignation in November 1999 and the Bank's withdrawal from the Structural Adjustment Participatory Review Initiative (SAPRI), a civil society-driven review of the impacts of structural adjustment on the poor.[9] These developments indicate the limits of the PWC in the World Bank – it cannot address NIE and NGO challenges because to do so would mean challenging Washington Consensus hegemonic principles and logic. These limits derived from internal Bank culture and external factors, in particular the US Treasury: when Stiglitz's questioning of the Washington Consensus went too far, the US Treasury flexed its control over the Bank to ensure he resigned (Ritzen 2005: 101).

A further component of the PWC is the Bank's interest in social capital, which was prominent in the Bank from 1996 to the early 2000s. The relevance of social capital for development was tested in several sites, including Indonesia. Its prominence was indicated by the development of a dedicated website, which has since been downgraded.[10] The original site defined social capital as:

> the *institutions, relationships, and norms* that shape the quality and quantity of a society's social interactions. Increasing evidence shows that social cohesion is critical for societies to prosper economically and for development to be sustainable. Social capital is not just the sum of the institutions which underpin a society – it is the *glue that holds them together* (emphasis added).

The Bank's approach to, and definition of, social capital derived from its adaptation of NIE. Its goal remained economic growth, and for a while social capital was seen as the missing link needed to achieve this. As is clear from the definition, it is an all-encompassing phenomenon; there can be 'bad' as well as 'good' social capital. As Fine (2001b: 158) argued, 'social capital fills out everything that is not already taken care of in terms of standard economic analysis. In principle, it could be anything'. Further, he pointed out that social capital's appeal was that, on the one hand, it allowed 'the formal results of the new economics to be expressed in non-economic terms' and, on the other hand, it allowed economics to appear interdisciplinary (Fine 2001a: 136).

Although social capital was introduced to the Bank by social scientists hoping to challenge the hegemony of neoliberal economics, development economists rather than social scientists 'won' the debate in the group set up to develop the Bank's social capital strategy. According to Anthony Bebbington *et al.* (2004: 43–45), the discussion and use of social capital bifurcated into an econometrically based one among economists and more social theory based among operation staff. Critics of the Bank's discussion of social capital tend to focus on the published work, which was mostly by economists. The discussion here looks at these critiques but the case studies subsequently critically explore their practical use by operations staff.

Social capital studies tend to find that there are many issues (variables) that need to be taken into account in analysis. However, in the development of theoretical models for social capital, the Bank's economists found that inclusion of more than a few variables resulted in the models being 'too complicated to be useful. It becomes a matter of focusing upon a few factors that are privileged by being chosen as the key to promoting development' (Fine 2001b: 141).[11] Fine's analysis (2001b: 160–63) of the statistical methods that have been used to determine the impact of social capital variables in the Bank suggested they are (mathematically) inadequate. His critique was far reaching as it took issue with the general problem of economic reductionism inherent in both neoliberal and NIE approaches. The key point here is that social capital research did expand the opportunities for non-economists but their opportunities ended at 'borders of the economy and the state', whereas economists were able to utilise social capital 'to address issues from which they have previously been excluded' (Fine 2001a: 149). By 2005–6, social capital was out of favour in the Bank and even those social scientists who introduced it seemed to find that its capacity to shift the Bank's analysis and position on social issues was limited (Harriss 2007: 163).

In August 2004, the Bank renamed Structural Adjustment Lending: Development Policy Lending. It also revised the relevant Operational Policy/Bank Procedures statement (OP/BP 8.60) (World Bank 2004a). The policy review was presented as the culmination of lessons learned about adjustment lending from practice and reviews over the past decade. It was also meant to reflect changes in policy and practice in this period. The OP/BP does not fundamentally change the rationale for this kind of lending, it is still justified as quick or rapidly disbursing policy-based financing to meet 'actual or anticipated' financing gaps. The new rationale does explicitly include domestic factors in addition to external factors as possible causes of gaps. Three key themes are visible in the revised OP/BP, these are increased flexibility and simplification, participation and reducing costs to borrowers.

In September 2004, the Bank released its yearly Doing Business report: Doing Business 2005: Removing Obstacles to Growth (World Bank 2004g). The report 'benchmarks regulatory performance and reforms in 145 nations'; in other words, the environment for business as measured by indicators such as business commencements, access to credit and legislation regarding hiring and firing workers, enforcing contracts, registering property and protecting investors (World Bank 2004g). The report's conclusions are not surprising: there are heavier regulatory burdens on business in developing countries than in developed ones;[12] the benefits of reform 'appear to be large;' and 'regulation and weak property rights exclude [sic] the poor – especially women and younger people – from doing business' (World Bank 2004g). They contrast to Ha-Joon Chang's work looking at the historical role of institutions in the now developed countries. Chang's (2002: 116–17) analysis suggested that the institutions of today's developing countries are, in general, far ahead of the now developed countries when they were at similar levels of development. While this is mostly a good thing, he pointed out that good institutions take time to develop, must be affordable for the country and must be socio-politically acceptable. He argued (2002: 135) that international standard property rights and corporate governance are the two areas that are most problematic for developing countries as they require large investments (large numbers of lawyers and accountants) for limited returns and, as a result, reduce the availability of funding for education or essential infrastructure.

Doing Business 2005 shows how the Bank is increasingly centralising and unifying the production of economic and political intelligence on states that was traditionally produced by firms and banks engaged in international investment. Does this activity assist private investment which, according to the dedicated website, 'is central to promoting growth and expanding opportunities for poor people'? (World Bank and International Finance Corporation 2004). Possibly, though there are certainly more convincing explanations for global investment patterns. And as Chang (2002: 137) also pointed out, investors seem to like China and India in particular, which have not followed the Bank's prescription on institutions. What it does do is reinforce the power of transnational corporations and global finance that has grown so dramatically since capital markets were liberalised in the 1980s (Gill and Law 1993: 98–99, 105). Equally, it reinforces the Bank's own policy prescriptions for economic development.

The year 2004 was probably when the PWC reached its zenith. Moreover, the replacement of Wolfensohn with Paul Wolfowitz in 2005 heralded the start of a shift in the Bank's direction. The year 2004 is also the final year of the case studies, so this is where the exploration of the PWC concludes.

Key Features of the post-Washington Consensus

The key features of the post-Washington consensus are the following.

- A fundamental continuation of the neoliberal approach to monetary and fiscal policy; however, the approach to financial liberalisation should be more cautious given concerns about market failure and applicability to local conditions. Interestingly, support for trade liberalisation remains largely intact in the Bank despite academic challenges regarding its theoretical and empirical outcomes (Broad 2004: 136).
- Following from above and the (supposed) abandonment of one-size-fits-all approaches to development, there should be greater attention to the specific country situation. This should include better-developed socioeconomic analysis of local conditions as well as consideration of global and regional impacts.
- Recipient government's should own their development programme and projects: in a strong version this would mean recipient government's initiate and control development assistance projects, a weak version is indicated by reference to proxies for commitment such as counterpart funding and expressions of support.
- A reduction in the Washington Consensus hostility to the state, allowing an expansion of its role to compliment, rather than compete with markets.

There remains signification variation in the view of the state's role – a weak form only promotes a state that provides a good policy environment for business, in other words an active, pro-capitalist state (Broad 2004: 136). A further step would allow more space for state institutions to engage with market imperfections (information and transaction costs). A strong version, which indicates a genuine engagement with the state as actor, would require an analysis of actors and interests in the society and the distribution of power and resources between them as well as analysis of who wins and looses from policy proposals (Broad 2004: 140–41; Cammack 2002: 5).

- Increased concern with *market* failure to complement existing focus on government failure; this would be indicative of a stronger version of the PWC. Practical indications of implementation include analysis of markets prior to promotion of privatisation. A related issue is increased attention to the sequencing of reform programmes, in particular the development of adequate regulatory frameworks relevant to local conditions prior to liberalisation.
- A greater concern for the social costs of adjustment and poverty in general.
- A seeming genuine appreciation of local knowledge and practices tempered by a concern about coherence and coordination (Wodsak 2002: 44). This may be presented as expanded participation in the planning, design and implementation of activities. Participation needs to be considered both in terms of the type of participants involved (bilateral and multilateral organisation, levels of government, levels of civil society and the private sector) and the extent and nature of the participatory process. A related concern is analysis of social capital – this likely extends to economists analysing social factors but not social scientists in the Bank analysing the economy and state.
- Increased attention to decentralisation as a policy prescription for supposedly increasing participation, ensuring local needs are met and improving governance.
- A slightly broader approach to health and education.
- A revitalised concern with corruption.

The PWC continues the Washington Consensus concern with corruption but on the basis of quite different assumptions – the Washington Consensus focuses on corruption derived from the NPE's cynical and almost malevolent view of states in the Third World (Toye 1993: 135). It sees politicians as driven by only self-interest, which is meant to explain both their failure to adopt the right (neoliberal) policies and problems of corruption, whereas NIE understands corruption as the result of government *and* market failures. This expands the possibilities for dealing with corruption beyond the Washington Consensus mantra of smaller government. Further, it makes corruption a less dangerous area for the Bank, as it transforms it from a political to an economic issue. Equally the focus on property rights and institutions (which comprise legal systems, conventions and norms and their enforcement) is rejuvenated;

as these are essential to minimising transaction and information costs and thus to economic growth, they are a prerequisite to 'getting the prices right' (North 1998: 23–25). Moreover, its analysis of the incorporation of conventions and norms in institutions suggests that simply transferring Western systems to the developing world is unlikely, on its own, to improve performance.

One final area demanding consideration is the Bank's project model and procurement practices. The Bank has historically been at the centre of project identification, development and appraisal, which became increasingly linked to poor outcomes. The Strategic Compact involved large-scale decentralisation of Bank staff to country offices and streamlining of bank procedures in order to improve the country ownership and quality of development programmes. These reforms were relatively successful because they fitted with the Bank's existing organisational culture with its focus on disbursing funds. However, the new management system did tend to undermine the commitment to social and environmental safeguards policies, and it did not improve the system of outcome monitoring (Weaver and Leiteritz 2005: 380–81; Nielson *et al.* 2006). Moreover, and not surprisingly, reforms did not address the Bank's requirement that project activities be tendered out. The Bank will not directly fund governments to run any project components, even, for example, a road safety campaign component of a road rehabilitation project. The Bank's project model is hostile to government and directed at expanding the space for private markets. Procurement must be undertaken to Bank standards through one of three methods: international competitive bidding (ICB), national competitive bidding (NCB) and local shopping. ICB has been the dominant form of Bank procurement. ICB does allow a margin of preference (generally 15 per cent) for local suppliers. Nevertheless, historically North American or European firms have won the majority of contracts, although over the last couple of decades the trend has been to work with national partners or through local offices of an international firm (Caufield 1998: 242–43). ICB needs to be seen as a way of ensuring national economies are internationally integrated. It has been another hegemonic principle in the Bank. Thus, the case studies also examine whether there has been any challenge to Bank project development and procurement methods.

Overall, there is limited evidence that the Bank has moved beyond its traditional concern with economic growth within a market capitalist framework. Indeed, it is clear that the concern with social issues ultimately rests on their impact on 'economic development or the functioning of markets' (Wodsak 2002: 98). However, it is equally clear that there has been a level of change, influenced in part by NIE and in part by NGO critiques. However, in the same way that most engaged with the NIE do not want to replace neoliberalism, but rather to supplement it, the PWC is best understood as an expansion and revision of the Washington Consensus. Thus the term *post*-Washington Consensus is appropriate, highlighting its intellectual, political and practical origins in what Paul Cammack has described as the Bank's 'constant commitment to the systematic transformation of social relations and institutions in the developing world, in order to generalize and facilitate capitalist accumulation on a global scale, and build specifically capitalist hegemony through the promotion of participation and ownership' (Cammack 2003: 3).

The book turns now to case studies of the World Bank in Vietnam and Indonesia. The changes in Bank lending in each country are explored with a focus on this list of the key features of the PWC in order to enable some empirically based conclusions to be drawn about the extent to which changes in lending have reflected PWC discourse.

Part II

The World Bank in Vietnam and Indonesia

5 Introduction to Part II

Case study selection

Part II of the book comprises two case studies of how the post-Washington Consensus (PWC) has translated into Bank lending. This section introduces the case studies and outlines the methodology used in the selection of case study countries. The case studies examine the Bank's overall relationship with the borrower but pay particular attention to Bank lending. This is a timely exercise because surprisingly, in the last decade or so – apart from the odd controversial dam project or the like – Bank lending has received limited critical focus. Further, investment lending receives even less than adjustment lending. Attention has in the main been focused on the Bank's development discourse. This focus is undoubtedly warranted and had been facilitated by the Bank's increasing disclosure of documents from 1993. The new disclosure policy, though, also applies to loans, thus making analysis of the Bank's lending significantly easier. However, there is now sometimes so much information available that it is difficult to analyse it.

Bank lending is more than just a way of maintaining the relationship with a country in order to influence its policy directions, as has on occasion been suggested (Kapur *et al.* 1997: 270). Rather, as is shown in the case studies, the Bank's lending programme involves the pursuit of an often long-term agenda. Moreover, the form and nature of Bank lending – project lending, design and implementation according to Bank standards, and procedures and international tendering – binds borrowing countries to market procedures and enmeshes them with international capitalism.

In terms of the timeframes studied, the Washington Consensus dominated the Bank from the early 1980s to the mid to late 1990s. Ideally, a case study of Bank lending in this period would have covered a period in the late 1980s to early 1990s. However, in 1993 the Bank relaxed its official disclosure rules for projects approved after that date (Caufield 1998: 266). Given the change in disclosure, the first case study starts in 1993 and it was considered that five year's analysis of new project approvals would provide a comprehensive overview of Bank lending and trends, so the first case study period runs from 1993 to 1997. For the PWC period, the latest period possible was chosen to allow its influence to have filtered through the Bank's pipeline of projects – the period studied is 2000–4.

In order to select the case study countries, a range of data was collected on eight developing countries across four regions with active Bank portfolios. In South-east Asia, Indonesia and Vietnam were explored, in South Asia, Pakistan and Bangladesh, in South America, Peru and Brazil and in Africa, Nigeria and Uganda. Given the focus of the project on changing lending practices, two factors were considered crucial for case study countries: first a fair-sized portfolio with the Bank (approximately $1 billion in gross disbursements over a five-year period) so that there are a range of loans to compare in the different periods. Second, borrowers should have at least a 'medium-sized' economy so that development policy and lending has not normally been seriously impacted by a single event such as a large fall in the price of a key export or a natural disaster. It was considered important that the countries have a strong relationship with the Bank and that it's lending is likely to be of notably economic consequence. Thus, although it is beyond the scope of the current research project to determine the impact of Bank lending (indeed this is a virtually impossible task), the project may in addition be of some use in indicating where Bank programmes have been most influential in case study countries and some of the possible implications of this.

Data collected on each potential case study country included:

- eligibility for International Bank for Reconstruction and Development (IBRD) and/or International Development Association (IDA) loans;
- total number of Bank projects and the cumulative lending;
- Bank approvals in 2003;
- type of loans (investment, adjustment and other non-project);
- gross and net disbursements over the period 1997–2002;
- net Official Development Assistance (ODA) received 1997–2002;[1]
- net Bank disbursements as a percentage of net ODA 1997–2002;
- ODA as a percentage of gross national income (GNI) *or* gross national product (GNP), 2001;
- foreign direct investment (FDI) flows 1997–2002; and
- ODA as a percentage of FDI, 1997–2002.

Data were obtained from official World Bank publications and its website, the UNDP Human Development Index and the OECD Development Assistance Committee website.

The South American countries were quickly excluded, as in both cases, although Bank funds are significant in relation to net flows of ODA, ODA as a percentage of GNI overall is minute (for Peru 0.85 per cent and Brazil 0.07 per cent). In addition, both countries only have access to IBRD funding and both, as of July 2004, had only environment and investment loans with the Bank, that is they had no adjustment loans. In Nigeria, ODA as a percentage of GNI was also small (0.47 per cent) and, in addition, Bank gross disbursements were quite low and net disbursements were negative for 1997–2002. Uganda had by far the highest ODA as a percentage of GNI of the countries studied (14.28 per cent); the Bank was a significant contributor of funds overall and there was a good mix of loans. However, Uganda had the smallest population examined and the high levels of poverty mean the economy is quite small, add to this the high dependence on primary commodities and the ongoing unrest in the northern border regions and it was not attractive for this study of Bank lending.

For both Pakistan and Bangladesh, ODA is a small but significant contributor to GNI – 3.37 and 2.12 per cent respectively. The level of ODA to Pakistan increased notably from 2001 – a direct result of its role in the so-called 'war on terror'. The instability in Pakistan and ongoing travel warnings essentially ruled it out as a case study country. World Bank gross disbursements to Bangladesh were over $2 billion for 1997–2002, a significant amount both in relation to total ODA flows and total FDI flows. However, as of July 2004, the active Bank portfolio contained only one adjustment loan. It was a possible case study.

ODA as a percentage of GNI in Vietnam was 4.42 per cent, a comparatively significant level. Between 1997 and 2002 gross Bank disbursements were over $1.3 billion, a significant amount in relation to both ODA and FDI flows. The Bank portfolio is made up predominately of investment loans; however, structural adjustment lending increased from almost 9 per cent of lending in 1993–7 to over 16 per cent in 2000–4. Although this is well below the Bank's current average of 33 per cent of loans in structural adjustment, it is a significant level for a country defining itself as socialist.

In Indonesia, ODA as a percentage of GNP in 2001 was approximately 2.5 per cent, which is a historically average level, although a spike in 1998–9, due to the Asian Financial Crisis, took it to over 4 per cent (Chowdhury and Sugema 2005: 189). Nevertheless, 2.5 per cent is a significant level for such a large economy. Gross Bank disbursements to Indonesia 1997–2002 were over $5.8 billion, although interestingly net disbursements were quite low, indicating a high repayment burden. This meant that net Bank loans as a percentage of net ODA were a low 3.7 per cent. However, the significance of the Bank to Indonesia is clear when the gross Bank disbursements (1997–2002) of over $5.8 billion are compared with FDI flows during the same period, which were *minus* $13.3 billion. As of July 2004, Indonesia had only one active adjustment loan out of a total of forty loans. Prior to the Asian Financial Crisis, Indonesia had only ever accessed one adjustment loan, since then it has had four, bringing the total to five out of its total of 317 loans.

There are a range of other reasons why Vietnam and Indonesia stood out as attractive options for the case studies: there has been relatively little study of Bank activity in these countries; they are both very accessible; and there is an interesting contrast between their forms of government and their relationships with the Bank. Further, Bank lending to Vietnam only resumed in 1993, during the period when the Bank was shifting away from the Washington Consensus. It seems reasonable to assume that the assigned staff would have fewer preconceptions about the 'right' policy actions, which may mean that new directions in the Bank's approach to development could be more apparent there.

Indonesia and Vietnam share a region and are now at similar levels of development – Indonesia's 2006 Human Development Index ranking was 108 and Vietnam's was 109 (United Nations Human Development Report 2006). Indonesia's GNI per capita is still significantly higher than Vietnam's (2005: $1280 versus $620) but Vietnam's life expectancy is higher (2004: 70.3 years versus 67.4 years) (World Bank Group Website). Both countries have an adult literacy rate of just over 90 per cent and similar levels of reported income inequality (2002 Gini Index Indonesia 34.3, Vietnam 37.0) (United Nations Development Report 2006). Of course, Indonesia has a much larger population than Vietnam, they are geographically very different and their development and coherence as 'nation-states' is quite distinct. They also have interesting and contrasting forms of government, levels of political stability and approaches to the role of the state in development. These contrasts were useful for the study in terms of analysing the Bank's changed approach to the role of the state in the economy and specificity to local conditions in two diverse settings.

The contrast continues with the impact of the Asian Financial Crisis – Indonesia was hit early and hard by the Crisis and is only just returning to earlier levels of GDP growth. Whereas the relatively insulated Vietnamese economy was only indirectly impacted and growth rates quickly returned to equal the previous high levels. Indonesia was an early favourite of the World Bank and their relationship through to the time of the Asian Financial Crisis was, if not always perfect, certainly strong. However, since then Indonesia has fallen out of favour with the Bank and the level of lending has decreased. Vietnam in contrast, after decades in the wilderness, has become a Bank favourite – one of it's proclaimed 'success stories'. Since the Asian Financial Crisis though, there have been hints of strains in the relationship.

There is one identifiable weakness in the suggested case studies, which is that both countries have a low proportion of adjustment loans compared with the Bank's overall portfolio. In 2003, adjustment loans accounted for 33 per cent of new lending commitments and for the period 1997–2003 they averaged 38.2 per cent. However, adjustment loans appear to be disproportionately concentrated in a few countries. A brief survey of loans in 30 countries confirmed this with 20 countries (including India, China and Thailand) having none or only one adjustment loan, while a few countries had a very high proportion of adjustment loans. For example, over 48 per cent of Turkey's loan portfolio by value was adjustment lending.[2] Overall the majority of Bank loans are project loans and relatively less analysis has been done on them, whereas structural adjustment has been the subject of much study.

Structure of the case studies

Each case study comprises two chapters. The first chapter focuses on the general background, starting with some information on the political, economic and social structures and policies of the country. The country's dealings with donors are outlined as are their relationships with the World Bank. The initial chapter also details the link between the policy framework of the country and the Bank's programme through an analysis of the Bank's key country planning documents: the Country Assistance Strategies and Poverty Reduction Strategy Paper.

The second chapter provides a detailed analysis of Bank lending structured by type of lending: adjustment or investment. Adjustment loans were studied together but analysis of investment lending was separated into sectors, utilising the Bank's own sectoral classifications of activities. Thus loans in say the transportation sector in the first case study period are compared with loans in the transportation sector in the second case study period. This generally worked well because, despite the broad nature of the sectoral classification, Bank projects in both case study periods tend to be similar. For example, in Vietnam energy and mining sector projects are made up only of activities in electricity generation, distribution and retailing. It did create some problems in sectors where Bank lending was small. For example, in Indonesia there is only one loan in each case study period in the information and communications sector and they are in quite different areas. This made any comparison impossible but such problems areas made up only a very small proportion of lending, so their exclusion or incorporation into other sectors is unlikely to have any detrimental impacts on the overall outcomes of the loan analysis.

The case studies are based on an analysis of key Bank documents, in particular Country Assistance Strategies, Staff Appraisal Reports (later renamed Project Appraisal Documents) and Implementation Completion Reports (where available). In addition, the analysis was informed by secondary literature available on the projects and by interviews in each case study country with World Bank officials, government officials, non-governmental organisations and academics.

6 Vietnam

An overview

This chapter commences with an overview of the structure of the Vietnamese government and an outline of key socioeconomic developments. It covers the period since reunification, although the focus is the post-1986 period, as this is when the process of socioeconomic reform or renovation, called *Doi Moi*, was initiated. Next, donor activity in Vietnam is highlighted, followed by an outline of the Bank's relationship with Vietnam and a detailed analysis of the changes in the Bank's country strategy for Vietnam over the two case study periods of 1993 to 2004. This analysis provides the structure for the analysis of Bank lending in Chapter 6. The primary and secondary literature on Vietnam is more limited than for Indonesia. Further, official Government of Vietnam (GoV) documents do not always accurately reflect policy. The GoV has been careful not to publicly challenge the views of international donors but that does not necessarily mean it shares their views. Thus, as Pietro Masina (2006: 3,17) argued, it is safer to analyse Vietnamese policy through what is implemented than what is sometimes said.

The political and administrative structure in Vietnam

The political structure of Vietnam is not easy to describe because the Communist Party of Vietnam, while not having a clearly defined role in the Constitution and elsewhere, parallels the formal structure of the state and the administration at every level (McCarty 2001; Van Arkadie and Mallon 2003). The Constitution indicates the importance of the Party rather than its role – it defines Vietnam as a socialist republic 'of the people, from the people, for the people' and notes that the Party represents the 'rights and interests of the working class, the toiling people … [It] is the force leading the state and society' (cited in Van Arkadie and Mallon 2003: 58–59). Membership of the Party, state administration and business interests overlap; generally the Party decides key administration appointments. However, a 1995 government reorganisation by the 'pro-reform' Prime Minister Vo Van Kiet and his faction (and supported by the IMF (International Monetary Fund) and World Bank) started a process of insulating government administration from the Party (Kolko 1997: 132–35). The Party seems to have largely acquiesced to this reduced role and, since the late 1990s, it has limited its role to policy-making and guidance and not directly managed activities (Nørlund *et al.* 2003: 53). This enabled the administration to develop property rights and increase the importance of the rule of law.

The Constitution provides for a unitary system of government operating at four levels: national, provincial, district and commune. At the national level, the Constitution provides for a National Assembly with 450 deputies elected for five-year terms. The National Assembly elects the President and Prime Minister, each for five-year terms; the President is the ceremonial Head of State and Commander-in-Chief of the armed forces. The Prime Minister selects the ministers or heads of the state's 22 ministries and 26 other agencies and heads the Council of Ministers.

The Prime Minister also selects the leaders of the Provincial People's Committees, which administer the 59 provinces and five municipalities. There is a separate provincial legislative arm, Provincial People's Councils, but membership of the two bodies often overlaps.[1] A similar structure operates at the district and commune level and villages are organised too. Despite the unitary structure and strong national control, provincial administrations have increasing autonomy with respect to budgeting and operations. The degree to which this has been utilised varies and depends in part, not surprisingly, on the standing of local leaders (Van Arkadie and Mallon 2003: 61).

Despite being a one-party and unitary state, Vietnam was never as centrally planned or controlled as other socialist countries. Stein Tønnesson (2000: 243) explained this as the result of necessary compromise between the many layers of the Vietnamese state: social, political–doctrinal, economic and geographic. Further, an important Viet Minh legacy is that key groups remain committed to social justice, which to an 'extent reduces the capacity of those Vietnamese decision-makers who want to combine social stability with market-oriented reforms'. Such doctrinal commitments can cut across regional differences (between the north, centre and south) and combine in various ways with the diverse but linked class grouping (for example, linking various groups focused on security concerns or commercial matters) and with Confucian and Vietnamese cultural traditions. As Adam McCarty (2001: 5) concluded, it is appropriate to describe Vietnam as 'a rather unique form of consensus governance' or a 'managed democracy' that allows mass representation under Party control.

The Grassroots Democracy Decree legislated in 1998 is a good example of the consensus process. The decree was partly a reaction to peasant uprisings, especially the disturbances in 128 villages in Thai Binh Province in 1997–8. They appear to have been caused by a combination of the reaction to economic reform in rural areas, local corruption and governmental unresponsiveness to these issues. The Decree gave people at the commune level specific rights to participate in decision-making, petition authorities and oversee local budgets; it was overlain with a commitment to promoting democracy at the commune level (Nørlund *et al.* 2003: 44).

The consensus system, a cautious leadership and the continuing perception that the Party and State are concerned about the welfare of the general population, means the Party and State have retained a fair degree of legitimacy in Vietnam (Masina 2006: 3,17). The process of reform or renovation, called *Doi Moi*, initiated in 1986 coupled with a willingness to admit to previous mistakes undoubtedly assisted with the retention of legitimacy. Gabriel Kolko (1997: 32–33) suggested that *Doi Moi* was strongly influenced by the IMF – or rather that IMF staff had strong influence on a few key Vietnamese policy-makers who were the key architects of the reform.[2] However, others disagree and point to Vietnam's strong political structure and culture that give it a notable capacity to resist donor pressure for political reform. McCarty (2001: 21–22) argues that aid dialogue has had only limited impact, partly because of the diffuse policy making process, which involves a high level of consultation and consensus with a range of actors. The capacity of Vietnam's historic bloc to resist the Bank's hegemony is a reoccurring theme of this case study.

Socioeconomic changes and policy in Vietnam since 1986

Academic debate about the nature of *Doi Moi* and the Vietnamese socioeconomic system more generally revolves around two central issues: first, the relative strength or weakness of the Vietnamese state and its contribution to the country's notable economic growth over the past two decades. The second issue is the level and pace of reform required to ensure continuing economic growth. Similar to the literature on East Asian development, a rough dividing line can be made between 'free market' (or neoliberal) and more critical ('statist') perspectives. The former group point to the weakness of the Vietnamese state and concurrently the need to speed up market-based reforms (Fforde 2004; Turley 1999; de Vylder 1995). Whereas the latter scholars highlight the relative stability, continuity of political institutions and decisive economic decision-making that the GoV has provided, which has been a key part of Vietnam's poverty reduction and economic growth performance (Kerkvliet 1998; Van Arkadie and Mallon 2003; Lee *et al.* 2005). Equally, critical scholars analyse the impact of regional and international geopolitical and economic developments on Vietnam's policy choices.[3]

Following formal reunification in 1976, economic growth was low and unable to keep pace with population growth. The demands of rehabilitation and reconstruction competed with security needs as Vietnam was forced to engage militarily with both Cambodia and China, and this led to a doubling of the size of the army. Difficulties were exacerbated by the US-backed UN economic embargo after Vietnam's intervention in Cambodia. Domestically, the attempt at collectivisation in the south generally failed, while in the north, collectivised agriculture performed poorly. The performance of manufacturing enterprises was highly variable. Already in 1979, a sporadic process of relaxing constraints on economic activity and decentralising of decision-making commenced. After initial gains, poor structures combined with high levels of military expenditure resulted in further economic deterioration. By 1986, inflation was 500–700 per cent per annum and the budget and trade deficits had escalated – a situation made worse by the cessation of Communist Bloc and Chinese aid in the following years (Van Arkadie and Mallon 2003: 51, 67). On an expenditure basis, over 70 per cent of the population were living in poverty and some areas were on the verge of famine (Nguyen 2001: 166–70). The resultant social unrest was a key impetus to *Doi Moi* along with the informal activities occurring in trade and exchange, which drove formal policy changes.

Dzung The Nguyen (2001: 166–70) described *Doi Moi* as comprising three main periods. The first period, 'Path Seeking' (1986–8), was driven by informal activity. A series of microeconomic reforms were undertaken to reduce the limits on private sector activity and domestic trade. This was followed by increases in official prices for non-essential consumer goods to bring them closer to market prices. Price reform was undertaken fairly systematically through to 1992, by which time prices for all but a few commodities were at market levels, lifting a significant burden from the state budget. In 1987, a law allowing private land-use rights was passed and the following year land was equitably reallocated to households. In combination with additional freedoms for farmers and new forms of support, the result was significant improvements in farm productivity (Van Arkadie and Mallon 2003: 70). These improvements were at the core of the dramatic reductions in poverty (Masina 2006: 3, 17).

Macroeconomic reform started in 1987 with the first currency devaluation, although a major devaluation of the Dong did not take place until 1989, which brought the Dong close to its market rate and resulted in positive interest rates (Van Arkadie and Mallon 2003: 70). From 1989 to 1993, the second phase of reforms systematically moved Vietnam towards a market-type economy and macroeconomic stabilisation took place (Nguyen 2001: 167). This period saw a formal end to the two-tier price system; increasing formal acknowledgement of the role of the non-state sector in production; a gradual reduction in foreign exchange and trade restrictions; legalisation of foreign direct investment and gold trading; development of a two-tier banking system; and legislation on land-rights trading.

Reform of state-owned enterprises (SOEs) got under way; between 1988 and 1992, their number was reduced from 12,000 to 6,000 and the SOE labour force was reduced by one-third. In 1992, the process of 'equitisation' was initiated, which the GoV explains as transforming the ownership of the mode of production, but it generally amounts to little more than privatisation (Evans 2004: 1). It can take place through maintaining the state capital value and issuing shares to attract new capital; selling part of the existing state capital value of the enterprise; selling part of the enterprise; and selling the entire capital of an enterprise and turning it into a joint stock company (Evans 2004: 6).

Commentators on both the 'left' and 'right' have characterised the programme of reform as equivalent to a typical International Monetary Fund stabilisation package. However, there is reason to be cautious with this interpretation and to consider the impact of indigenous influences on *Doi Moi.* As Stefan de Vylder (1995: 37–38) pointed out, in Vietnam microeconomic reforms preceded macroeconomic reform – the reverse of the standard IMF approach. Despite reductions in the SOE sector and tight monetary and fiscal policy, government expenditure actually increased during the reform period, in stark contrast to standard IMF prescriptions of reducing government expenditures (Nguyen 2001: 174). The Vietnamese also opted for a gradual process of reform, with much 'learning by doing' – it cannot be characterised, regardless of IMF preferences, as a 'big bang' approach (Turley 1999: 278). As a result, Vietnam was not able to meet IMF or World Bank requirements to receive adjustment loans between 1995 and 2001. The process was more than mere 'adjustment' of the economy, it 'revolutionised the entire set of development concepts and strategies' (Nørlund *et al.* 2003: 78). And this 'revolution' has been as much influenced by socialism and the model of the East Asian 'developmental states' as it has been by neoliberalism (Masina 2006: 28). It is a process in which Vietnam is still engaged.

The positive economic developments – economic growth jumped to 5.1 per cent in 1988 and inflation stabilised – cannot be explained only by the *Doi Moi* reforms. A key factor was the end of the war in Cambodia.[4] By 1993, growth reached close to 10 per cent and remained at high levels until mid-decade. Much of the early growth was attributable to the farm sector, which employed around 70 per cent of the working population. Given the egalitarian land distribution, growth had a strong impact on poverty; by 1998 the poverty rate had fallen to around 37 per cent of the population (Joint Donor Report to the Vietnam Consultative Group Meeting 2003: 9).

Prior to 1986, Vietnam was performing better than countries with similar levels of per capita income, assessed by development indicators such as levels of literacy (1980: males 91 per cent, females 78 per cent), primary schooling (gross enrolments in 1980: 108 per cent of age group) and maternal mortality (200 per 100,000 live births) (Nguyen 2001: 200). Thus the existing social welfare structure underpinned the ongoing reductions in poverty. Serious problems remained: malnutrition affected 52 per cent of under-five year olds in 1980–5; in 1997–2000 it still affected 37 per cent of under-fives, which is high by regional standards (World Bank 2002a, Annex 5).

While Vietnam progressed on most human development indicators between 1986 and 1992, the overall social welfare system – covering health, education and social support – was largely neglected. In education, lower and upper secondary enrolments actually declined until 1995. In health, the number of beds, medical assistants and nurses declined, accompanied by reduced access to the formal health care system (Nguyen 2001: 200). The introduction of user-fees meant that by the year 2000, households directly covered approximately 43 per cent of the costs of education and 35 per cent of public hospital costs. A public hospital visit cost a household from the poorest population quintile on average around 45 per cent of their annual non-food expenditure (Nguyen 2001: 251–54). From the mid-1990s state allocations to health and education increased and these combined with the income from user fees to produce quality improvements (Masina 2006: 26).

Other forms of social welfare such as transfers and poverty reduction programmes were severely neglected. Under the old system, the provision of housing, food, utilities, health, education, etc., was organised around cooperatives, SOEs and the arms of the state. But cooperatives largely disappeared and SOEs had most social obligations removed in the transition to market operations. Only after 1992 were steps taken to adjust social services to the new economy.

Dzung The Nguyen argued that the third period of *Doi Moi*, 1994–2001, focused on consolidating reforms. Tight fiscal and monetary policy was maintained and incremental reforms continued, including decentralisation of budget management and a general focus on public sector management from 1995 (Nguyen 2001: 200). Irene Nørlund *et al.* (2003: 59) saw the incremental process as the government's attempt 'to set up rational and harmonious development structures before creating a common playing field for all economic components'.

Since 1994, further steps have been taken to integrate Vietnam into the world economy, including tariff reductions, removal of various quantitative restrictions and quotas, further liberalisation of export and import licensing requirements, and in 2000 a stock exchange was established in Ho Chi Minh City. Some of the steps were requirements for accession to the World Trade Organization, which occurred in January 2007. The GoV hopes to complete planned equitisation of SOEs by 2010, but the pace has been relatively slow and this deadline might not be met, despite World Bank pressure.

The Asian Financial Crisis reduced GDP growth, although not nearly as heavily or as long as in neighbours such as Thailand and Indonesia. This was in part due to the continuing controls on foreign investment and exchange, which meant funds were long-term investment oriented not short-term and speculative. FDI to Vietnam did decline in the lead up to the Crisis but this was not, as the World Bank argued, due to foreign investors concerns about slowing down of reform. Rather, it was due to a decline in real estate investment and fluctuations in oil and gas investments (Masina 2006: 67–68). The decline during the Crisis was mostly because over 60 per cent of Vietnam's FDI came from East Asia, that is from other countries affected by the Crisis (Masina 2006: 79). The Crisis also appreciated the value of the *Dong*, reduced exports and hit government revenues. In 1998, growth dropped to 5.8 per cent and in 1999 to 4.8 per cent. However, the government acted to maintain macroeconomic stability by controlling imports, devaluing the *Dong* and adopting conservative monetary policy (Masina 2006: 84–86). By 2000, growth had recovered to 6.8 per cent, and in 2004 it was 7.7 per cent. Poverty continued to decline significantly – from 37.4 per cent in 1998 to 28.9 per cent in 2002 and 20 per cent in 2004. However, the gap between the rich and poor in Vietnam is steadily increasing (Joint Donor Report to the Vietnam Consultative Group Meeting 2003: 12–13).

From 1992, steps were undertaken to adjust the social services to the new economy, including the extension of social insurance to non-state employees in formal sector enterprises with more than 10 employees, meaning it covered only around 11 per cent of the workforce (Nguyen 2001: 214–15). Combined with existing veterans' pension and state obligations, social insurance accounted for 90 per cent of the 3 per cent of national expenditure that was directed to social welfare at this time. Most of the benefits go to upper and upper-middle income groups. The other key development was the creation of a national programme of poverty reduction assistance. Some of the components of this programme were already in existence, but in 1998 nine programmes were consolidated into the National Target Program for Hunger Eradication and Poverty Reduction (Nguyen 2001: 224–28).

The final component of the social protection system is social assistance, comprising two funds: a social guarantee fund, and the contingency fund for pre-harvest starvation and disaster relief. These funds are the main safety net for the bulk of the population yet they were equal to only 0.1 per cent of GDP in the mid-1990s. They provide benefits that leave recipients living below the poverty line (Nguyen 2001: 218–23). Dzung The Nguyen's (2001: 235) analysis of the overall social welfare system concluded that, despite some improvements, 'Vietnam's social protection system provides its benefits to those who appear to be least in need'. Yet, since Nguyen's study, poverty reduction expenditures have been increasing and there was a big drop in poverty between 2002 (28.9 per cent) and 2004 (20 per cent), which indicates that the overhaul of social expenditures is proving effective (World Bank Operations Evaluation Department and IMF Independent Evaluation Office 2005: 94).

Development assistance to Vietnam since 1993

Prior to 1993, Vietnam had only limited engagement with non-communist donors. There were some international advisers present, coordinated through the United Nations Development Programme (UNDP), which had a small programme in Vietnam along with UNICEF (United Nations Children's Fund). The IMF maintained a limited programme but Vietnam defaulted on repayments in the mid-1980s and the United States vetoed the rescheduling of its arrears until 1993, thus preventing any new programme (Freeman 1993: 10). The Bank made one loan to Vietnam in 1978 but a self-imposed ban stopped further activity until 1993 (see the following section for further detail). In addition, the Swedish International Development Cooperation Agency and a number of NGOs, such as Oxfam and Save the Children, had small programmes prior to 1993 (Nørlund *et al.* 2003: 75–76).

Non-communist donors re-engaged with Vietnam only after the debt with the former regime in the south was settled. According to Chossudovsky

(1997: 147), Vietnam was only allowed to rejoin the Bank after the 1993 agreement in which Hanoi took over the debts of the South Vietnamese regime; this was the costs of access to new credit and an end to the US embargo. At one level then, it is surprising how dependent the GoV is now on Western aid. As Painter (2003: 32) pointed out: 'between 1994 and 1999, annual overseas development assistance (ODA) averaged 20 per cent of central government expenditure, rising from 17 per cent in 1997 to 27 per cent in 1999'. There are now over 20 countries and organisations providing ODA to Vietnam; however, over 80 per cent of funding comes from just three sources: Japan, the World Bank and the Asian Development Bank (ADB). Given the sources of ODA, not surprisingly most is in the form of concessional loans not grants – in 2002, 84.8 per cent of ODA was in the form of loans requiring repayment (Duc 2004: 46). As a consequence, '[a]bout four-fifths of debt in Vietnam is with multilateral and bilateral donors, on concessional terms' (Painter 2005).

In terms of sectors of support, according to the OECD Development Assistance Committee (2005) categories, just over 40 per cent of ODA in Vietnam is for economic infrastructure and services, 17.5 per cent is allocated to programme assistance and the remainder is divided fairly equally among education, health, production, multisector and other assistance. Japan is overall the largest donor of ODA – in 2002 alone it disbursed $429 million. On average, 73–82 per cent of Japanese ODA has been loans: 45.5 per cent went to the electricity sector, 32.3 per cent to transportation and 16.8 per cent to rural and urban infrastructure projects (Duc 2004: 48). By the end of 2004, ADB (2005) cumulative commitments to Vietnam were $3.15 billion. Its sector profile was somewhat more diverse than the World Bank or Japanese ODA. The agriculture and transport sectors led its priorities – each receiving just over 19 per cent of loans in value terms. The energy sector was also a major focus, receiving 12.6 per cent of flows, while the finance and water sectors each received 10.8 per cent. The remaining funds were divided among education, multisector, law, health, and industry and trade. There is a significant convergence visible between the three major donors in the sectors of electricity, transport, and water supply and sanitation, yet they have received little critical attention and analysis from NGOs and academics.

Since the rescheduling of arrears in 1993, the IMF and Vietnam have had a rather tumultuous relationship. It resumed lending to Vietnam in 1994 and made further commitments in 1995 and 1996. However, after a falling out in 1997 regarding the timing of reforms, loan disbursements were withheld and there were no loans until 2001, and the programme was formally suspended in April 2004 when Vietnam failed to meet IMF standards for central bank accounting and auditing (Anon. 2004a). According to Porter and Craig (2004: 400), use of such standards has become a standard IMF mechanism for deepening fiscal discipline. They are also a broad 'post-conditionality' mechanism similar to that employed in Bank PWC adjustment lending.[5] The IMF maintains its office in Hanoi and continues a programme of technical advisory work in the financial sector, including banking supervision, state-owned commercial bank equitisation, monetary policy and anti-money-laundering initiatives (Consultative Group Meeting for Vietnam 2004: 39).

The World Bank in Vietnam

With the support of McNamara, the World Bank made its first loan to Vietnam in 1978 – the Dau Tieng Irrigation Project. The loan was made despite the US government's disproval, and it proved costly to the Bank – a campaign against the loan led by Congressman C. W. Young led to inaction on an agreed capital increase for the Bank. Young also called for a cut to the US replenishment of the International Development Association (IDA) and inclusion of a proviso preventing US funds being used for loans to Vietnam and a handful of communist states (Shapley 1993: 568–71; Bello *et al.* 1982: 34; Gwin 1997: 225–26). In late 1979, McNamara signed a letter to Young stating that the Bank would not again lend to Vietnam, in return Young agreed to end his campaign and support the capital increase and Bank replenishment. The letter was leaked and caused an uproar because it violated the Bank's rules on political involvement and on negotiating with member governments only through specified channels (Shapley 1993: 571). Nevertheless, the self-imposed ban remained in place until 1993.

Between 1993 and 2004, the World Bank committed just over $5.12 billion to Vietnam. Between 2000 and 2002, it committed significantly less than average at $270 million per annum, but remained Vietnam's second largest donor. The Bank's 2002 Vietnam: Country Assistance Strategy (Vietnam CAS) indicated that loans would increase in 2003–6; its base scenario ('base case') for loan commitments was an average of $581 million per annum (World Bank 2002a). In 2003, the base case was met and in 2004, loans moved to the Bank's high-case scenario with loans totalling over $744 million. So in 2004, the Bank actually topped Vietnam's donor list. The Bank's priority sectors have historically been energy and mining (electricity), which between 1993 and 2004 accounted for 22 per cent of the value of Bank commitments, and transport, which was 20 per cent. The three sectors of agriculture, fishing and forestry, law, justice and public administration, and water supply and sanitation each accounted for 13 per cent of the value of Bank loans.

The Bank also administered $44.6 million in trust funds specifically for Vietnam between 1993 and 2004. Trust funds have been a key mechanism for extending Bank influence since their inception in the 1970s. In Vietnam, the Bank's use of trust funds indicates how it has sought to be at the front of donor coordination. Its donor coordination role increased after 1999, when Vietnam agreed to join the pilot Comprehensive Development Framework process and the associated Poverty Reduction Strategy Paper process. The Bank also chairs the Consultative Group for Vietnam (CGV). The combined effects of a shared development agenda and the Bank's influence on donors resulted in the CGV making additional aid in 1998 and 1999 conditional on

Vietnam undertaking World Bank prescribed reform (Masina 2006: 67–68). The Bank's role in the CGV gives it influence broadly over the geographical spread and sectors of a donor's ODA.

The Bank also encourages joint funding of its loans; for example, under the 2004 structural adjustment loan, called Poverty Reduction Support Credit III, the Bank lent $100 million; co-financing by other donors was $73 million. The Bank plays a lead role in pushing a 'development' agenda, which was confirmed in a study by Irene Nørlund (2001: 6). However, the response from the GoV and others to the role of the Bank was generally positive as it was seen as having a 'very open attitude in Vietnam'. Further, the Bank has generally adopted a 'tolerant and longer-term view of the relationship' with Vietnam, in contrast to 'the IMF's preference for imposing stricter conditions and timetables' (Painter 2005: 274).

The Bank has used alliances and networks to further its objectives, most prominently it aligned itself with the so-called 'pro-reform' factions in the party and bureaucracy. At times, it has linked with private business interests, for example to assist in its campaign for business licensing reform. The Bank's vast array of technical advisers employed to develop reports, designs, legislation and policy recommendation assist in making the Washington Consensus hegemonic principles 'common sense'. The Bank trains bureaucrats and party cadres in neoliberal principles through particular projects and specific training programmes. It even trains private businesses in Vietnam in how to operate in a market economy by training them how to tender for Bank-financed activities.

The World Bank's key planning documents: the Country Assistance Strategy and Poverty Reduction Strategy Paper

There are references to a first CAS dated September 1994; however, despite requests the documentation remains unavailable. Prior to 1998, the Bank tended to keep its country programming documents confidential (even from recipient governments). The first available Vietnam CAS is 1998–2002. However, the first Structural Adjustment Credit (SAC I) provided to Vietnam in 1994 does give some indications of earlier Bank priorities. While available documentation is limited, the brief 'Programme Information Document', was very supportive of the *Doi Moi* reforms that had taken place. The reforms were described as the start of a Washington Consensus structural adjustment package, regardless of whether this is an accurate description. Thus it emphasised conservative monetary and fiscal policy combined with price liberalisation to control the budget deficit and inflation and to 'get the prices right', currency devaluation and financial sector reforms, reform of SOEs, openness to foreign direct investment, decollectivisation and property rights, as well as limited and highly targeted social programmes (World Bank 1994l). Conditionalities on the loan were focused in the areas of government budgeting, the programme of SOE reform, the legal framework for property rights, and commercial transactions and banking reforms – in other words, core Washington Consensus concerns.

While SAC I praised 'ownership' by the GoV of *Doi Moi*, the 1998–2002 CAS (World Bank 1998a: ii) already noted differences between the Bank and the GoV on the pace of reform, with the Bank urging a faster programme. This issue frequently reappeared in Bank documentation. It is not an exaggeration to suggest that it is at the centre of Bank–GoV relations. The Bank's overarching focus was on the pace of reform despite the significant inroads made into SOE reform and cuts in the labour force pre-1993 and the evidence from other countries that quick privatisation often results in a significant decline in production with high social costs and a strong likelihood of insider privatisation. Thus it indicates the limited extent to which the Bank has taken on board New Institutional Economics (NIE) concerns about the pace and timing of reform over the Washington Consensus concerns with government failure and rapid adjustment.

Yet, the Bank and other donors have supported an increased focus on poverty reduction in Vietnam. The Poverty Task Force and Poverty Working Group were established in 1999 and involved the government, donors and NGOs. The smaller Poverty Working Group was the initial vehicle for participatory poverty assessment and living standards surveys. While this was clearly an innovative process for Vietnam, it was largely driven by donors, in particular the World Bank (Nørlund 2001: 2).

The GoV requested involvement as a pilot CDF/PRSP (Comprehensive Development Framework/Poverty Reduction Strategy Paper) country because it was a precondition for access to structural adjustment lending. But, in the wake of the Asian Financial Crisis and the downturn in FDI, producing a PRSP was a signal to both the donor community and international financiers that Vietnam was continuing its reform programme (Nørlund *et al.* 2003: 131–32). The interim-PRSP, released in March 2001, drew on the results of the Poverty Working Group and, in particular, a report it released in December 1999, Attacking Poverty (Poverty Working Group 1999). However, the interim-PRSP was produced quickly in order to maintain access to structural adjustment lending and involved little public participation (Wolff *et al.* 2002: iii). In a separate process, the Government's own key planning documents were concurrently drafted and debated by political/civil society across the country. The 'Five Year Plan for Socioeconomic Development 2001–5' and 'Ten Year Socioeconomic Development Strategy 2001–10' were approved in April 2001 by the Party Congress. They did not mention the PRSP process.

The Bank and IMF approved the interim-PRSP but their Joint Staff Assessment identified issues that had to be addressed in the full PRSP including improving poverty data and monitoring, sector strategies for addressing poverty, costing and prioritisation of programmes, improving the participatory process and increasing attention to vulnerable groups (Wolff *et al.* 2002: 24). The list of concerns certainly suggests a shift from the Washington Consensus yet it contrasts with the process whereby, until 2005, the Bank and IMF's Executive Directors approved PRSPs.

The GoV had a relatively strong degree of ownership of the full PRSP; indeed their very renaming of it as the Comprehensive Poverty Reduction and Growth Strategy (CPRGS) may indicate a desire to distinguish it from Bank processes (Payne 2005). Released in May 2002, it involved significant consultation with various levels of government, some local NGOs, international NGOs and donors, organised through the Poverty Task Force (now the lead body for poverty assessments). Yet, the participatory processes were not country driven, the World Bank 'mobilised an immense effort to facilitate the process', following it at every step and ensuring that research could be transformed into policy (Nørlund *et al.* 2003: 92; World Bank Operations Evaluation Department and IMF Independent Evaluation Office 2005: 93). This intervention expanded the Bank's level of on the ground involvement in Vietnam and, 'at a more political level, the greater presence on the ground by the Bank and the Fund and more intensive and widespread relations may well be further smothering local officials, reducing "ownership" rather than fostering nationally owned initiatives' (Woods 2006: 190).

An evaluation of the overall process concluded that to start with it had little impact on the GoV or the broader community; indeed, the document remained 'unknown at the provincial and communal levels, and even foreign to members of the Vietnamese development research community' (Nørlund *et al.* 2003: 23). This obscurity is largely because the CPRGS process was kept separate from the Government's existing planning process, which involves debate across civil and political society (including party cells and mass organizations) and final approval by the National Assembly. The CPRGS has progressed to becoming 'a "second-track" policy forum, paralleling government and party policy' (Nørlund *et al.* 2003: 7). Despite the Bank and Fund's preference to have the CPRGS as the main policy planning mechanism, in future the PRSP plan will be subsumed under the Government's Five Year Plan. This should largely address problems such as the fact that participatory processes have not been mainstreamed.

That the CPRGS is not mainstream is conceded by the Bank; however, a Bank staffer suggested that 'the strength of not being a mainstream document is that is has the space to discuss sensitive issues that are not normally tackled in a direct way in the mainstream documents of government' (Turk 2005). This may have some truth, yet the Bank-organised participatory processes did not include any discussion of macroeconomic policy settings or structural reform, which must be one of the most 'sensitive' components of any country's development programme (World Bank Operations Evaluation Department and IMF Independent Evaluation Office 2005: 93).[6] Failure to include discussion of macroeconomic policy in participatory processes seems to be a common feature of PRSPs (Panos Institute 2002).

In summary then, the CPRGS process contained notable elements of Bank and IMF control, for example the Bank direction of the participatory process and the requirement that the IMF and Bank Boards approve the final document to gain funding access. However, the GoV took increasing control of the drafting process and the content and seems to have come to regard it as an action plan for the Five and Ten Year Plans (Nørlund *et al.* 2003: 97; Wolff *et al.* 2002: 33–34). In terms of the underlying development theory it largely reflects the PWC conception of 'growth with equity', as it prioritises economic growth as the key to poverty reduction. What is new for Vietnam is the use of poverty language and analysis, and here tensions are visible between neoliberal self-help ideas and the emphasis on the role of the state in development and equity.

The 2003–6 Vietnam CAS (World Bank 2002a) claimed to be based on the CPRGS and sets out three broad objectives derived from it:

(1) high growth through a transition to a market economy;
(2) an equitable, socially inclusive and sustainable pattern of growth; and
(3) adoption of a modern public administration, legal and governance system.

Although these three themes did appear in the CPRGS, the report was not organised around them, and the way they are presented differs subtly but significantly from the CPRGS. The CPRGS, drawing from overall objectives in the Government's Five Year Plan, aimed to:

> [b]ring about a significant improvement in the people's material, cultural and spiritual life, lay the foundations for the country's industrialization and modernization, build a prosperous people, strong country and a just, equal, democratic and civilized society, and establish the institutions of a *socialist-oriented* market economy.
>
> (Socialist Republic of Vietnam 2002: 6, emphasis added)

The Bank's version ignored the *socialist* orientation of the market economy and changes the 'people's material, cultural and spiritual life' into an equitable '*pattern of growth*'. The Bank's approach can be read in two main ways, a generous reading suggests the Bank has made a significant concession to country ownership in supporting a country operating on other than a market basis (Wolff *et al.* 2002: iv). A more critical reading asks why the Bank would find it so difficult to accept the idea of a socialist-oriented market economy given the level of redistribution and public ownership in many of its (democratic) member states (Payne 2005). Of course, the situation is made more complex by the lack of a consensus on the meaning of a 'socialist-oriented market economy' within the government and party in Vietnam.

In terms of public administration and the legal environment, the Bank's key descriptor was 'modern', the CPRGS (2002: 7) on the other hand referred variously to a fair, level, transparent and efficient system. 'Modern' is clearly a synonym for a Western capitalist system, which translates in the lending programme as assistance in the design of key laws consistent with a 'market-driven economy' in areas such as land, gas and electricity.

The CAS examination of Vietnam's historic bloc is revealing: social aspects received little attention accounting for only one paragraph out of 14. The economic analysis was also brief and made up largely of broad claims and truisms. The focus was on the need for a faster pace of policy reform connected to building a market economy. The short section on the medium-term outlook focused on the (presumed) link between continued policy reform and economic growth. Monetary and fiscal policy analysis was limited but emphasised prudence and soundness, which fits with the analysis of the PWC as maintaining the Washington Consensus approach. There was no consideration of the potential impact of the external environment, which is surprising given that the Asian Financial Crisis must still have been fresh in people's minds.

The 2003–6 CAS (World Bank 2002a: iii) contained three scenarios for lending volumes; the outcome was linked only to the 'pace of progress on the Government's policy and institutional agenda'. It was *not* linked to poverty outcomes or to the potential impact on Vietnam of regional or global events. There was also no suggestion of alternative scenarios in case the economy and poverty reduction did not respond to the proposed policy prescriptions. So, although the Bank needs and wants to be more 'organic' in the PWC period, its structures as a Bank and commitment to the hegemonic principles of *pax americana* expressed in the Washington Consensus ultimately prevented it from moving beyond superficial interventions and issues.

Yet, there have been substantial reductions in poverty since the PRSP process began, although until 2000 the rate of reduction was slower than in the early 1990s. Can these be attributed to the PRSP process? Probably not, as the GoV itself, reflecting the demands of local social forces, made a decision prior to joining the PRSP process to overhaul its social welfare system and to increase and redirect poverty reduction expenditure as indicated by the introduction in 1998 of the National Target Program for Hunger Eradication and Poverty Reduction.

Conclusion

Vietnam had a stable and quite 'strong' government over the case study periods. It has managed to maintain quite high levels of growth and poverty reduction during a period of significant economic transition. Its strength enabled the GoV to work closely with the World Bank yet still maintain a fair degree of autonomy. In other words, the Bank was by no means always able to impose its 'common sense' on Vietnam. The next chapter explores this relationship in more detail through an examination of Bank adjustment and investment lending.

7 World Bank lending in Vietnam

This chapter commences with an analysis of changes in the overall lending programme in terms of sectoral lending and loan size and then embarks on a detailed exploration of all Bank loans to Vietnam in the two case study periods by sector, commencing with structural adjustment lending. Investment loans are analysed by Bank sector, starting with energy and mining and water, sanitation and flood protection, which are grouped together because of the common approach in these sectors. Transportation is dealt with separately; finance lending is combined with the law, justice and public administration sector, as four out of its five credits were structural adjustment loans. Health and education are also combined because of the small number of loans in each sector.

A sectoral analysis of World Bank lending to Vietnam

Looking at the two case study periods, 1993–7 and 2000–4, this section explores the evolution of Bank lending in terms of sectoral focus and the size of loans. The analysis utilises the Bank's own sector classification system. In 1993–7, transportation and energy and mining were clearly the focus of Bank lending (see Table 7.1). Together they accounted for almost half of total new Bank lending commitments. Transportation comprised mainly projects to rehabilitate highways and ports; the energy and mining sector in Vietnam is restricted to projects in electricity generation, distribution and management. Finance, the third largest sector focused predominately on microfinance and banking reform projects. Health and education received scant attention in either period. Indeed, despite the focus on poverty reduction in the post-Washington Concensus (PWC), the Bank's overall levels of lending for education, the environment and health remained fairly stable across the Bank after 1996 at a level lower than the first half of the 1990s. Social 'sector lending has only increased marginally following the record low of 2.5% of Bank lending in 1996' (Wodsak 2002: 90).

The 1998–2002 Vietnam Country Assistance Strategy (CAS) stated that the Bank would shift its focus towards poverty, social issues and rural development. There are indications of a shift through such projects as the Northern

Table 7.1 World Bank new loan approvals to Vietnam by sector, as a per cent of total country lending: 1993–7 and 2000–4

Sector	*1993–7 (%)*	*2000–4 (%)*
Transportation	29	16
Energy	20	23
Finance	16	7
Law, justice and public administration	9	18
Health and other social services	9	1
Agriculture, fishing and forestry	7	11
Water, sanitation and flood protection	6	18
Education	4	6

Source: World Bank Website, Projects & Operations, Projects Database.[1]

Mountains Poverty Reduction Project and the targeting of power project to rural areas. Yet, looking at Table 7.1, the negligible expenditure on health and education speaks for itself. Transport and energy (electricity) are the key sectors in both case study periods, although law, justice and public administration and water, sanitation and flood protection moved into equal second place in 2000–4. The increase in the share of Bank commitments in these last two sectors was suggested by the analysis of the PWC, given its renewed emphasis on government's facilitating the provision of infrastructure to enable economic growth, as well as its focus on property rights and on business and regulatory frameworks to reduce market and government failures. Overall there was a strong focus on infrastructure – water, transport and energy accounted for 57 per cent of new commitments in 2000–4. In an interview, a Bank staff member explained the strong focus as the inevitable result of Vietnam's pending graduation from International Development Association (IDA) to International Bank for Reconstruction and Development (IBRD) loans: 'the reality is that countries like to borrow IBRD money for infrastructure, and the Bank has to be able to lend that money otherwise it is going to run out of money sooner or later' (Turk 2005).

The Bank has been criticised over many decades for its focus on project quantity rather than quality and loan size as the key indicator. Ranis argued that the fact that average Bank loans are still around $100 million indicates the continuing 'trade-off between the quantity and quality of lending' (Ranis 1997: 86). Vietnam does not deviate from this model. The average loan size shifted only slightly in the case study periods, in 1993–7 it was $105 million and in 2000–4, $124 million. The mean moved from $100 million to $110 million.

Structural adjustment lending in Vietnam

Structural adjustment lending increased from almost nine per cent of the value of new commitments in 1993–7 to over 16 per cent in 2000–4, which is notably less than the current bank average of 33 per cent of lending (World Bank 2003r: 36). Until 2004, Vietnam only accessed four adjustment loans: there was one Structural Adjustment Credit (SAC) in the 1993–7 period and three – called Poverty Reduction Support Credits (PRSCs) – in the 2000–4 period (Table 7.2).

There is limited information available on the 1994 SAC; however, it supported the initial programme of *Doi Moi* undertaken by the Government of Vietnam (GoV) and emphasised those aspects that fit the Washington Consensus – conservative monetary and fiscal policy, devaluation, price liberalisation, land use rights, foreign trade and investment, etc. The objective of the credit was to assist the transition to a market economy. It included some discussion of the social costs of adjustments and concluded that the Bank should focus on a 'broader' approach to aiding the vulnerable rather than direct support for social policy (World Bank 1994l: 5). The meaning of broader support becomes clear when loans in the finance sector are analysed. Conditionality seemed to be focused on regulation and competition policy, tax policy and administration, and debt management and fiscal sustainability. Brian Van Arkadie and Raymond Mallon (2003: 131) suggested that the SAC was the driving force behind the 1993 Law on Bankruptcy and the 1995 State Enterprise Law, both of which were developed with little consultation and have been poorly enforced.

The gap in adjustment loans until 2001 paralleled the gap in the IMF programme in Vietnam. The failure to reach a consensus continued throughout the Asian Financial Crisis, which negatively impacted economic growth and poverty reduction efforts in Vietnam. This gap, and the low level of adjustment lending in general, indicates the relative strength of the Vietnamese historic bloc – because, despite the impact of the Crisis on the economy and the state budget reliance on donor flows, the GoV rejected access to quick-disbursing loans in favour of some domestic policy freedom. These policy decisions, outlined in Chapter 5, involved conservative monetary and fiscal policy but also trade (import) restrictions. They were clearly preferable to the GoV over the liberalisation and privatisation programmes being pushed by the World Bank and IMF. Equally, the Bank's position is evidence of its commitment to hegemonic principles over country ownership of macroeconomic policy settings or over mitigating the impacts of crisis on the poorest (World Bank 2001i: 1). During the gap in lending, the Bank attempted to implement aspects of its structural reform programme through a combination of sector

Table 7.2 Word Bank adjustment lending to Vietnam: 1993–7 and 2000–4

Project name	*Year approved*	*Approved amount (US$ millions)*
Loans 1993–7		
Structural Adjustment Credit	1994	150.0
Loans 2000–4		
Poverty Reduction Support Credit I	2001	250.0
Poverty Reduction Support Credit II	2003	100.0
Poverty Reduction Support Credit III	2004	100.0

programmes and a large programme of analytical studies (see, in particular, the power sector).[2] As noted earlier, the Bank-chaired Consultative Group for Vietnam (CGV) also pressured Vietnam by offering additional funding, subject to Vietnam following World Bank reform prescriptions (Masina 2006: 67–68).

Despite its title and the analysis of poverty in the report, the policy reforms in PRSC I do not directly address poverty (Porter and Craig 2004: 402). PRSC I proposed action in five areas: the private sector climate; state-owned enterprise (SOE) reform; banking reform; trade reform; and public expenditure management – in other words, largely the Washington Consensus areas about developing markets and global integration. The connection to poverty requires two leaps of faith, first that making such reforms increases economic growth and second that economic growth decreases poverty. However, Van Arkadie and Mallon (2003: 104–5) found that in Vietnam, 'improvements in enterprise performance have usually preceded changes in the legal framework'.

There is a significant shift from PRSC I to II/III, as the later loans incorporate some of the issues in Vietnam's interim PRSP released between PRSC I and II (World Bank 2001h, 2003h, 2004h). From PRSC II the policy reform agenda was expanded mostly around social issues. New issues included health, education, land use and transferability, environmental sustainability, government planning and legal reform. However, the five sectors from PRSC I that conform to the Washington Consensus agenda continued to receive the most attention. Decentralisation and corruption appeared in PRSC II and became more prominent in PRSC III; these are part of the PWC focus on governance and provide new grounds for the Bank to propose 'reforms' to Vietnam's legal and regulatory system.

The number and types of conditions also changed – PRSC I for $250 million contained 24 conditions for the two tranches in the five sectors mentioned above. By PRSC II ($100 million), conditions were dropped in favour of 'policy actions', 19 of them. In addition, PRSC II included a list of 14 'triggers', which are additional targets to be achieved prior to PRSC III being negotiated. By PRSC III ($100 million) only triggers remained – 15 of them. Conditionality has been a controversial area for the Bank, particularly in relation to structural adjustment loans (later renamed Development Policy Lending). The Bank claims that triggers 'are not conditions', however the explanation of what they are suggests otherwise: '[p]rogress on most triggers and no backtracking on any of them leads in principle to the preparation of the next PRSC operation' (World Bank 2004h: 17). The triggers in PRSC III (for PRSP IV) included both broad directives and specific actions, for example Vietnam had to draft new 'Enterprise and Investment Laws in accordance with the Guiding Concepts and Principles date April 26, 2004' (World Bank 2004h: 32). As Penny Griffin (2006) noted, these broad 'post-conditionality' mechanisms often increase the Bank's 'encroachment into the day-to-day governance of developing countries'. The Bank's argument (Turk 2005) that PRSCs are merely a retrospective of what the country has done over the last 12 months is not convincing, they need to be seen as an opportunity for the

Bank to influence the government's agenda or as a way of continuing conditionality in a more expansive form. The GoV demonstrated its strength by only negotiating a limited number of structural adjustment loans. Further, it has not always met structural adjustment loan (SAL) conditions, particularly when conditions have conflicted with the needs of the historic bloc. For example, where equitisation of SOEs or trade liberalisation measures threatens the interests of powerful groups, they tend not to be implemented (Masina 2006: 26).

One of the most controversial aspects of the PRSCs was the requirement for equitisation of SOEs. From 1992 to 2000, there was pilot equitisation of about 450 firms. PRSC I required adoption of a five-year SOE reform programme covering one-third of SOEs. The second tranche included five conditions (of 12) on equitising SOEs: streamlining the equitisation process, completing equitisation of 200 major and 200 minor SOEs, equitising non-core assets of General Corporations and modification of a redundancy fund for equitising SOEs (World Bank 2001h: 41–42). It is surprising to see the use of single numerical targets in the PWC period. This is a simplistic and inadequate form of conditionality, which leaves the Bank with only a pass or fail outcome. Where a target is likely to be missed, it provides no incentive for getting close to the target and it offers no leeway in case of unforeseen events.

In PRSC II, the Bank shifted from broad numerical targets to a programme listing enterprises and target dates for equitisation. This is an even more coercive (but likely even less effective) form of conditionality pursuing a Bank hegemonic principle. In PRSC III, the Bank finally dropped numerical targets for SOE equitisation, although the section analysing or outlining current government policy supported the government's plan to equitise, sell or liquidate around 2,400 SOEs between 2004 and 2006.

The Bank/GoV debate on equitisation needs to be understood in the context of the reform and performance of SOEs during *Doi Moi*. Significant rationalisation of SOEs was undertaken prior to the Bank's engagement in Vietnam. Perhaps for this reason, despite variable performance of individual SOEs, as a group they outperformed domestic private enterprises in terms of growth until around 2001. They remain a very important source of stability and government revenue. Van Arkadie and Mallon (2003: 112–13) found little evidence to support the idea that SOEs have 'crowded out' growth in private enterprise. Further, the experience of rapid privatisation in Eastern Europe provided good reasons not to undertake 'big bang' privatisation. At least six other factors influence and/or constrain the GoV position on SOEs.

(1) Equitisation is a sensitive process impacting on multiple interests and involving many actions including: 'state business interests, state bureaucrats, party leaders and other state actors' (World Bank 2004h: 22).
(2) Connected to the above, there remain substantial and explicit political commitments to retaining state ownership of SOEs in strategic parts of the production chain, as well as for key utilities, some military production and in a range of other 'sensitive' areas of the economy.

(3) SOEs are central to government revenue generation; it is difficult to replace them with other sources given that it is difficult for developing countries to effectively tax private businesses (Kolko 1997: 56).
(4) Equitisation is administratively and managerially complex and has stretched the regulatory capacity of the government in Vietnam.
(5) The 'considerable labour retrenchment' involved is politically sensitive (World Bank 2004h: 37).
(6) The government has made some progress on hardening the budget constraint faced by SOEs (limiting subsidies and preferential access to cheap credit in particular), thus they are not the drain on government resources they have been in the past.

Combine these factors with the tendency for consensus decision-making in Vietnam and the GoV approach to SOE reform can be better characterised as 'successful management and containment of the conflicting ambitions of' various domestic social forces, with the aim of improving performance of SOEs and maintaining key state interests (Painter 2003: 23).

As seen in the PRSCs, such social, political and economic considerations appear to have had little impact on Bank enthusiasm for privatising the ownership of enterprises, and the pace of equitisation was a significant source of tension between the Bank and the Government until at least 2004, when the Bank seemed to slightly relax its attitude – long after the Bank had supposedly shifted away from simplistic Washington Consensus programmes. Nevertheless, privatisation is still on the Bank's agenda (Rohland 2004). The reasons for the Bank's cooling on the topic are not clear – it tends to tread carefully in Vietnam to avoid backfire, or it may have felt that pro-reform voices had gathered enough support to push the reform agenda without the Bank's explicit support. Further, World Trade Organization accession, according to one Bank staffer, covered much of what would have been on the conditionality agenda (Turk 2005). Ultimately though, as Martin Painter (2003: 34) argued, Vietnam has accepted the resources of donors and even made public pronouncements on timetables for equitisation but these co-exist 'with other policy pronouncements that speak of another trajectory altogether – the entrenchment and strengthening of the state sector'.

In terms of the actual process of SOE reform, one of the biggest issues is valuation of enterprises and land. Early on, to speed the process, the Bank pushed successfully to have the required independent audit prior to equitisation dropped. A decade later, there are still concerns that firms are not appropriately valuing assets, in particular land, which is not surprising given that the land market remains underdeveloped (Gainsborough 2003: 24–28; Hung 2005: 34). Managers have utilised undervaluation in order to gain control over enterprises (Evans 2004: 13; Höông B 2004: 4; Sam and Hai 2004: 4–5).

Workers receive priority access in purchasing shares, so the lack of reliable information also makes it more difficult for them to make judgements about the value of the company. Given their limited knowledge of share owning in the first place (the process ignores the issue of worker education), it is not surprising that one survey indicates that, at best, 55 per cent of workers are taking up shares and only 24 per cent are retaining them (Höông B 2004: 1). The point of this is that the Bank's continuing pressure on the Government to equitise SOEs quickly, despite its own judgement that 'insider privatization' (cited in Sam and Hai 2004: 3; Painter 2005) is taking place, is indicative of its judgement regarding the relative importance of government versus market failures. Clearly New Institutional Economics (NIEs) 'lessons' about market failure and the pace and sequencing of reform and the experience of equitisation in Vietnam to date are secondary to the Washington Consensus agenda on privatisation.

The Bank policy for redundant workers also sheds light on the PWC. As part of PRSC I, the Bank negotiated additional support for redundant workers under a specially established fund for SOEs. The fund provided more generous assistance than the Labor Code in the form of lump-sum compensation plus a six-month vocational retraining voucher. Its purpose was undoubtedly to defuse the growing discontent over redundancies, which could have threatened the process of equitisation. It is adjustment welfare and other than the voucher, a passive approach to labour market policy (Hai 2003; Sam and Hai 2004). The Bank's review of this programme claimed it was a success but an independent review highlighted a number of problems emerging after redundancy, particularly among vulnerable groups. Around 75 per cent of workers made redundant are women, most of whom have limited skills and education. Over 70 per cent end up in the informal sector without any protection and as a result 'their family's living standards decline dramatically as a consequence' (Evans 2004: 10). The survey also found problems in the administration of the fund, whereby more than half of the retrenched workers had only received half the compensation owed to them a year after retrenchment.

The form and implementation of the redundancy package is indicative of the Bank's view of a limited role for the state in social issues. Contrast this to the Bank's view of the government's role in private sector development in Vietnam – in justifying the inclusion of the number of new private enterprises registered each month as a trigger, it is argued that '[e]ssentially private sector development is the combined outcome of policy actions in many areas, from financial sector reform to better governance and public administration' (World Bank 2004h: 17). This is the PWC with a weak conception of the role of the state, limited to providing *adjustment* welfare not redistributive justice and to promoting business.

Investment lending in Vietnam

Energy and mining, and water, sanitation and flood control

Energy and water and sanitation and flood protection are grouped together for the analysis as there is a clearly discernible common model to the Bank's activities, underpinned by the goal of privatisation. The approach to privatisation is organised around the dual Bank policies of decentralisation and 'unbundling'. Rudolf Nsorwine *et al.* (2005) succinctly outlined this model in their study of water privatisation in Ghana, which I have adapted for understanding the Vietnamese experience. Before outlining this model, how privatisation came to be applied to utilities is briefly explored – as it was not an original part of the Washington Consensus, rather it was added in the early 1990s.

According to Xu Yi-chong (2005: 651–52), three broad sets of developments in the 1980s combined to facilitate the application of structural adjustment to utilities by the World Bank. First, in the 1980s the globe was flush with capital due to petrodollars, financial deregulation and the like, which needed to be invested in revenue-generating activities. Second, the rise of neoliberalism gradually reduced support for state involvement in all sectors of the economy. The Thatcher government started the trend of privatising utilities and expanding private investment in the sector. Yet, other than new privatisations, the utilities market in developed countries was largely saturated while that in developing countries was constrained by lack of investment. Third, in the 1980s, economists developed a theory of utilities that combined the 'grand story' of neoliberalism with a view of utilities that changed them into a commodity like any other that can, and should, be traded in markets. In this view, utilities operated in the same way across the globe, thus the same model for restructuring their ownership could be applied everywhere (Yi-chong 2005: 652). The narrative about utility privatisation was generally well received by politicians and bureaucrats in developed and developing countries, as many already were committed to neoliberalism; the story also fitted the new 'common sense' and offered a 'solution' for countries facing difficulty in meeting the increased demand for utilities because of their severely constrained resource position. Often the financial position of utilities themselves was poor, privatisation offered a 'solution' here too (Yi-chong 2005: 658).

For the Bretton Woods twins, privatisation of utilities offered a new project and a new way of facilitating the shift of American private capital to developing countries. They certainly took up the project with gusto and privatisation of utilities quickly became a hegemonic principle of the Washington Consensus. The Bank developed a model of utilities privatisation with two core steps: first, separation of profitable urban components of utilities from unprofitable rural ones – this effectively removes the capacity to cross-subsidise; and second, separation of the different business components of the utility. In electricity, this means separating generation, transmission and distribution; private operators are then introduced in each sector starting with generation. In the water sector, the separation of business components means unbundling the more profitable water supply sector from the less profitable, or unprofitable, sewerage sector. In its earliest days, the Bank saw this as a gradual process with an emphasis on introducing private participation rather than privatisation. However, no sooner was it adopted than more radical requirements for restructuring and privatisation became standard (Yi-chong 2005: 655–56).

The PWC claim that privatisation based on decentralisation, by definition, improves community participation supposedly strengthened the Bank's privatisation rationale. Decentralisation also reduces central government fiscal expenditures (by transferring responsibility to regions or municipalities) – a key concern of the Washington Consensus that remains central to the PWC. Participation is, of course, a supposed key differentiation of the PWC, although as we shall see in the utilities sector it is reduced to little more than willingness to pay. Most importantly, however, decentralisation facilitates unbundling of utilities, which separates the profitable and the unprofitable sectors (Amenga-Etego and Grusky 2005: 279).

Utilising Amenga-Etego and Grusky's (2005) five-step schema, I have developed an eight-step model to explain the Bank's approach to water and electricity privatisation in Vietnam. The steps are listed below.

(1) Grant funds are provided for international consultants to study and develop plans for sector. Subsequent grants are provided to 'assist' with developing a legislative framework, industry pricing, etc.
(2) National utilities are dissolved into geographically based entities with responsibility generally devolved to provinces or communes.
(3) Business components are separated. In electricity generation, transmission and distribution are separated, in water it is water supply and sanitation.
(4) Devolved urban utilities are corporatised; in rural areas corporatisation is trialled.
(5) Private providers are introduced in generation and in water supply.
(6) Subcontracting of maintenance, etc., to private providers is trialled in all business components.
(7) A national regulatory agency and agency/ies to support rural utilities are created.
(8) The final step, which has not yet occurred in Vietnam, is to privatise urban corporations.

The specific approach of the Bank in each sector is outlined below.

The energy and mining sector

The World Bank's principal goal, since its first loan in the energy and mining sector in early 1995, has been a fully privatised electricity sector. It pursued this through six loans and one guarantee in the sector, numerous linked technical assistance grants, trust fund operations and conditions in PRSCs.[3] There were two loans during 1993–7 and three plus the guarantee during 2000–4. The Bank's programme in Vietnam is similar to that it pursued in other Asian countries – it started with studies to restructure the industry and followed quickly with support for the introduction of Independent Power Producers (IPPs) in the generation side of the industry (Beder 2003: 86–100). The preconditions for IPPs were set by the 1995 Power Sector Rehabilitation

Table 7.3 Word Bank energy sector lending to Vietnam: 1993–7 and 2000–4

Project name	*Year approved*	*Approved amount (US$ millions)*
Loans 1993–7		
Power Sector Development and Rehabilitation Project	1995	165.0
Power Development Project	1996	180.0
Loans 2000–4		
Rural Energy Project	2000	150
System Efficiency Improvement, Equitization and Renewables Project	2002	225
Vietnam Guarantee Project	2004	75.0
Rural Energy II	2004	220.0

and Expansion Project and associated technical assistance grants, which 'assisted' the power sector's move towards a more commercial orientation and promoted unbundling of generation, transmission and distribution functions. Conditions on the loan included the GoV implementing the outcomes of studies (funded by the Word Bank and Asian Development Bank (ADB)) on industry structure and legislative requirements, financial management and electricity tariffs (World Bank 1995d).

The introduction of an IPP (called Phu My 2–2) at the Phu My power generation complex outside Ho Chi Minh City was a condition of the 1996 Power Sector Development loan. The World Bank's Staff Appraisal Report (1996f: 20) hailed this development as a 'breakthrough in the introduction of private power in Viet Nam'. The loan funded the development of the technical, commercial and legal structure of the IPP and an associated technical assistance grant created 'a legal and regulatory framework for the power sector that would be conducive to private sector participation' (World Bank 1996f: 32–33). Moving to 2000–4, the construction of Phu My 2–2 by foreign investors was assisted by a US$75 million guarantee from the World Bank; much of the other capital was sourced from the ADB and the Japan Bank for International Cooperation (World Bank 2002e). The Bank guarantee was, in turn, guaranteed by the GoV. Further, the state-owned electricity company, EVN, signed contracts to purchase the power produced by Phu My 2–2 under a 20-year Power Purchase Agreement. In this way, risk was transferred to the GoV and EVN, who must continue to purchase power at a set price even if technological or other breakthroughs result in a significant decline in the costs of generation. The project contracts are all denominated in US dollars, meaning that the GoV and EVN assume most of the exchange rate risk as well.[4] In other words, private investors assumed minimal risk for the project and were not exposed to competition after the contract was signed. This leaves one asking why have private companies in the first place.

Phu My 2–2 was constructed by the Meco Energy Company Ltd – a consortium of EdF International, Sumitomo Corporation and Tokyo Electric

Power Company (TEPCO).[5] A quick search on the internet revealed the following information about these companies: EdF International is a wholly owned subsidiary of Electricite de France, a French public enterprise. It is the largest nuclear power station operator in France and has been watched by Greenpeace in relation to concerns regarding its storage of nuclear waste. EdF has been heavily subsidised by the French government for years, but according to the *Economist* (Anon. 2004b: 77) has nevertheless rarely been profitable. Further, they consider it has 'questionable accounting practices' and has made 'imprudent use of funds set aside for nuclear decommissioning and waste-management'. Sumitomo is part of the Japanese Sumitomo *keiretsu*; in 1998 it offered a settlement of US$150 million to the USA Commodity Futures Trading Commission because of the Commission's concerns about its manipulation of copper trading in 1995/96 (USA Commodity Futures Trading Commission). TEPCO, another Japanese firm, was shown in October 2002 to have falsified inspection data on leak rates during containment tests in its nuclear power station to the Japanese regulatory agency. It was also shown to have concealed damage in three of its power plants.

The Phu My 2–2 Guarantee is a powerful statement of the Bank's position on the relative importance of state and market failures. Further, given that the project was approved two years before the new National Electricity Law was passed by the National Assembly, it is also indicative of the lack of concern with the pace and sequencing of reform when it conflicts with the ongoing privatisation agenda.

Two of the Bank's three loans during 2000–4 were in rural electrification (RE). These aimed to expand access to power in rural areas via grid extensions and alternative energy sources. The expanded access of rural households to energy could have a significant impact on living standards. There are, however, a couple of catches in the projects that show the more coercive side of Bank hegemony. Connection to the national grid – the largest part of the programme – was only provided to communes that demonstrate adequate rates of return from connection (World Bank 2000d, 2004l). So, poverty reduction was clearly second place to economic efficiency. The distribution model in the projects promoted Washington Consensus hegemonic principles.[6] In rural areas, EVN has not been historically responsible for electricity distribution, it has been undertaken by a variety of commune and district level enterprises. The RE projects formalised this system of well over a thousand communal and provincial electricity distributors and provided them with funds to address technical and managerial deficiencies. One condition of the RE projects (also a condition of the System Efficiency project) was the commercialisation and subsequent equitisation of distributors (and the equitisation of EVN assets as well) (World Bank 2002d). These projects show the Bank promoting fairly radical and fast equitisation for rural utilities, suggesting a continued prioritising of Washington Consensus themes over those of the PWC. The RE appraisal documents contained little analysis of the technical and financial viability of small operations across different parts of the country. Indeed, there was little mention in Bank documentation of problems with either the privatisation process generally or specifically of electrical utilities across the globe, from California and the UK to India and Brazil (Beder 2003; Yi-chong 2005).

A theme that runs across all of the loans in both periods was electricity tariffs. The Bank consistently pursued the GoV to raise tariffs. The Government actually slowed the pace of increase in 2001 after concerns about the slowed economic growth following September 11 (and with the Asian Financial Crisis and some civil disturbances still a recent memory). The Bank responded by changing its performance rating on two loans from satisfactory to unsatisfactory. This was only lifted after the GoV agreed to a Tariff Implementation Plan in May 2002 (World Bank 2002e: 24). The number of conditions in relation to tariffs went from two in each of the two loans in 1993–7 to five, four and two in the three loans in 2000–4. This suggests that the concern with 'getting the prices right' that was so central to the Washington Consensus was not tempered by analysis of, or concern for, the social and economic impacts of price adjustments. It demonstrates that the PWC is a modification of the Washington Consensus and does not challenge its hegemonic principles.

The loans in 2000–4 included additional conditions on resettlement. This indicates the Bank's knowledge of, and sensitivity to, policy and implementation differences with the GoV on the issue. Resettled people, particularly those with no 'legal' claim on the land they were occupying are often left worse off under GoV resettlement procedures. Further, cultural and socio-economic sensitivities have not always been taken into account. For example, people whose livelihood involves street enterprise have been resettled into high-rise flats, where they cannot conduct business and take care of household responsibilities simultaneously. Although the new housing may have been of better quality, many people have left redeveloped areas and moved in order to resume their occupations. The Bank worked with the GoV on this issue and in 2004, the GoV revised their policy.

There were two notable new concerns in the loans in the second period of study, namely decentralisation and participation. Decentralisation was a key policy prescription in all three loans in the second period. It is a policy that, on the surface, responds to critics of the one-size-fits-all view of Bank programmes and also is assumed to provide more local participation in decision-making. However, as in Hadiz's (2004: 700–01) analysis of decentralisation in Indonesia, the decentralised structures are not the product of political or social forces on the ground, rather they are an issue for supposedly apolitical technicians who will determine how to efficiently manage and administer electricity enterprises. So, in Vietnam there was no social analysis of local political and power conditions to determine where and how grid extension should take place, rather decisions were based on the estimated economic rate of return.

Participation made a welcome appearance in the three loans in 2000–4, although its purposes were limited. In RE projects, communities were consulted to 'determine the need for electrification', in other words to assist in the assessment of the economic rates of return and to confirm that 60 per cent of the local population were willing to pay for the service. This supports Cammack's (2003: 12) argument that the Bank's vision of civil society participation has been a deliberate strategy 'to induce people to experience tightly controlled and carefully delimited forms of market-supporting activity as empowerment'.

What was visible in the power sector was the Bank pushing a radical model of privatisation in both case study periods. The GoV seem to have adopted a more gradual approach to reform and accepted and adapted those components of utility privatisation that suited its approach. Thus we saw a gradual introduction of IPPs in generation, a slow approach to legislative reform and utilisation of Bank funds to develop the already decentralised distribution arrangements in rural areas.

Water, sanitation and flood control

The first loan in the sector was the Water Supply Project for four cities, approved in 1997. The project was a response to a *1991* request from the GoV to undertake a water supply *and* sanitation project. The Bank's Staff Appraisal Report (1997d: 7) argued that it was separated into two projects, a water supply project to be followed by a sanitation project, because 'the great number of involved institutions with various financial objectives would make the project very complex'. However, separation of water supply from sanitation is a strategy the Bank has employed in numerous countries as a key step in achieving privatisation of the more profitable water supply business.

Much of the process of unbundling of the sector was already carried out under the impetus of the GoV's decentralisation programme and with help from an ADB technical assistance project (World Bank 1997d: 26). Water Supply Companies (WSCs) were formed under the responsibility of Provincial People's Committees. Sewerage is controlled at the municipal level by

Table 7.4 Word Bank water, sanitation and flood control sector lending to Vietnam: 1993–7 and 2000–4

Project name	*Year approved*	*Approved amount (US$ millions)*	*International competitive bidding (%)*
Loans 1993–7			
Water Supply Project	1997	98.61	93.8
Loans 2000–4			
HCMC Environmental Sanitation Project	2001	166.34	90.8
Urban Upgrading Project	2004	222.47	53
Urban Water Supply Development Project	2004	112.6	48.55

Sewerage and Drainage Companies or by Urban Environment Companies. The Water Supply Project included training and capacity-building measures to make the WSCs 'commercial companies in a market economy' that are 'attractive for private sector participation' (World Bank 1997d: 28 and 4). The largest component of the project was design and construction, and it was here that private sector involvement was firmly established via the Bank's requirement for international competitive bidding (ICB) for materials and construction, which in this project accounted for a high 93.8 per cent of the Bank loan.

Poverty got very little attention in the Water Supply Project, indeed the Bank (1997d: 9) cited its global experience as a justification for ignoring it: '[t]he principal lesson is that sector projects should not be used as vehicles to pursue subsidiary objectives at the expense of the main objective. Thus tariffs should not be distorted to satisfy poverty alleviation objectives'. This is the kind of argument the Bank made regarding water projects from its first forays into the sector in the mid-1960s and its residual suspicion of such 'social' projects meant that cost recovery or revenue raising was promoted in the sector from the outset (Kapur *et al.* 1997: 199–200). The project contrasts starkly to the three projects in the second case study period that all focus heavily on poverty reduction as an objective. However, these projects maintained the push for privatisation. In the Ho Chi Minh City (HCMC) Environmental Sanitation Project, amid technical discussion of wastewater and drainage components was a plan to divide the maintenance units of the Urban Drainage Company (UDC) into five self-financing business centres which, by 2002 must have entered into management contracts with the UDC. By 2004, three of the five maintenance units must be fully separated from the UDC, with two remaining inside the UDC as a baseline and to provide flexibility in case of emergencies. Operation and maintenance for new wastewater facilities built under the project must be fully contracted out (World Bank 2001d: 4). Over 90 per cent of the value of the Bank's loan was for works contracted via ICB. Of the remaining $15.3 million, $14.3 million was for consultants.

The Urban Upgrading Project (2004) stepped out of the mould; it had a poverty focus and participatory components, although participation was still reduced to the 'willingness and ability-to-pay' of communities (World Bank 2004m: 7). All of the activities had to be contracted out; however, only 52 per cent of the value was subject to ICB procedures. Forty-five per cent were reserved for NCB and the remainder was consultancy service.

The Urban Water Supply Development Project (World Bank 2004n) returned to the traditional Bank mould of projects expanding private participation; however, it focused on district centres. The Bank loan funded components one and two of the project, respectively entitled the Competition Route and Performance Route. Under the Competition Route, contractors were used to design and build water supply facilities in unserviced district towns. A separate round of bidding was then planned for contracts to operate the facilities. Component two, the Competition Route provided funds to existing WSCs that were performing well, defined as meeting criteria on staffing, unaccounted for water and financial ratios. The funds could be used to subcontract work on construction or rehabilitation of systems. The only concession to the projects being outside major urban centres was that slightly over 50 per cent of funds were reserved for NCB (World Bank 2004n: 43).

The water tariff was a theme and condition in all of the loans, with the Bank focused on increasing tariffs to levels that fully cover costs. The Bank's (1997d: 3) attitude to tariffs was clear in this statement on key challenges for the sector, which were:

> reorientation of the enterprise management to providing water and sanitation services as a business rather than exclusively as a social obligation, to the gradual replacement of subsidies by user charges, and to the increased ability of enterprises to make rational business decisions without unnecessary political control.

Tariffs are not a simple issue in water supply. Those not connected to water supply systems (normally the poor) sometimes pay substantially more absolutely and relatively for their water than those who are currently connected, who are more likely to be wealthy (McIntosh 2003: 1–2). Thus higher tariffs for piped water can be justified if they fund expansion of networks. However, high tariffs often result in the poor switching to cheaper water sources (e.g. groundwater) and increases can cause political disturbances. Moreover, historical experience is that 'network extension in the water sector has only ever been achieved through cross-subsidisation implemented through central government' (Bayliss and Hall 2002: 10). Water is a very 'political' issue because it has implications for poverty, health and the environment and it is clear that private sector involvement has not, and cannot by itself, guarantee provision of safe water to the poor (McIntosh 2003: 39–40). The Bank's view of water tariffs as being simply a business decision reflects a weak analysis of actors and interests in society and a weak version of the PWC.

Transportation

Transportation has been one of the largest areas of Bank lending in Vietnam. There were seven loans, mostly large, over the two case study periods (Table 7.5), supported by an extensive programme of analytical and advisory services. Despite being one of the least contentious areas of Bank activity, three issues stood out for attention: procurement; road standards; and the socioeconomic impact of transport projects and their poverty implications. These issues address the core issue for this study – the nature and extent of the Bank's shift from the Washington to post-Washington Consensus.

Standard Bank procedures relating to procurement apply to transport loans; thus the Ministry of Transport cannot carry out work, rather it must be contracted out. The only area of flexibility relates to whether procurement is open internationally or restricted to national bidding or shopping. Table 7.5

Table 7.5 Word Bank transportation sector lending to Vietnam, 1993–7 and 2000–4

Project name	*Year approved*	*Approved amount (US$ millions)*	*International competitive bidding (%)*
Loans 1993–7			
Highway Rehabilitation Project 1	1993	158.5	N/A*
Rural Transport Project 1	1996	55.0	1
Second Highway Rehabilitation Project	1997	195.0	73.9
Inland Waterways and Ports	1997	73.0	67.1
Loans 2000–4			
Mekong Transport and Flood Protection Project	2000	110.00	89.5
Community Based Rural Infrastructure Project	2001	102.78	0.7
Road Network Improvement Project	2003	225.26	53.6

Note:
* International competitive bidding procurement was used in the project but no figures are included in the available reports on the project. Presumably levels were similar to Second Highway Rehabilitation Project.

indicates the percentage of each project that was subject to ICB. Rural projects, in both periods, show a higher component of non-ICB. This may indicate more flexibility from the Bank. However, pragmatically, it is unlikely that international capital would (currently) be interested in small operations in rural Vietnam. Therefore, from the Bank's perspective, local capital and competition is required. Thus, the Bank sought to assist in the establishment of local private contractors and the project set aside funds for training firms in 'bid preparation, cost accounting, and contract management' (World Bank 1996e: 15).

Given the experience of the Rural Transport Project where 'too many' SOEs were winning contracts, in December 2000 SOEs connected to the Ministry of Transport and relevant provincial governments were banned from bidding (World Bank 2004t: 16). The Bank explained this decision on the basis of removing potential conflicts of interests. However, it also effectively excluded many firms with relevant skills and experience from competing for work. The Bank's Implementation Completion Report on the Second Highway Rehabilitation Project (2004c: 18) was critical that this project had not done enough to promote equitisation:

> there remain a large number of SOEs to which reform has not been applied ... The equitisation process could have continued through this project with a programmatic approach that would have created the right incentives for [Ministry of Transport's] MOT's innovation, supporting successful case models for future application, focusing on equitisation of profitable enterprises and extending the reform to large SOEs.[7]

Note the way the Bank explicitly connected reform of procurement, equitisation of SOEs and deregulation of the construction industry (see also World Bank 2002h: 6). In rejecting a mixed economy model, the Bank aimed to systematically transform Vietnam to a neoliberal, mediated yet individual and market-driven form of capitalism.

The Inland Waterways and Port Rehabilitation Project (1997) aimed to establish a framework for the privatisation of 'commercially-viable transport services' in the Mekong and the Mekong Transport and Flood Protection Project (2000), in the second case study period, continued this goal. According to the Bank (2000e: 4, emphasis added), the Vietnam Roads Authority must 'gradually disengage from force account operations, and focus on performance-based long-term contract management and quality control. The road construction industry *will have to develop correspondingly, by first divesting state-owned construction enterprises*'. The Road Network Improvement Project moved the focus from private participation in road construction to private participation in road maintenance. Its goal of creating a 'large number' of road maintenance enterprises across Vietnam again required encouragement for local capital. Therefore, the level of ICB bidding for the project was only 53.6 per cent of the value of the Bank's credit (World Bank 2003l: 10).

Road standards have been an issue of some contention in all Bank-funded projects, in relation to the Highway Rehabilitation Project 1 the problem lay in rehabilitation versus expansion. Some sections of highway that were rehabilitated by the Bank needed, shortly after completion, to be expanded and or bypasses needed construction, due to traffic growth. According to the Bank's Project Performance Assessment Report, both the Bank and the GoV ignored lessons from other countries in post-conflict or transition stages that road transport is often an area of pent-up demand (World Bank 2004t: ix).

Standards on rural roads have been even more controversial; on the basis of a cost–benefit approach, the Bank limited upgrades on many rural roads to spot upgrading and gravel surfacing. In many cases, however, both the community and the relevant local authority pushed for bituminisation. Key reasons for this were that, as in the case of highways, upgrading often leads to increased traffic volumes, which increase the impact of externalities on the many communities living along the roads. The Bank's Project Performance Assessment Report (2004t: 13) recommended that such externalities be taken into account in analysis. This report appears to have had little impact on the Bank's approach – at an interview a Bank officer noted: 'I know we've been having a big debate internally and with the government about gravel paving versus rural roads. I think the modus operandi seems to be we finance a gravel road and then they pave it later on' (Gray 2005). When I asked the officer about the implications of the Bank's position in terms of government and local ownership, the response was to cite the issue of costs – the GoV cannot fund all the infrastructure projects they wish and the Bank needs to work with them to establish priorities.

On transport investment and socioeconomic development generally and, more specifically poverty reduction, the World Bank and other donors in transport presume a connection between increased investment and a range of socioeconomic benefits, for example improved access to markets, health and education facilities and off-farm income generation possibilities.[8] This analysis resulted in a generally implicit correlation being posited between transport (and roads in particular) and poverty reduction. Rural Transport I (World Bank 2004t: 13) makes the link explicit in referring to data from a national survey that purportedly 'shows that people who live near an all-weather road have higher living standards than those who do not'. There is, however, little analytical work to explain the correlation.

Philip Taylor's (2004: 255) work on the Khmer Krom ethnic minority in the Mekong delta does not question this correlation per se, rather the reasons for it. He found that road transport projects have driven the Khmer Krom away from better-located land and that the primary effects of road infrastructure have been 'to open new opportunities for those who are already advantageously placed'. The Khmer Krom are primarily rice farmers who, after initial gains in living standards in the late 1980s and early 1990s, have suffered under the decreasing price of rice. Further, the price of many of their key crop inputs has increased, as have the costs of health and education, often resulting in high levels of debt. Taylor (2004: 261) found that when Khmer Krom landowners were offered seemingly good prices for their land (from those with knowledge of forthcoming projects), they often accepted and either relocated to more remote areas where land was cheaper or they became (landless) agricultural labourers. The implication is that people who already have high living standards are able to advance their position by purchasing land near roads to be upgraded and this can result in impoverishment of people from lower socioeconomic strata.

The Bank appeared to recognise this problem in the Community Based Rural Infrastructure Project (World Bank 2001b: 13), stating in the lessons learned section that it is necessary to transparently target the poor 'and minimize opportunities for influential people to favor the non-poor or preferred location'. The project implementation model was more participatory than earlier projects; it involved community capacity building prior to projects. This change is strong evidence of a PWC model of development. However, a note of caution is required – the necessity for scale in Bank projects meant the project did not include a differential analysis of its impacts on minority and other disadvantaged groups. Further, as outlined in more detail in the section below on loans in agriculture, fishing and forestry, the Bank has not been overly successful in implementing participatory projects. The changes visible in the Community Based Rural Infrastructure project are not applicable to the two other loans in the second case study period. Overall then, it can be concluded that the PWC had a minor impact only on rural transportation projects.

Finance and law, justice and public administration

Four of the five credits in the law, justice and public administration sector were structural adjustment loans analysed above. Thus the remaining credit in

Table 7.6 Word Bank finance and law, justice and public administration sector lending to Vietnam: 1993–7 and 2000–4

Project name	*Year approved*	*Approved amount (US$ millions)*	*Microfinance (%)*
Loans 1993–7			
Agricultural Rehabilitation Project	1994	96.0	51
Payment System and Banking System Modernization Project	1995	45.65	–
Rural Finance Project I	1995	122.0	100
Loans 2000–4			
Second Rural Finance Project	2002	200.0	100
Public Financial Management Reform Project	2003	54.3	0
Forest Sector Development Project*	2004	39.5	51**

Notes:
* Project sector as classified by Bank is agriculture, fishing and forestry.
** See Note 9.

this sector, the Public Financial Management Reform Project, is included with finance sector activities. The Bank classified the Agricultural Rehabilitation Project (World Bank 2002g: 2) as a finance project because 51 per cent of the loan value was for a form of microfinance – supervised credits to private smallholder farm households across ten provinces to provide access to farm inputs. The non-microfinance aspects of the credit are analysed with agriculture, fishing and forestry loans. The Forest Sector Development Project, which is classified by the Bank as 100 per cent agriculture, fishing and forestry, includes a similar microfinance component for smallholder plantation forests valued at 51 per cent of total project funds (and a greater portion of World Bank loan funds). The microfinance component is covered in this section.

These two loans with specific agricultural credit components are somewhat surprising, as agricultural credit became unfashionable in the Bank in the 1980s because of a combination of poor performance and a shift in paradigm regarding rural credit (Kapur *et al.* 1997: 428–36). The new paradigm, outlined in more detail below, is to mainstream microfinance services and operate them on commercial lines. This was the model for both Rural Finance Projects, with an addition of targeted funds for the rural poor (accounting for 9.8 and 14 per cent respectively of the first and second Rural Finance Projects) (World Bank 1996d, 2002c). The new paradigm was also the reason for the switch from using a single institution for microfinance (sub-project) loans (the Vietnam Bank for Agriculture and Rural Development), to using one wholesale bank and multiple, competing banks and organisations for sub-project loans. Overall, microfinance was the dominant theme in finance sector loans, comprising three of the four activities and accounting for 89 per cent of loan funds in the sector.[10]

Microfinance has been part of the World Bank 'toolkit' since the 1980s, when a so-called 'revolution' took place, shifting 'from the old paradigm of subsidised credit delivery to the new paradigm of sustainable commercial microfinance' (Robinson 2001: 46). From this shift, we can see that microfinance is sympathetic to the Washington Consensus supporting its faith in individualism, entrepreneurship and banking liberalisation, especially in relation to control over interest rates. By the early 1990s, the Bank was publicly supporting microfinance as an approach to poverty reduction – an approach that eschews the need for social safety nets as 'a welfare-biased approach to poverty alleviation that disenfranchises the poor and establishes new dependency relations' (Gibbons *et al.* 2000: 266). The Bank's theory is that empowering the poor requires the appropriate 'enabling environment' thus giving them the opportunity to be entrepreneurial. As Heloise Weber (2004: 362) pointed out, the enabling environment in policy terms becomes in essence an issue of access to credit, which in a neoliberal context has the effect of placing financial sector liberalisation as a central issue in poverty reduction. Thus, she concluded that microfinance is more than merely sympathetic to the Washington Consensus, as a poverty reduction strategy its goal is 'to both advance and legitimize neoliberal restructuring' (Weber 2004: 360).

The administration of microfinance projects is often presented in ways that imply a need for financial sector liberalisation. This is evident in statements from the Bank-sponsored group responsible for mainstreaming microfinance, the Consultative Group to Assist the Poorest (CGAP), who state that necessary financial sector reforms to support microfinance include

> removal of ceilings on interest rates, removal of competing subsidized credit schemes, less restrictive banking laws to encourage new entrants, and prudential regulation and supervision to accommodate non-bank financial institutions, particularly those involved in savings mobilization and uncollateralized credit to individuals through solidarity groups.
>
> (Cited in Weber 2004: 374)

The strategy of promoting multiple, competing banks for loans was a part of the Bank's overall project of reforming finance in Vietnam – the Second Rural Finance Project (World Bank 2002c: 17) justified IDA involvement in the loan because it facilitated restructuring of state-owned commercial banks, improved banking competition and created 'a framework within which there can be substantial private development within the financial sector'. Further, the project was supposed to 'strongly complement' banking sector reforms supported under the PRSCs, which aimed to create a private, liberalised finance sector. Subsumed under the conditions on the contents of a policy manual for both the first and second rural finance loans was a requirement for commercially sustainable interest rates acceptable to IDA (World Bank 1996d: 37, 2002c: 30). Indeed, there was a high level of conditionality on both the Rural Finance Projects – 29 conditions on the first loan and 45 on the second. These are the second and third highest numbers of conditions in the two case study periods in Vietnam; the average number of conditions was 20.9 and the median was 19.[11]

Weber argued that microfinance is a key policy response to crises that follow from structural adjustment programmes –it is 'a neo-liberal safety net *for* neoliberal political restructuring' (Weber 2004: 362). In Vietnam, microfinance loans were among the first organised by the World Bank. This was at a time when, following a period of restructuring broadly along neoliberal lines, the rate of reduction in poverty had declined and the social welfare system, which had been neglected since the mid-1980s, was in a state of disrepair. Even in education and health, where Vietnam had achieved above-average outcomes, user-fees and neglect resulted in declining performance. This produced increasing levels of unrest, especially in the countryside. Given the Bank's commitment to neoliberalism, microfinance loans in Vietnam should be seen, as Weber's analysis suggests, as part of the neoliberal policy response to problems arising from economic adjustment.

The model of microfinance used in the Bank loans also sheds light on the PWC. It was what is called a minimalist approach to microfinance and involved credit provision only for those accessing sub-projects (Weber 2004: 364). That is to say, there was no training or skills development involved for the poor. There were, however, significant programmes of institutional strengthening for the wholesale bank and the participating financial institutions. There was a substantial administrative burden on participating financial institutions and little flexibility for them to modify operations to suit local conditions and needs. The paradox of this approach was that microfinance operations were initially established precisely because traditional banks and financial institutions were not flexible enough to serve the poor. The Bank's model required participating financial institutions to follow the management and institutional arrangements of mainstream financial organisations (Weiss *et al.* 2005: 250; Gibbons *et al.* 2000: 260).

There can be little doubt that what has kindly been called the 'mission drift' towards commercialised credit operations will significantly impact on microfinance operations (Weiss *et al.* 2005). A review of rural lending in Vietnam by Pham Bao Duong and Yoichi Izumida (2002: 333) found that the Vietnam Bank for Agriculture and Rural Development (VBARD), which accounts for 84 per cent of formal lending for rural households, lends primarily to the non-poor. VBARD lending is primarily determined by a household's reputation in the village (a measure of both economic position and prestige), a low number of dependents and by the amount of credit applied for. In other words, VBARD follows traditional commercial banking practices that make it difficult for the poor to access formal credit. Further, differential in access to credit is, according to A. Haroon Akram-Lodi (2005: 84–87), contributing to a stratification of peasant landholdings in rural Vietnam, which in turn is contributing to the creation of landless wage labourers. The percentage of landless rural households jumped from 8.2 in 1993, to 9.2

in 1998 and 18.9 in 2002 (Akram-Lodhi 2005: 84–85). It may well be that World Bank microfinance (and other) activities are contributing to the development of a landless proletariat in Vietnam.

There was little information in the loan documents on the way the microfinance activities operated; however, a couple of references suggest a relatively standard microfinance model. This involves the formation of small savings groups of approximately five people; after a few weeks of demonstrating their savings capacity a limited number, generally two, members of the group are eligible for loans. If these loans are repaid in line with the rules, other members of the group become eligible for loans. The key feature is the collective or group responsibility for loan repayment; this collective responsibility also serves as 'collateral' for the loan (Hassan 2002: 208). Jude Fernando (1997: 160), in a review of microfinance in Bangladesh, found that the group system results in range of pressure tactics to ensure repayment including control and regulation of household consumption. Difficulties meeting repayments can increase the conflict within a household too.

Other research has shown that microfinance loans are often not used for the purpose for which they were made, instead they are used for consumption (e.g. medical costs, school books, etc.). As Weber (2006: 195) pointed out, donors responded to this finding by changing the objectives of microfinance to include consumption 'smoothing'. Where loans are used for income generation activities, the requirement for immediate weekly repayment means income generation activities need to provide returns from day one. Often new loans are taken to repay existing ones, which can result in debt dependency (Fernando 1997: 161).

The Second Rural Finance Project (World Bank 2002c: 15) referred to results from a socioeconomic study of the first project reporting that there was a high repayment rate of loans (98 per cent) and that the bulk of funds went to projects in cultivation and animal husbandry (74 per cent of loans). There was no detail on the impact on poverty, despite the project being classified as a Poverty Targeted Initiative. On gender issues, the assessment was limited to noting that only 30 per cent of borrowers were women.[12] The study does not indicate the level of access of ethnic minorities (who suffer the highest levels of poverty in the country) to the programme, but it claimed that there was no negative impact on them (World Bank 2002c: 15).

The Second Rural Finance Project (2002c: 18) posited that '[f]inancing viable initiatives of the rural poor and providing them with better access to financial services would increase their chances of getting out of the poverty trap'. Despite the growing literature on microfinance, there is little solid and uncontested evidence to support this argument. The Bank's claim is an example of the belief that microfinance has 'intrinsic value' and the 'general expectation' that it will assist the poor (Weber 2004: 365; Weiss *et al.* 2005: 262). More to the point, though, the argument reframes social vulnerability as economic potential and thus can be seen as 'a form of social disciplining aimed at commanding compliance' with Washington Consensus restructuring

(Weber 2004: 356). The Bank's continuing reliance on microfinance demonstrates the PWC's neoliberal core. Further, this individualistic, self-help approach to economic growth is increasingly being marketed to the poor themselves and to the developed world as *the* appropriate way of achieving development (Weber 2006: 195).

The final two loans examined here are the Payment System and Banking System Modernization Project from 1995 and the 2003 Public Financial Management Reform Project. The Payment System Project aimed to establish a national inter-bank payment settlement system, a commercial intra-bank payment system and provide institutional strengthening for commercial banks. It was designed to undertake precursor actions for the commercialisation and equitisation of the domestic financial sector and as a 'step toward the gateway for global markets' (World Bank 2004b: 8).

The Public Financial Management Reform Project provided hardware, software and training for a management information system for Treasury. It piloted the use of Medium Term Fiscal Frameworks and Medium Term Expenditure Frameworks (MTEFs). Because these were to be linked to achieving the goals of the CPRGS, the Bank (2003k: 15) claimed that 'the poor should benefit disproportionately' from the project. This may be the case, but accounting and planning methods were the reason that Vietnam has not been able come to terms with the IMF since 2001. More to the point, these standards are an effective way to deepen PWC fiscal discipline and global transparency; MTEFs in particular 'provide one, comprehensive device through which global agreements, national intersectoral budgeting and highly localized investments are bound together in ways that were never possible' with older style national development planning (Porter and Craig 2004: 400). Further, in an exercise of hegemonic control, such standards are used to keep the public out of economic decision-making, making it instead the realm of technocratic experts (Crawford 2006: 125). This project may have been sold in poverty terms but it was clearly about other Washington Consensus priorities.

On the central question of whether and how the PWC differs from the Washington Consensus, this section has demonstrated that finance and public administration sectors remained dominated by Washington Consensus thinking.

Agriculture, fishing and forestry

Two things are surprising about loans in the agriculture, fishing and forestry sector: first the lack of change in the language and content of projects over the two case study periods and, second, the number of projects that can best be described as area development or integrated area rural development projects. These developed during the McNamara presidency as poverty lending but became unfashionable in the Bank in the early 1980s. The ongoing use could be because they fulfil the Bank's need to be seen doing something about rural poverty through their focus on geographical areas with high poverty

Table 7.7 Word Bank agriculture, fishing and forestry sector lending to Vietnam: 1993–7 and 2000–4

Project name	*Year approved*	*Approved amount (US$ millions)*
Loans 1993–7		
Agricultural Rehabilitation Project*	1994	96.0
Irrigation Rehabilitation Project	1995	100
Forest Protection and Rural Development Project	1997	21.5
Loans 2000–4		
Northern Mountains Poverty Reduction Project	2001	110
Water Resources Assistance Project	2004	157.8
Forest Sector Development Project	2004	39.5
Avian Influenza Emergency Recovery Project	2004	5.0

Note:
* World Bank sector classification is finance 51 per cent, non-finance components included in this section.

concentrations. In terms of language and content, participation of local communities was incorporated by 1997 – in the Forest Protection and Rural Development Project – and maintained a strong presence thereafter. Decentralisation was discussed more explicitly in the second case study period loans, not enough though to suggest significant change. This may be because given their nature, all projects adopted decentralised management and implementation systems (with the exception of the avian influenza loan).

In the Northern Mountains Poverty Reduction project (World Bank 2001c: 25), the Bank claimed that its key 'value-added' to the project was its direct support for 'true and full participation during design, implementation, operation and maintenance, and monitoring and evaluation'. However, a brief analysis of the project design reveals that most project implementation responsibility lay with districts rather than communes and that participation essentially involved representation from existing GoV structures and connected organisations (e.g. Women's Union, Youth Union and Farmers' Association). Participation in this form is likely to reinforce existing power relations. This design indicates why the Bank's own Operations Evaluation Department (2002: 1) concluded that in general 'the language of NGO/CBO involvement in Bank-supported projects outstripped the reality'.

Both forest sector loans claimed to be focused on biodiversity protection; however, they can be better understood as rural area development projects – in the Forest Protection and Rural Development Project (World Bank 1997e) $10.46 million of the $21.5 million loan was directed to rural infrastructure projects in the two project areas, a further $1.77 million was for agriculture support services and $1.62 million was for *land allocation*. In the Forest Sector Development Project (World Bank 2004j), $38.02 million of the $39.5

million loan was for development of smallholder plantation forests in four sites (including the microfinance component discussed earlier).

The Northern Mountains Poverty Project (World Bank 2001c) was also an area development project – it targeted 368 poor and remote communes across six provinces and funded a range of community-selected rural infrastructure projects and some associated 'software'. Informal feedback indicated that this and other community development projects in Vietnam did not perform particularly well. The Project Appraisal Document (World Bank 2001c: 23) acknowledged some problems the Bank has encountered with both community development and area development projects, noting they have 'not been entirely successful in terms of impact or sustainability'. Specifically it highlighted project complexity as a problem and acknowledged this project has 'above average complexity' and will place significant demands on local institutional capacity. This concern with administrative and procurement complexity is one that could be applied to all the area development projects as well as the two irrigation projects.

Both forest sector projects supported provision of land-use certification as a way of increasing stability, access to credit and sustainable land use. There was little sign here of the impact of NIE which would caution that: 'partially complete "real" markets are capable of being "regulated" by dominant economic agents that can take advantage of asymmetrical information and bounded rationality to shape the operation of markets to their own advantage' (Akram-Lodhi 2005: 79). Akram-Lodhi found that partial land markets are a central cause of 'differentiation in access to land' contributing to the stratification of rural households. Land-use certification is more than a reflection of core Washington Consensus concerns, land markets as a way to create and reproduce private property are a hegemonic principle of the liberal capitalist Bank.

The water resources/irrigation projects were designed to rehabilitate, improve and expand existing large irrigation schemes. Neither made substantial claims regarding poverty impact, rather the Water Resources Assistance Project (World Bank 2004o: 2), for example, supported 'transition to a more market-based economy by promoting changes in infrastructure and management that will encourage and underpin further agricultural diversification'. Wealthier farmers tend to already and increasingly have access to irrigated land (poor households in contrast are more likely to have a high portion of forested land). According to Akram-Lodhi (2005: 94), the Bank was correct in pointing to the growth potential of diversified (i.e. non-rice) agriculture; however, the resulting accumulation process 'may be inequalizing'. Support for rehabilitation of existing irrigation schemes was likely to contribute to the stratification of rural landholders that is (as the Bank itself acknowledges) already occurring and thence to increasing landlessness (as was the case with microfinance).

Overall, loans in the agriculture, fishing and forestry sector provided linkages to the pre-Washington Consensus Bank expressed largely though PWC rhetoric. These commitments combined with core Washington Consensus principles of private land ownership and economic growth regardless of its distributive impacts seem to form the basis of the PWC version of poverty reduction.

Education and health

There were only three projects in each of the health and education sectors; to facilitate comparison between the two case study periods, the sectors were combined. Education and health care were also the two sectors with least World Bank lending activity, which is, in itself indicative of the relative priority these sectors have been given in the Bank's programme for Vietnam. Loan volumes to the two sectors dropped only slightly from $221.2 million in 1993–7 to $206.1 million in 2000–4; however, the weighting shifted significantly towards education projects, despite the ongoing problems in Vietnam's health sector.

In terms of the structure of the projects, there was a notable tightening of focus and goals in the 2000–4 loans – they shifted from generic projects covering a range of issues and many regions to more tightly focused and geographically limited projects. This may have been a response to the Bank's own evaluations of the earlier projects, which indicated that they were too complicated and imposed too many administrative burdens on ministries not used to working with donors.[13] Ministries were required to establish specific structures, entities and accounting and reporting systems for Bank projects, whereas this was not a requirement for the integrated rural development projects. In education, projects had a strong focus on construction of infrastructure – in the Primary Education project, rehabilitation and construction of primary school infrastructure accounted for 58.6 per cent of the loan at completion; in the Primary Education for Disadvantaged Children, 91.8 per cent of the Bank commitment was for infrastructure.

Table 7.8 Word Bank education and health sector lending to Vietnam: 1993–7 and 2000–4

Project name	*Year approved*	*Approved amount (US$ millions)*
Loans 1993–7		
Primary Education Project	1993	70.0
Population and Family Health Project	1996	50.0
National Health Support Project	1996	101.2
Loans 2000–4		
Primary Teacher Development Project	2001	19.84
Regional Blood Transfusion Centres Project	2002	47.5
Primary Education for Disadvantaged Children Project	2003	138.76

There was relatively little change in justification or analysis for projects between the two case study periods, apart from increasing concern with the regressive effects of user fees on the poor (only) in education but *not* in health care. This change may reflect the impact of the non-governmental organisation (NGO) lobby and poorer Vietnamese regarding growing inequality. In education, the Bank (2003j: 13) proclaimed it had undergone a 'fundamental shift' in its understanding of equity from one focused on inputs to one aimed at achieving 'equity in outcomes'. This focus on outputs is another way of making the 'non-poor' responsible for education themselves and equally limiting government social expenditures on education by targeting them to the poorest – thus this approach effectively increases the burden on the so-called non-poor in meeting the costs of education (Puiggrós 2002). This outcome supports Porter and Craig's (2004: 412) finding that the PWC may aim to get people above one dollar a day but it does not aim for much more and that the PWC is 'fundamentally not redistributive in any substantive sense'.

In health care, the early Bank loans focused on support for the communal health system, which was undermined by the end of the cooperative system. The communal system is the centre of preventative health care in Vietnam and World Bank health policy has, since at least the early 1990s, focused on allocating government health resource on so-called low-cost, high-return activities that target the poor, that is preventative public health interventions (Laurell and Arellano 2002: 192). The corollary to this focus has been a programme to reduce government expenditure on curative health care services and promote market forces, initially in curative services. This is a neoliberal agenda proscribing health as a private activity and concerned with limiting state intervention and expenditure, but one tempered in the early 1990s by political backlash engendered by its socioeconomic impact (Laurell and Arellano 2002: 192–93; Brunet-Jailly 1999; Patnaik 1999).

The unbundling of the curative and preventative health sectors has the added advantage that the curative sector can then be subject to market forces and the extraction of profit. There is an interesting parallel here in the separation of profitable and non-profitable components of utilities. For Asa Laurell and Olivia Arellano (2002: 193, 204) the problematic consequence of Bank health policy is that it 'recreates a modern version of 19th century charity: the state intervenes in response to popular demands but the benefits provided are regarded as concessions rather than rights'. Indeed the Bank 'also covertly seek[s] to destroy the very concept or idea of social rights, a critical condition for the privatization and commodification of health financing and provision'.

In curative health, Bank policy in Vietnam followed this model as part of encouraging the transition to a market economy. The reasoning was quite seductive, the Bank argued that curative services were disproportionately accessed by non-poor households meaning that relatively too much GoV expenditure was devoted to them, particularly though hospital care. However, making curative services subject to market forces only makes such services even less accessible given that, as a study in Vietnam demonstrated, the poor already tend to 'forgo inpatient treatment because of the expense' (Segall *et al.* 2002: 501). The Bank's argument about access was premised on a simplistic, non-specific distinction between the 'poor' and 'non-poor'. It assumes that when households are no longer poor they have the capacity to pay for curative services. This focus on making the 'non-poor' pay for health services also supports Porter and Craig's argument that the PWC only aims to get people above one dollar a day and no more.

There are alternatives: a study of health services in Vietnam recommended, in the first instance, exempting the poor from user-fees in both primary and hospital care (Segall *et al.* 2002: 503–4). In general, such exemptions are administratively complex and generally do not effectively target the poor, which the Bank acknowledged in relation to education exemptions. Thus, in the longer term, the study recommended that exemptions be replaced with more comprehensive support. Ensuring good public health outcomes requires, in the first instance, maintaining the strong public health system built under central planning. This is in contrast to the Bank's approach of pushing the sector towards market mechanisms.

Overall, it is difficult to determine if the Bank's approach to health care has shifted under PWC (or other) influences, as there was only one loan in the later period. The lack of projects in itself indicates that the Washington Consensus approach of 'marketising' health care, which is apparent during the first case study period and was linked to poorer health outcomes in Vietnam, remains dominant. In education, while there was support for private providers, there was a greater concern for equity.

Conclusion: a weak post-Washington Consensus

This analysis of the Bank's programme in Vietnam demonstrated that the impact of the PWC on country programmes and lending has been more limited than it appears from Bank policy documents and research output. In terms of country ownership – perhaps the feature that is meant to distinguish the PWC most from the Washington Consensus – we saw that Vietnam's CPRGS did involve country ownership but that the process was significantly Bank driven and controlled and has been at best a second-track policy forum. The Bank's CAS liberally reinterpreted the CPRGS to focus on neoliberal priorities. In terms of loans, there were few changes in administration and procurement requirements that ceded greater control or authority to the GoV. Project personnel, implementation manuals and accounts all must be 'acceptable to the Association'. Project accounting and procurement must be done according to Bank guidelines and, if anything, the attention to Vietnam's procurement arrangements increased in the second case study period.[14]

In terms of sectoral priorities, as suggested in the 2002 Vietnam CAS, Bank lending has prioritised regional development projects but these address welfare only indirectly at best through provision of infrastructure, especially roads.

There remains limited support for health, education or more direct forms of social welfare. Indeed, the Bank's main support for 'social safety nets' was in the form of microfinance – which really cannot be described as a safety net, even if prefaced by the term neoliberal. A number of Bank interventions may be increasing landlessness in a context where, by all accounts, the equitable distribution of land provided the basis for rapid and relatively equal growth out of poverty. The Bank's rural development activities seem remarkably similar to those that dominated the second phase of the McNamara presidency. And these projects, as Caufield (1998: 108) argued, were based on the 'conviction that the best way to create new wealth is to invest in the wealthy, not the poor'.

The increased focus on law, justice and public administration through structural adjustment lending, seemed to be the product of the PWC priority on good governance and reducing corruption. Structural adjustment loans showed an expansion of the development agenda, some of which were poverty focused, but equally the revitalised PWC agenda on governance was visible with the focus on land titling and government administration. The approach to health and education remained focused on increasing the space for markets and on maintaining fiscal restraint on the state. Public administration reforms equally were focused on state expenditure, indeed in a more invasive and expansive way than during the Washington Consensus period. Further, when PWC ideas conflicted with those of the Washington Consensus, the latter inevitably prevailed. All of this demonstrates a weak version of the post-Washington Consensus at work.

The Bank's lending and technical advice during the Washington Consensus can be seen as a Gramscian 'war of position' designed to impose at least the key features of a capitalist system – private property and markets, connected to an unequal distribution of wealth and the expansion of a class of landless proletariat. The PWC was a passive revolution whose aim was to continue the Washington Consensus project through compromise regarding the social costs of adjustment. What this analysis demonstrated is that the PWC's added focus on poverty reduction is a minimalist one, concerned to get people out of absolute poverty but not much more.

This Gramscian analysis of the Vietnamese historic bloc and its relations with the World Bank highlighted both the acceptance of, and resistance to, the imposition of Washington Consensus policies. The case study showed that the state has notable capacity to resist outside pressure for reform. Thus, in the case of SOE equitisation, to date Bank funds have essentially been co-opted to further the process as far as acceptable to the mix of interests in the historic bloc. What is not yet clear is whether the Bank has successfully helped change the underlying terrain on which debates about equitisation occur in favour of market interests. The Ninth Party Plenum gave some indication; it committed to expanding the scope of equitisation to include the large general corporations but not all SOEs. It also committed to ensuring enterprises were properly evaluated before sale, including land-use rights and transparency in the equitisation process (Hung 2005: 32).

In areas not subjected to much public scrutiny – energy, water supply and transportation sectors – the Bank seems to have had a greater measure of success in introducing market 'reforms'. The Ninth Party Plenum committed to expanding the scope of SOE equitisation to include electricity (Hung 2005: 32), although the Vietnamese have generally conducted such processes at their pace rather than the Bank's, and the GoV's involvement in these projects helps them to (re-)assert central state and party control in what is a quite decentralised country (Painter 2005: 276). Thus, the new Electricity Law, the drafting of which was funded by Bank technical assistance grants, took over nine years to pass the National Assembly. The Bank envisaged a two- or three-year timetable and was not fully happy with the final content.

Looking at Vietnam's record on poverty reduction, economic growth and social stability they seem to be doing something right – Vietnam was one of the countries in Asia least affected by the Financial Crisis in 1997 and quickly returned to high growth rates. Growth in 2003 was 7.2 per cent and was slightly higher in 2004. The incidence of poverty has declined from 58 per cent of the population to 20 per cent in 2004. There are still huge challenges in poverty, education, health and infrastructure to name a few, but the largely cautious programme and the reinvestment in the social sectors, for the most part contrary to Bank advice, has been more successful than most other former communist countries undergoing transition (with the notable exception of China).

8 Indonesia

An overview

In parallel with the case study on Vietnam, this chapter outlines the structure of the Indonesian government and its principal socioeconomic policies from 1966 to the end of 2004. The political and socioeconomic background starts with the New Order Government of Suharto, which came to power via a bloody coup in 1965, but focuses on the period from 1993 to the end of 2004. The chapter briefly explores the history of Official Development Assistance (ODA) in Indonesia, including the World Bank programme, which approved over $30 billion in loans between 1968 and 2004. The macro-analysis of the Bank's involvement in Indonesia continues with an analysis of shifts in sectoral lending and size of loans. Chapter 9 is a detailed exploration of all Bank loans to Indonesia in the two case study periods. As we shall see, this second case study provides not only a different context but also a distinct pattern of lending through which to understand World Bank lending under the post-Washington Consensus.

The political and administrative structure in Indonesia from 1966

Indonesia continues to be governed by the 1945 Constitution, which, as its name suggests, was instituted at the beginning of the revolution for independence as a temporary measure. It was replaced in 1949 when sovereignty from the Dutch was ceded. In 1959, it was reinstated as part of Sukarno's 'Guided Democracy', again as an interim measure. The 1945 Constitution is short, open to varied interpretation and concentrated power in the President. Thus when Suharto overthrew Sukarno, he was able to utilise it 'as a suitable vehicle for a strong presidential rule' in what was essentially an authoritarian and patronage-based regime (Kingsbury 2005: 41). During the Suharto era, the formal political process was largely subsumed to a project of nation-building or development. However, later in the New Order, the focus shifted to shoring up Suharto's economic and political control (Bourchier 2001: 116–17).

The political structure under Suharto: 1966–98

In Indonesia, full executive authority is vested in the President, who until 2003 was elected by, and responsible to, the People's Consultative Assembly

(MPR). Legislative power is predominately in the hands of the House of People's Representatives (DPR). The MPR is formally the highest constitutional body, although it had little power before constitutional reform commenced in 1998. Its main responsibility was electing the President and Vice President but, under Suharto, the President was selected by consensus. The MPR included appointees from the President and, after reforms in 1992, representatives of provincial-level legislative assemblies. Given that Suharto controlled the DPR, the 'MPR was, in effect, beholden to the president' (Kingsbury 2005: 66). The DPR had primary responsibility for legislation, although the executive was also able to initiate legislation and, under Suharto, virtually all legislation came from the executive.

The bureaucracy, civil society groups and political parties were linked through the Joint Secretariat of Functional Groups (Golkar), which became in effect the key political force and a central organising body for the state (Vickers 2005: 161). Golkar was not a formal political party until 1999 but still won between 62 and 73 per cent of the votes in the (rigged) elections between 1971 and 1993 (Kingsbury 2005: 64). All government officials (and government-connected organisations) had to be members of Golkar. From 1992, officials had to get permission to vote for other parties. Golkar was used to organise and control civil society – it incorporated official groups organising labour, peasants, fisherman, young people and women. This corporatist structure was expanded over time to encompass a range of other occupations and groups in order that they could be controlled and monitored by the dominant historic bloc. As Andrew MacIntyre (1990: 27) notes, the *de facto* role of these groups under the authoritarian corporatist structure 'was to absorb and contain the demands of extra-state groups ... They were, in short, a means of social and political control'.

Cabinet's role in the New Order, like Parliament's, was restricted. Detailed policy debate usually took place through working groups at the ministerial level. The President's view on controversial issues was sought through private meetings (MacIntyre 1990: 30). Individual cabinet members could, and often did, wield significant power. The entire parliamentary structure was framed by the state ideology of *Pancasila* – its five principles are belief in one God; a just and civilized humanity; the unity of Indonesia; democracy guided by the wisdom of deliberation and representation; and social justice for all the people of Indonesia. *Pancasila* is important, as Richard Robison (1993: 44) pointed out, because, beyond its 'bland generalisations', it 'legitimates authoritarianism as a mechanism that achieves the common will of society through consensus under the tutelage of a state'. Moreover, it defines 'liberalism, laissez-faire capitalism, communism or any exclusive claim to represent a religious, ethnic or class interest' as illegitimate in the Indonesian state (Robison and Hadiz 2004: 49). These were hegemonic principles of the New Order historic bloc. *Pancasila* remains a defining feature of the constitution in post-Suharto Indonesia, although its formal role in guiding political parties and other organisations ended in 1998 (Robison and Hadiz 2004: 228).

Until 2001, despite the existence of provincial and local level government, Indonesia was largely centrally controlled and run. Through most of the Suharto era there were 27 provincial-level units: 24 provinces (called *propinsi*), two special regions (Aceh and Yogyakarta) and the special capital city region (Jakarta). Provinces elected Regional People's Representative Councils (DPRD), which could recommend appointments for governors from a shortlist prepared by the Minister of Home Affairs, but the President had the final choice. Beneath provinces are districts; during the New Order there were 241 districts (*kabupaten*) and 40 municipalities/city governments (*kota*). The Department of Home Affairs appointed district heads. Districts are divided into subdistricts (*kecamatan*) and further into villages. Provincial and local government implemented Jakarta-determined policies and programmes. Jakarta also controlled budgets and personnel appointments and there was little capacity for feedback to the centre. The overarching goal of this centralised structure was to ensure national integrity and integration, which was projected as requiring significant redistribution of wealth from resource-rich outer provinces to the more population-dense areas (in particular Java and Bali). This had the added benefit of giving the central government control of national wealth.

No discussion of Indonesian politics is complete without reference to the military. Under Suharto, the army had a key role in politics – officials could be appointed to all levels of administration down to the village level. The army played a coercive role similar to that in most authoritarian states. Military influence has fluctuated over time and there is disagreement regarding its current significance and the extent of its recent apparent decline. Some commentators point to its declining economic significance both in budgetary and non-budgetary terms, its reduced operational capacity and its lack of political unity in post-New Order elections (Rieffel 2004: 100–102). Others point out that its territorial structure has remained intact; military support has been important to the presidencies of Megawati Sukarnoputri and Susilo Bambang Yudhoyono, and the events of 11 September 2001 and the bombings in Bali and Jakarta assisted the police, and to a lesser extent the military, in regaining international standing (Kingsbury 2005; Robison and Hadiz 2004).

The late 1980s saw a brief period of political 'openness' in Indonesia but this ended in 1993–4 (Vickers 2005: 198–201). The New Order was in decline by the mid-1990s. However, it took the economic upheaval of the Asian Financial Crisis to finish the Suharto regime. The story of his downfall has been extensively covered elsewhere and is not repeated here; rather, the chapter turns to an overview of the political reform process in the post-Suharto era (Aspinall *et al.* 1999; Eklof 1999).

Constitutional and political reform: 1999–2004

Doctor Jusuf Habibie became President of Indonesia in May 1998. As Suharto's chosen successor and a New Order insider, he surprised many by his political reformism. His earliest reforms were the vote on independence in East Timor, removal of controls on press and release of political prisoners. In terms of Indonesia's political society, Habibie removed laws restricting the number of political parties, although limits were retained on the number of small parties – parties require representation in nine provinces and within the nine provinces in half of the districts. Elections became open and a series of reforms changed the constitution, introduced checks and balances on presidential power and increased the influence of the legislature. The MPR now comprises the DPR and a Regional Representative's Council (DPD), both fully elected. Since 2004, the President and Vice President have been popularly elected and limited to two five-year terms. The role of the MPR is limited to swearing-in the President and Vice President, removing them for specified constitutional violations and amending the constitution.

The DPR has strengthened legislative responsibilities, including the right to submit legislation, although the President is still in charge of promulgating government regulations in the implementation of law. The DPR has increased power to review the executive, military and bureaucracy; however, it has shown limited interest in using its review or legislative powers (Fealy 2001: 105–6). Radical decentralisation accompanied the reforms and resulted in national political and executive authority being limited to 'international policies, defence and security, judicature, monetary and fiscal policy, religion' and other fields requiring national planning and policy-making (Turner *et al.* 2003: 24).

The DPD manages relations between the regions and the central government. It participates in debate, and can submit bills to the DPR on regional issues, for example finances and relations between Jakarta and the regions. It considers DPR bills on the budget, taxation, education and religion and is empowered to supervise their implementation. Members of the DPD are elected by DPRDs, whose members are directly elected. The creation of the DPD was the logical outcome of the radical decentralisation of formal political power and government administrative responsibilities that commenced in 1999, as were amendments recognising the role of provinces, *kabupaten* and *kota* in regulating and managing their own governmental matters. Reform led to fully elected DPRDs and elected local leaders (governors, *bupati* and mayors). The constitution now states that regional administrations 'exercise the broadest possible autonomy'. Though, of course, the reality is more complex.

Decentralisation was the product of two laws, no. 22/1999 on regional governance and no. 25/1999 on fiscal balance between the central and regional governments. Law no. 22/1999 aimed to democratise local government and devolve central government responsibilities to the provinces, *kabupaten* and *kota*. *Kabupaten/kota* are given equal status with provinces and, along with the provinces, are given explicit responsibility for 'public works, health, education and culture, agriculture, communication, industry and trade, capital investment, environment, land, cooperative and manpower affairs' as well as for managing natural resources (cited in Turner *et al.* 2003: 24). But even within these areas, national government retains some responsibilities, particularly for coordination activities. The division of responsibilities both between the centre and provinces and between the provinces and *kabupaten/kota* continues to lack clarity. This has given international donors and various elements of the historic bloc room to influence outcomes in directions they see fit.

Decentralisation is a key issue for this and the following chapter, because the World Bank claimed it was 'catalytic in getting the Government to focus on' it. Further, decentralisation was a major area of financing during both case study periods (World Bank 1999a: 1). The core issue here is the impact of decentralisation on post-New Order power structures. Hadiz (2004: 699, 711) argued that decentralisation has not challenged existing networks, they quickly reconstituted themselves under the decentralised system, creating 'newly decentralized, predatory networks of patronage' that 'are relatively autonomous of central state authority'. For this reason, decentralization has done little for the most disadvantaged in Indonesia. This equally applies to the reform process overall. Thus, Robison and Hadiz (2004: 250) noted that, apart from decentralisation, the Suharto-appointed DPR controlled the reform process. The voting system they agreed upon for the DPR – candidates are elected by proportional representation organised around provinces but allocated by party performance at the district level – allowed incumbent politicians to utilise their existing party structures, giving them an advantage over newly formed parties. All this suggests that the transition from the New Order was, in Gramscian terms a passive revolution. That is, it is a way already dominant groups confronted with changing social relations, manage this change using the instruments of the state to ensure that their dominance is maintained or indeed extended. In Indonesia, the elite continued their domination of the political process and furthered their own private interests (Robison and Hadiz 2004: 245).

Socioeconomic developments in Indonesia since 1966

Socioeconomic developments under Suharto

As noted above, under Suharto there was a strong commitment to nation-building and an explicit development project. Growth was strong through the 1970s, slowed in the early 1980s but returned to respectable levels after 1987. In the early 1990s, many commentators including the World Bank, labelled Indonesia as a new Asian 'tiger'. Following the Asian Financial Crisis it was more commonly seen as the epitome of 'crony capitalism'. With hindsight, it is possible to dismiss some of the economic growth under Suharto as a proverbial 'house of cards'. However, such an approach, neglects the substantial changes that did take place.

There is a debate about the extent to which the Indonesian economy is market based. In the early years of the regime – with the background of the

Cold War and Western hostility to the previous Sukarno regime – Indonesia was presented as a market-based economy. This was possible because, in contrast to Sukarno's closed and increasingly socialist-oriented policies, Suharto pursued more mainstream policies. With the assistance of a group of US-trained economists labelled the 'Berkeley mafia' or technocrats, he controlled inflation and pursued conservative monetary and fiscal policy (including a 1000 per cent devaluation of the *Rupiah*), restructured and reduced debt (with the assistance of the West via the Inter-Governmental Group on Indonesia) and liberalised the foreign investment regime (Hill 2000: 30–64). Western aid is discussed in more detail later in the chapter but it is worthwhile to point out the haste with which bilateral donors became involved with Indonesia after Suharto's brutal take over, and they were followed quickly by the International Monetary Fund (IMF) and World Bank.

Beneath the liberal surface though, the regime was committed to a high level of state involvement in the economy. The level of intervention shifted with the changing configurations of the New Order historic bloc. During the early years, a relatively open economic stance was adopted reflecting the New Order's need to distinguish itself from the previous regime in order to attract Western investment and debt restructuring. At the same time, the regime itself was relatively weak so the 'Berkeley mafia' had significant influence over fiscal and monetary policy and over economic and social planning more broadly.[1]

The economy responded to the stability and relative openness to capital and these combined with development expenditures, available largely because of oil wealth produced gross domestic product (GDP) growth of 10.9 per cent in 1968 (Hill 2000: 15). From 1971 through to 1981, economic growth continued at a high average of 7.7 per cent, despite growing political and economic turbulence. In 1972, poor rice harvests led to price hikes and unrest. In 1973, the international oil shock and growing discontent among domestic Islamic businesses contributed to the Malari riots in 1974 (Hill 2000: 16; Robison and Hadiz 2004: 51). However, the New Order was, by this point, hegemonic and it responded to the instability with both coercion – repression of dissenting forces – and consent – populist policies in the form of a resurgent nationalist economic agenda. Thus, from 1973–4 a range of controls over foreign investment, trade and other economic policies were introduced.

In the 1980s, economic growth slowed to around 4 per cent. An increasing proportion of oil production was being consumed domestically and this combined with decreased prices for oil exports to erode valuable export earnings (Hill 2000: 16).[2] Debt was also accumulating at a fast pace. This contributed to increased unemployment and some social unrest and prompted policy reforms from the early 1980s, particularly to reduce government expenditure and reform the banking system. However, it took the international recession of 1986–7 and leverage from the IMF and World Bank to initiate more substantial 'adjustment' and even then liberalisation was not systematic (Robison and Hadiz 2004: 73).

The reform, linked to a period of increasing political openness, was enough to kick-start the economy and economic growth averaged 6.7 per cent between 1987 and 1992. But economic growth and increasing corruption made the regime complacent so by the early 1990s the reform programme slowed substantially, followed in 1994 by an end to the period of political openness. Nevertheless, economic growth remained strong at 7.8 per cent between 1991 and 1995. In the years leading up to the Asian Financial Crisis, there were no significant fluctuations across a wide range of macro- and microeconomic indictors (Hill 2000: 262–64). The debt to GDP ratio was stable at around 54 per cent and it comprised more private than public sector debt, with an increasing portion of debt being short term. The influence of the technocrats in the regime was again on the wane and corruption intensified (Hill 2000: 281–82). Social and political turbulence increased from 1996 with Suharto's ousting of Megawati from the opposition Indonesian Democratic Party (PDI) leadership, which led to widespread ethnic violence in early 1997.

The extent of change in the Indonesian economy is indicated by the change in the structure of its GDP. In 1966, agricultural output accounted for over 50 per cent of GDP, by 1992 it was 36 per cent. Industry grew from a few per cent of GDP in 1966 to around 40 per cent, although oil was the major source of growth until 1987. Shares of employment by sector have not changed as much as GDP, but agriculture dropped from 73 per cent of employment in 1961 to around 50 per cent in 1990. Industry increased from 8.1 per cent to 17 per cent and services grew from 18.9 per cent to 32.9 per cent. Though, as Hal Hill (2000: 19–23) points out, these averages hide strong variations between Java and the rest of Indonesia.

New Order economic policy needs to be situated within the complex network of business, political, bureaucratic and military relationships that formed the Indonesian historic bloc. Business and political interests increasingly merged as the Suharto family expanded its business interests in the 1980s and 1990s. They were also fused with the New Order-controlled bureaucracy (Robison and Hadiz 2004: 51). The military played a role in business too – initially directly but over time it was through an indirect network built around *yayasan* (charitable foundations) and interconnected business interests. These complex social forces created a delicate balance between economic growth, social objectives and entrenching the (economic and political) interests and power of the politico-business families that controlled the economy (Robison and Hadiz 2004: 53). Fundamentally though, Suharto legitimacy was underpinned by economic performance, in particular improving living standards for ordinary Indonesians. For most of the New Order, the regime succeeded in improving living standards and social indicators. When it could no longer do this, the regime fell.

Between 1970 and 1996 the proportion of Indonesians living below the poverty line dropped from 60 to 11 per cent, this equalled a drop from 70 to 22.2 million people (World Bank 2003q: 3). However, the poverty line used in these measurements is lower than used by the poorest countries in the world.

If the World Bank's measurement for near poor (US$2 per day) is used, in 1996 some 50 per cent of the population were still living in poverty (Thee 2001: 171–72). This measurement makes the large number of people who fell into formal poverty as a result of the Asian Financial Crisis more explicable.

Growth was achieved without large increases in relative inequality as measured by income inequality (Fig. 8.1), although initial inequality was higher than in other countries in the region. Moreover, there are no reliable figures available for wealth or asset inequality, which may well be high (Thee 2001: 174–75; van der Eng 2001: 193–97). There were significant disparities in growth between urban and rural areas and between Java (and some other resource rich regions) and outlying regions, in particular West and East Nusa Tengarra.

Universal primary education was achieved in the early 1980s and here gains were also impressive in rural areas (World Bank 2003q: 3). Health care improved – as an example, the infant mortality rate dropped from 118 per 1,000 live births in 1970 to 47 in 1997; however, this is significantly higher than regional averages and the percentage of the population with access to safe drinking water was much lower than regional neighbours. In general, as Thee (2001: 169–70) concludes, social development was less impressive than economic growth and compares 'unfavourably with the gains made in Malaysia, Thailand and the Asian "Tigers"'.

The Asian Financial Crisis and beyond: economic and social impacts

According to Thee (2003; see also Chang *et al.* 1998; Haggard 2000), there have been two main economic explanations of the Crisis. The first or 'fundamentalist'

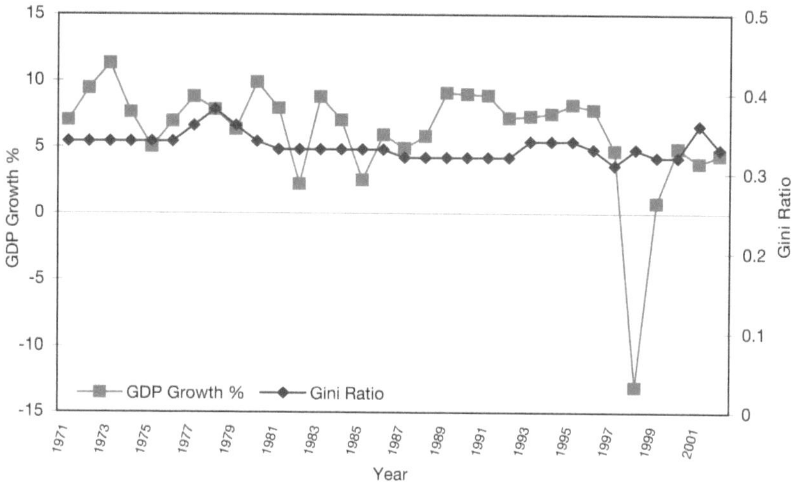

Figure 8.1 GDP growth and Gini ratio Indonesia: 1971 – 2002[3]

explanation saw that the Crisis was caused by deep-seated economic weaknesses in affected countries. It pointed to domestic factors as the primary cause and argues that the affected countries' good economic indicators in some areas 'masked serious structural problems and policy shortcomings that rendered these countries vulnerable to the crisis' (Thee 2003: 185). 'Fundamentalists' focused on the large short-term external debt, large and volatile private capital flows, problems of the quasi-fixed exchange rate system, weak and poorly regulated banks, corruption and poor governance. This was the position of the international financial institutions, in particular the IMF.

The second explanation focused on the panic and 'self-fulfilling pessimism of international lenders' (Thee 2003: 185–86). Under this analysis, economic fundamentals were not as important as the lack of market maturity and the structure and denomination of foreign and domestic debt. The two explanations are not mutually exclusive but as a rule it is political scientists who have tended to give more weight to political and social factors or to the role of international institutions, in particular the IMF's (mis-?)handling of at least the early response to the Crisis. This last aspect, though, is generally regarded as more an explanation of the length and depth of the Crisis rather than its origins (Stiglitz 2002).

The bulk of commentators on the Crisis do seem to agree that, in the case of Indonesia (as well as Malaysia and the Philippines), the trigger was (at least in part) 'contagion'. Equally though most of the factors that Thee's 'fundamentalists' point to were present in Indonesia. While macroeconomic indicators were stable (low budget deficit, moderate inflation and broadly accepted exchange rates) there was a growing level of short-term unhedged debt – unhedged in part because of the security provided by the quasi-fixed exchange rate system. Banks were poorly regulated and there had been a significant build up of corporate debt and some asset price inflation, although none of this had received much attention from economists (Harvie 2000). Poor governance and corruption were obviously issues, although Hill (2000: 279) questions whether their levels actually increased in the 1990s – while the wealth of the Suharto family had undoubtedly increased, the relative size of the SOE sector had fallen and the trade regime was more open. There were few indications that the market's perceptions of levels of corruption altered notably in the period leading to the Crisis.[4] Nor were there signs of a change in confidence in the regime's economic credentials. Domestic governance was, however, a factor in the severity and length of the Crisis: the government handed down an unrealistic budget shortly after the onset of the Crisis, it signed an overly ambitious programme with the IMF and mishandled bank closures (Hill 2000: 280). In addition, Suharto was seen to be protecting the interests of his family and its cronies. This contributed to the way the Crisis intensified.

The programme of liberalisation in the 1980s left the Indonesian government with limited levers with which to respond to the Crisis. For more radical critics of the neoliberal development agenda, liberalisation was the key factor behind the Crisis, as it facilitated uncontrolled build up of short-term debt (Pincus and Ramli 1988: 732). For those influenced by New Institutional Economics, it was the sequencing of reform that was the key failure – financial liberalisation should not have taken place prior to freeing up exchange rates, appropriate prudential supervision of banking, etc. (Stiglitz 2002: 64–67).

The impact of the Crisis on Indonesia was severe and long lasting. Economic growth in 1998 was *minus* 13.6 per cent and inflation soared from 6.5 per cent in 1996 to 65 per cent in 1998 and took time to be brought under control (Thee 2003: 186). The current account actually went into surplus because imports collapsed but exports declined too, despite the huge devaluation in the *Rupiah* after it was floated in August 1997 (in 1998, it was 28 per cent of its US dollar-denominated value from pre-crisis). Devaluation contributed substantially to the exploding debt. Private capital switched from a net inflow in 1996/97 of $13.5 billion to a net outflow of $11.8 billion in 1997/98, the capital account returned to positive in 1998/99 only because of the high level of official flows (Hill 2000: 264–68).

Official unemployment increased only slightly, to around 6 per cent, because formal unemployment is essentially not an option in Indonesia – workers were absorbed into less productive sectors, in particular agriculture. As a result, underemployment, which was always high, increased. There was also a substantial decline in real wages. According to the World Bank's conservative estimates, the incidence of absolute poverty more than doubled to 27 per cent in 1999, but declined again to 15–16 per cent by 2000 due primarily to a decrease in the price of food, especially rice (World Bank 2003q: 3). However, the overall vulnerability to poverty has increased significantly since the Crisis (Suryahadi and Sumarto 2003).

Growth returned in 2000 and between 2000 and 2004 averaged 4.6 per cent, still two percentage points below even the poorer phases of the Suharto era (World Bank 2006a). Inflation seems to be back under control; in 2004, it was just over 6 per cent, despite a spike in 2001–2. Foreign direct investment remains very weak, the major outflows continued into 2000–1 but levelled off in 2002–3 before some modest growth in 2004 (just over $1 billion). Formal unemployment jumped to 9.9 per cent and poverty remains higher than in 1996.

Official Development Assistance to Indonesia after 1966

According to James Soemijantoro Wilson (2001: 153), Cold War aid practices were central to perpetuating a post-colonial political economy in Indonesia built around 'a wealthy indigenous class that reaped its primary economic rewards from neither feudal nor market structures, but from transfer payments from a foreign government'. These practices, he suggests, continued throughout the Suharto regime and only with its fall did the façade collapse, revealing facts that donors had never properly taken into consideration. The Cold War context was central to the US and Western support for the New Order's murderous takeover of Indonesia. Once it had taken legal control and aligned itself publicly with the West it received 'unprecedented' Paris Club debt rescheduling and a very large aid package – $300 million in credits was provided in 1966 and $200 million in 1967 (Wilson 2001: 148). Aid was coordinated through the Inter-Governmental Group on Indonesia (IGGI) – which later became the Consultative Group on Indonesia (CGI). From 1967, when Indonesia rejoined the IMF and World Bank, the Bretton Woods twins became key avenues of support. The Bank's first loans were approved in September 1968 – a quick turnaround for the Bank. The support for Suharto was clearly politically motivated, reflected in the initial form of aid from the IGGI – over 80 per cent of aid was programme (or adjustment) not project aid – a quick disbursing, direct and relatively untraceable form of support for a pro-US and Western regime (Chowdhury and Sugema 2005: 188–89; Hill 2000: 79).

By 1974, aid was predominately in project form and shortly thereafter, programme aid accounted for only a tiny portion of aid flows (Chowdhury and Sugema 2005: 188). As oil revenue increased, aid flows declined in importance to Indonesia, measured both as a percentage of GDP and as a percentage of government revenue. The need to conform to the agenda of donors and to attract foreign capital declined and, as outlined earlier, a range of more nationalist economic policies were introduced. From 1977, aid flows slowly became more important, peaking in 1986–89 with the decline in oil and gas revenues impacting government receipts and an economic downturn. Aid accounted for only 1.5 per cent of GDP in 1977 and for almost 6.5 per cent in 1988. So from the early 1980s, the technocrats and international donors again had more influence on New Order policy. This influence was visible in significant trade liberalisation, devaluations in the *Rupiah*, relaxations in the foreign investment regime and some liberalisation of the finance sector – all Washington Consensus prescriptions.

After 1989 the proportion of aid to GDP declined slowly, averaging 2 per cent in 1995–97. However, as a percentage of government revenue, ODA remained significant – it comprised between 15 and 30 per cent of (official) revenues between 1982 and 1997 (Robison and Hadiz 2004: 72). During the Asian Financial Crisis, aid flows peaked at over 4 per cent of GDP in 1998–99 (Chowdhury and Sugema 2005: 189).[5] What was different after this crisis was how quickly aid declined – by 2000 aid was back down to 2 per cent of GDP. During both 1986–89 and 1997–99 the proportion of programme/adjustment to project aid increased significantly and declined quickly as each crisis subsided.

Historically, Indonesia has received aid from a range of agencies and countries. The most important sources have been the World Bank, the Asian Development Bank (ADB) and Japan's JBIC; other notable sources are the United States (USAID), Germany, France and the Netherlands. Since the 1990s, Japan has been the largest bilateral donor; the World Bank and ADB remain the major multilateral donors. According to Anis Chowdhury and Iman Sugema (2005: 192), in the first half of the 1990s the largest sectors of aid were mining and energy, transportation, agriculture, education and national defence. Since the Asian Financial Crisis,

> [t]he aid share of the mining and energy sector declined from around 20 per cent to less than 10 per cent. But the share of education, health and social welfare sector increased significantly and that helped cushion the poor to some extent from the adverse impacts of the crisis. The share of regional development, too, increased markedly. This shows the importance the donors are giving to the decentralization process that Indonesia undertook in 2001 following the crisis. There have also been significant increases in aid allocated to national defence since 2003.
>
> (Chowdhury and Sugema 2005: 192)

Interestingly the law, justice and public administration sector received only a minor increase in funding under the sectoral categorisation used by Chowdhury and Sugema. However, as we shall see, the World Bank boosted funds in this area significantly. The discrepancy may partly be due to categorisation – Chowdhury and Sugema used Indonesian Ministry of Finance data that includes a regional development and transmigration category, which the World Bank does not. Nevertheless, it seems that other donors have not had the focus on this area that the Bank has. Debt relief was also a major component of bilateral donors' contributions to Indonesia after the Crisis (OECD Development Assistance Committee 2005).

Indonesia's relationship with the IMF was historically based more on technical assistance and advice than on a large lending programme. From 1970 to the end of 2004, Indonesia accessed IMF loans on only six occasions – 1972, 1983, 1987, 1997, 1998 and 2000; notably three of the six occasions were during the Asian Financial Crisis (IMF 2005). The first Crisis loan was under the IMF's stand-by arrangement (SBA) and involved a fairly standard set of conditions, including reductions in government social expenditures and cuts to food and fuel subsidies, despite the fact that the budget was broadly in balance. It specified closure of 16 banks, which led to a run on other banks, and a rise in interest rates that did little to attract international investors while squeezing domestic creditors. Subsequent loans were under the IMF's Extended Fund Facility (EFF), indicating its determination to pursue a programme of structural adjustment for a now full-blown Crisis. However, as Chowdhury and Sugema (2005: 196–97) pointed out, Indonesia did not require the full SBA package. Despite paying interest and charges on the loan, Bank Indonesia only drew down 44 per cent of it. Indonesia's reserves were at a healthy level when the assistance was requested; its purpose was psychological – part of the attempt to restore market confidence. Of course, it did no such thing. Rather the IMF was seen as pushing for accelerating political as well as economic change in Indonesia.

As the IMF assumed a larger role in Indonesia, relations with the World Bank were not always smooth. Mallaby (2004: 193) contended that it was not disagreement regarding the appropriate policy response behind the poor relations. Rather, it was Wolfensohn's anger at the Bank's failure to respond quickly to the crisis, which resulted in it being seen in a poor light against its Bretton Woods twin. The Bank (2003q: 5, emphasis added) has acknowledged the tensions stating in one report that it '*eventually* developed a productive working relationship, playing a key role in the government's Extended Arrangement with the IMF'. It took until around January 2000 for the Bank, IMF and ADB to agree on a division of responsibilities for Indonesia's recovery period. This gave the IMF the lead in macroeconomic policy; the Bank the lead on structural and social policies, including corporate restructuring; and the ADB responsibility for privatisation and SOE reform. In addition, all three agencies agreed to support bank restructuring and financial sector reform (World Bank 2001a: 8). The Indonesian Government eventually terminated its arrangements with the IMF and it has returned to its more traditional role of advice and monitoring.

The World Bank in Indonesia

Indonesia rejoined the Bank in 1967 and they quickly formed a close relationship. After Suharto took control, high-level World Bank visits culminated in a visit from President McNamara in mid-June 1968. McNamara had set out to expand the Bank's presence and his visit 'may have been the most consequential that a Bank president has paid to a borrowing country. It galvanized the president into making Indonesia, from the Bank's side, an instant special case' (Kapur *et al.* 1997: 469). The unique operations in Indonesia involved the establishment of the Bank's first resident mission – its largest and most significant for many years with very broad terms of reference and, initially, direct responsibility to the President of the Bank (Hettne 1982: 58–60). This direct relationship may have been more to do with the Cold War than anything regarding Indonesia per se. It resulted in fundamental agreement on macroeconomic policy bound by 'intimate, ongoing' dialogue with Indonesia's technocrats (Kapur *et al.* 1997: 469–70). The Resident Mission worked most closely with BAPPENAS, the Indonesian National Development Planning Agency, but also with other core central government agencies.

Indonesia's honeymoon with the Bank was coming to a close by 1972 due to tensions between the Bank's Washington and Jakarta offices over the close personal relationships between the Jakarta office and the Suharto administration (Kapur *et al.* 1997: 489). By this time, the Bank was also concerned about corruption and the large-scale, public sector development programme being funded by oil revenues parallel to the government budget. Bank staff aligned with Indonesia's technocrats to oppose the expenditure, but they had lost political influence as oil revenues and the economy grew. As the technocrats' influence declined so too did that of the Bank (Winters 1996: 95–96). Yet the Bank's public response to the Pertamina scandal was to express confidence in

Indonesia (Kapur *et al.* 1997: 491–92). They did not speak out publicly on corruption until late in McNamara's term, which may only have been because a 1977 *Wall Street Journal* report stated that corruption increased the cost of Bank projects in Indonesia by 10–15 per cent (Caufield 1998: 246). In 1980, a World Bank mission produced a 600-page report critical of the bureaucracy and corruption. However, Indonesian officials 'refused to accept it' and the World Bank:

> blinked first – perhaps realizing that the country's oil revenues greatly diminished the bank's structural leverage and fearing that a decade and a half of good relations with Indonesia might be jeopardized if it pushed too hard in such circumstances. Said the World Bank's top official in Jakarta, 'They didn't need our money and they didn't listen to what we said'.
>
> (Winters 1996: 147)

The report was rewritten extensively but it was submitted to the 1980 IGGI (and the story leaked to the *Far Eastern Economic Review*) along with a recommendation of no increase in ODA – the first since 1967. There was also an ongoing problem with slow disbursement of loans that indicates some curtailment of the relationship (Kapur *et al.* 1997: 493–94, 322–23).[6] However, the Bank quickly returned to it's softly-softly approach and the level of change in the relationship should not be overstated in the light of the large ongoing lending programme and the 'miracle' economy tag. Indeed, it seems more accurate to conclude that Bank staff in Indonesia closely identified with the New Order regime and were largely 'captured' by it (Pincus 2001: 189–202).

Loans to Indonesia increased through the 1980s, when it was one of the World Bank's biggest borrowers. From 1981 new loans were only IBRD funded as Indonesia graduated from IDA funding, although after the Crisis in 1998 it again became eligible for IDA funding. The oil slump in 1982 increased the technocrats and Bank's influence and they were behind much of the structural adjustment that took place from 1986, outlined earlier (Winters 1996: 155–56). Lending peaked in 1988–91 with $6.2 billion in new loan approvals. Thereafter lending declined 'partly because the Bank was reaching its exposure limits and the Bank shifted its approach to smaller, diversified projects' (World Bank 2003q: 5). However, lending still averaged $1.3 billion per annum between 1990 and 1997.

During Wolfensohn's tenure it seems that the Bank's resident mission became divided between two factions: one trusting the Suharto regime and another that Mallaby (2004: 180–81) labelled 'corruption fighters'. During a visit by Wolfensohn in mid-1996, he privately expressed concern over corruption but the corruption fighters were losing the internal debate as the 'Bank's old Indonesia hands refused to alienate their star client'. This was partly because, at the time, the only notable mechanism for responding to corruption was cutting lending. Given Bank lending to Indonesia had already been reduced, this option was unpalatable both to many individual loans officers, whose jobs depended on lending, and to their managers who were focused on the Bank's perpetuation, which requires ongoing increases in lending.

The World Bank plays a key role in coordinating donor programmes in Indonesia – across the case study period, it chaired the CGI and it was represented in the Partnership for Governance Reform.[7] The Bank leads many projects that receive grant financing and/or co-lending from other donors. It has a close partnership with the United Kingdom and the Netherlands. The Bank (2001a: 18) itself notes:

> [e]ven where it is not in the lead, Government and donors rely on it for strong analytical and advisory support (decentralization, SMEs, corporate governance, privatization). The Bank plays a key role in Government's Extended Arrangements with the IMF ... And its relationship with key policymakers continues to be good – although where it differs on policy it tends to do so more openly than in the past.

As Fig. 8.2 shows, in terms of sectors of lending the Bank's historical focus has been on energy (electricity), agriculture fishing and forestry and

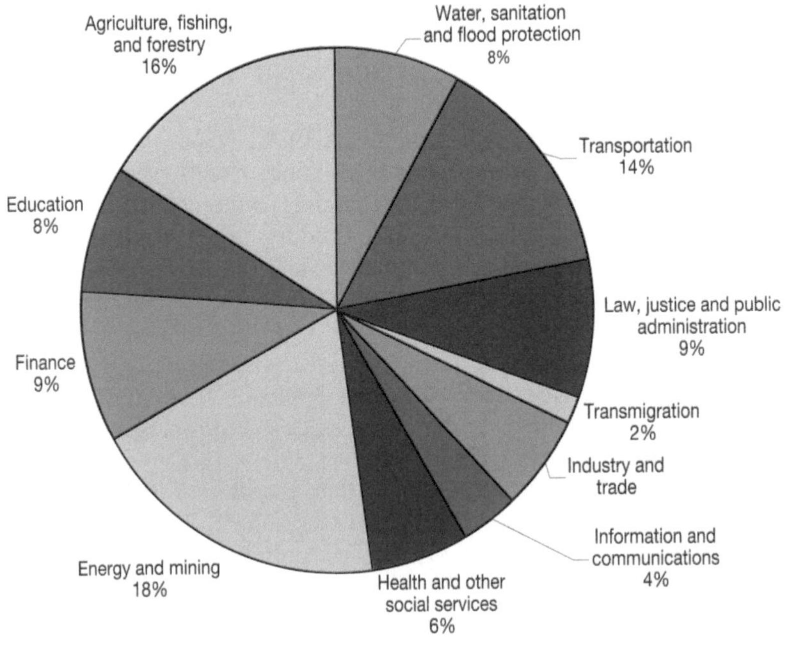

Figure 8.2 World Bank approvals to Indonesia 1968 – 2004, by sector
Source: World Bank projects database[8]

transport. Though, as we will see, there was a dramatic shift in Bank lending in the post-Washington Consensus (PWC) period.

The World Bank's key planning documents: the Country Assistance Strategy and Poverty Reduction Strategy paper

The first publicly available Country Assistance Strategy (CAS) is 2001, but references in other Bank literature indicate that the 1994 CAS (World Bank 1994c: 9) had the following objectives:

(1) maintaining economic growth with macroeconomic stability;
(2) reducing poverty and enhancing human resource development;
(3) enhancing private sector development and competitiveness;
(4) improving public sector management;
(5) improving environmental management.

The framing of the objectives around economic growth and macroeconomic stability indicates the predominance of the Washington Consensus. In terms of lending directions, there was a major shift from agricultural lending towards infrastructure, education, health and water supply and sanitation during the 1990s that was not envisaged in the 1994 and other CASs. Actual allocations for agriculture were 'consistently far below the amount in the CAS' (World Bank 1999a: 13). Nevertheless, the Bank lending programme fits within the themes outlined by the Bank; given the breadth of the themes this is hardly surprising.

The Bank's Board approved the 1997 CAS eight days after the Thai Baht was floated and it presented an essentially optimistic assessment of Indonesia's economic prospects. The 'objectives of the Bank's 1997 country assistance strategy remained broadly unchanged from those of the previous 1995 strategy, focusing on macroeconomic stability; increasing efficiency and productivity in the public and private sectors; reducing poverty; and sustainable management of natural resources' (World Bank 2003q: 6).

The July 1997 CAS had only a meagre discussion of the PWC theme of governance, and it relegated poverty to third on the agenda behind the efficiency and productivity of the public and private sectors. This is unsurprising given that poverty had not received adequate attention in general in Indonesia since 1990. This may have been because absolute poverty had substantially declined; nevertheless, prior to the Crisis over 20 million people were living in absolute poverty and around 50 per cent of the population lived on less than $2 a day. The CAS did note the fragility of the Indonesian banking system but did not consider a crisis likely. Even in mid-August after the *Rupiah* depreciated 20 per cent 'the Bank did not revise its strategy or develop a contingency plan for addressing the deteriorating situation'. Rather, they reported to the Bank Board that the Crisis was under control (World Bank 1999a: 6). The Bank's first solid response to the Crisis was a technical assistance loan in the finance sector (Banking Reform Assistance Project, $20 million); it was not approved until December 1997. This is the only direct Crisis response loan that comes under the first case study period. It took a further seven months for the Bank's large Structural Adjustment Loans (SALs) to be approved.

The Bank is now relatively frank regarding the failures of the July 1997 CAS and the failure to develop contingency plans after the Crisis started. Surprisingly though, a 1999 Operations Evaluation Department Country Assistance Note classified Bank performance in Indonesia over the 1990s as 'marginally satisfactory' (World Bank 1999a: 25). Mixed messages are apparent in relation to corruption: on the one hand, the Bank has acknowledged that a significant portion (30 per cent is the commonly cited figure) of Bank funds were misappropriated by the Suharto regime. On the other hand, the 1999 report referred only on page 10 to 'past allegations of improprieties in Indonesia'. Its review of sectoral achievements utilises old project evaluations without questioning their integrity. The report translates the 'special relationship' with Indonesia into an argument that Bank operations there were fully client driven and that this was the reason for it not pursuing 'unwelcome' policies (World Bank 1999a: 15–16). This reticence and lack of leverage may have predominated in some sectors (in particular finance) but the idea that the Bank did not pursue an agenda or possess any leverage is equally absurd.[9]

The 2001 CAS contained a more substantial analysis of social, political and economic forces than the earlier CASs, or indeed the 2002 CAS was Vietnam. It focused strongly on the PWC themes of participation, decentralisation, poverty and governance. The Bank claimed that the CAS was informed by consultation with 'civil society organisations', but it actually revealed a Bank vision of civil society as something requiring structuring into organisations that can be trained, evaluated and finally legitimated by the very process of their incorporation into Bank consultation. Bernadette Whitelum's (2003: 199–200) study of World Bank/NGO relations in Indonesia found that this was precisely what the Bank was doing with the NGO sector, which it regards as lacking capacity, maturity and an appropriate view of the Bank and of Indonesian development. Whitelum (2003: 188) demonstrates that the Bank 'has assigned itself a role *in shaping* Indonesian NGOs in order to further *its* vision of Indonesia'. Perhaps because of this view, it struggled to find NGOs willing to engage with it on its own terms.

On decentralisation, the Bank (2001a: 1) believed it 'makes good economic sense' but was concerned about implementation of such radical change. Decentralisation also offered the opportunity for selective support for provinces implementing appropriate reforms, that is for introducing competition among provinces. However, as Tania Li (2005: 11) pointed out, there is a tension between the project to 'institute competitive practices at various levels' and the Bank's supposed mission of poverty reduction. Thus where provinces have been performing poorly, the Bank leaves open the option to support 'bottom-up' reform via community development projects (World Bank 2001a: 26).

On levels of lending during the CAS period, the Bank (2001a: 11) forecasted a base case 'muddle-through' scenario with core lending at around $400 million per annum. This was what transpired and, as a result, net Bank disbursements have been negative since 2002. The CAS (World Bank 2001a: iii) also notes the 'significant *possibility of a crisis scenario*'. If this were the case, the Bank's planned response was to *cease all lending*. This is a surprising position because it would not have suited the needs of international capital or the poor (Whitelum 2003: 328); but the group that would have been most effected was Indonesia's political society. The Government's resources were substantially reduced by the Crisis and a stop to Bank lending would likely have produced a drying up of private capital flowing to the state. It may even have prompted further capital outflows. The impact on the relatively weak presidency of Abdurrahman Wahid (which lasted just six months after the CAS's release) would have been major. This then is quite a formidable example of the Bank's coercive power undoubtedly designed to ensure that the Wahid Administration undertook Bank-supported 'reform'.

The Washington Consensus themes visible in the 1995 and 1997 CASs dominated the 2001 CAS as well – its first theme of 'sustaining economic recovery and promoting broad-based growth' was little more than a reformulation of the 1994 CAS's economic growth and macroeconomic stability theme. The second priority was 'national institutions for accountable government', again a new expression for an old theme of efficiency and productivity in the public sector. However, the theme was given new legitimacy by the international financial institution's reading of the Asian Financial Crisis that focused on Indonesia's institutional weakness and corruption. This justified a more interventionist role for the Bank. The third theme, 'delivering better services to the poor', also rehashed the public and private sector efficiency theme, but for the newly decentralised service delivery environment. It was the component that covered the Bank's series of *Kecamatan* Development Projects and Urban Poverty Projects, which actually operate outside of local government administration. Yet the justification in the CAS for this theme was support for the government 'to maintain service delivery through the transition' to decentralisation (World Bank 2001a: 26).

The 2003 CAS was thematically similar to 2001. Theme one was refocused in PWC terms, where the state has a role in creating an enabling environment for business; it became: 'improving the climate for high quality investment'. Services for the poor were relegated to second on the list. The national institutions theme from the 2001 CAS became in 2003: 'the core issue of governance'. The forecast for lending remained at the base case, although evidence 'of decisive momentum in implementing the reform package could lead to an "enhanced" base case, in which the Bank would *offer* an adjustment loan in late 2004' (World Bank 2003f: ii). The Bank did offer the adjustment loan, the First Development Policy Loan, which is analysed in the following chapter. Regarding adjustment lending, the 2001 CAS gave a sense of a new Bank view, which was comprehensively stated in the 2003 CAS. In this view, adjustment lending does not offer good leverage in countries that have widespread governance issues and lack 'deep' commitment to governance reform (World Bank 2003f: 11). This is now precisely how the Bank views Indonesia, thus it proposed restrictions on the use of adjustment lending, making it a reward for 'good' past behaviour.

Indonesia is not a Highly Indebted Poor Country and thus was not required to prepare a Poverty Reduction Stratey Paper (PRSP) to gain IDA access. However, developing a PRSP was part of the 2001 CAS's conditions for moving to a higher lending scenario. An interim PRSP was completed in early 2003 and submitted to the World Bank Board in March of that year. As in Vietnam, the interim document was produced fairly quickly with limited public participation (International NGO Forum on Indonesia Development 2004: 7). The full PRSP process was due for completion in mid-2004 but was only finalised and released in October 2005. There is remarkably little information available on the PRSP or the process for its completion. The PRSP itself is not on the World Bank website; indeed there is barely a mention of it. According to Rudsi Tagaroa (2006), the PRSP proposes a strong rights-based approach to development, derived from a participatory process. The Government of Indonesia has committed to integrating the PRSP action plan into its medium-term expenditure framework; however, there is little commitment from most portfolios, and indeed they have refused to implement it (Tagaroa 2006).

Conclusion

Indonesia is an important case study because for most of the first period examined here, 1993–7, it was relatively stable, showed generally steady economic growth and progress and it was a Bank 'favourite'. Early in 1998 things changed: the often brutal and certainly authoritarian reign of Suharto and the New Order finally collapsed and were replaced by a series of relatively weak governments. The Bank seemed to support the first of these led by Habibie, who was a New Order crony turned reformist. Its support waned during the Governments of Wahid and Megawati. Yudhoyono's Presidency from October 2004 seemed to herald a return to relative stability. Even though it has not challenged entrenched interest in Indonesian society more than other post-New Order presidencies, it has seen some rebuilding in Bank support.

The next chapter explores the Bank's lending practices in Indonesia in detail, which will give more insight into how the Bank's underlying development philosophy has progressed and the tactics it has utilised to achieve its goals.

9 World Bank lending in Indonesia

In 1993, the start of the first case study period, the Bank and Indonesia were in a 'business as usual' phase of their relationship. Indonesia was one of the Bank's bigger lenders but the Bank's influence on the New Order was not particularly strong. This relationship is clear in the sectoral analysis of Bank lending that leads this chapter. What also becomes clear is the profound impact that the Asian Financial Crisis had on the Bank's programme with Indonesia. It resulted in both a large decline in the size of the Bank's programme and in major shifts in its sectoral support. The underlying rationale of these changes and how strongly they are connected to the post-Washington Consensus versus other factors are opened up as the chapter analyses Bank adjustment and investment lending in Indonesia.

A sectoral analysis of World Bank Lending in Indonesia

This section examines the evolution of Bank lending in terms of sectoral focus, types of loans and the size of loans in the two periods, 1993–7 and 2000–4 and provides an overview of lending during the Asian Financial Crisis. Like the case study on Vietnam, the analysis broadly utilises the Bank's sector classification system of new loans approved during the case study periods. More so than in Vietnam, there were a significant number of multi-sectoral projects and projects with anomalous Bank sector classifications. For example, *Kecamatan* Development Project (KDP) I was classified transport, its extension was classified as health and other social services and KDP II was classified as law, justice and public administration. Therefore, the loan analysis does not strictly follow the Bank's sectoral classification, rather it groups similar projects. These anomalies make the sectoral analysis somewhat problematic – it least affects sectoral classifications in energy and mining, education, transport and health (with KDP I as an exception) and is most prominent in agriculture, fishing and forestry, water sanitation and flood protection and law, justice and public administration.

Between 1993 and 1997 a total of $5.35 billion in new loans was approved – a little over $1 billion per annum. There was *no* structural adjustment lending. As per Table 9.1, the key sectors of lending were energy and mining – comprising

Table 9.1 World Bank new loan approvals to Indonesia by sector, as a percentage of total lending: 1993–7 and 2000–4

Sector	*1993–1997 (%)*	*2000–4 (%)*
Energy	24	6
Water, sanitation and flood protection	20	4
Transportation	15	18
Education	13	5
Agriculture, fishing and forestry	10	6
Law, justice and public administration	7	47
Information and Communications	6	<1
Health and other social services	4	14
Industry and Trade	1	0
Finance	<1	0

Source: World Bank Website, Projects & Operations, Projects Database.

totally power projects – and water, sanitation and flood protection – predominately urban development projects. Transportation projects were mainly road projects while education lending covered the junior secondary school level and above. Agriculture, fishing and forestry lending was focused on irrigation and water management projects, two area development projects and the first Village Infrastructure Project.

Between the case study periods, 1988–99, Bank new loan approvals were over $1.67 billion per annum, of which just over 70 per cent was structural adjustment lending. Indonesia has only ever received ten Structural Adjustment Loans (SALs): five between 1987 and 1990, four in 1998–9 and one in 2004 (note the parallel to International Monetary Funds (IMF) loans). The overall average of 13.8 per cent of loans being SALs is largely due to the large-scale loans of 1998/99. Net World Bank disbursements between 1997 and 2002 were only $322 million, because of repayments of older loans and delays or cancellation of tranches from active loans that were tarnished by New Order corruption (and World Bank complicity).[1]

Bank lending dropped dramatically in 2000–4 to $2.18 billion. With only one large structural adjustment loan, adjustment lending was 13.8 per cent of the value of loans. In contrast to the limited changes in the scale, type and sectors of lending in Vietnam, in Indonesia there were major shifts not just in volume but also in the sectoral focus. Most prominently, lending in the law, justice and public administration sector shifts from 7 per cent of lending to *47 per cent*, of which KDP projects account for just over 56 per cent. International Development Association (IDA) loans constitute 27.6 per cent of the value of all new loan approvals. In the 2001 Indonesia Country Assistance Strategy (CAS) (World Bank 2001a: 40), the Bank estimated that Indonesia's eligibility for IDA lending would phase out in four to six years.

On the average and median size of loans – an indicator of the Bank's trade off between project quantity and quality – in 1993–7 there were 54 loans with an average and median size of $99 million. In 2000–4, the average loan approval remained around the Bank's standard at $108 million but the median declined to $77 million. However, if the two small (less than $5 million) learning and innovation loans are discounted, the median was $100–103 million. The average number of conditions jumped dramatically from 15.5 (median 13) in the first case study period to 25.5 (median 24) in the second.

Structural adjustment lending in Indonesia

As noted earlier, structural adjustment lending in Indonesia is, as with Vietnam, well below the Bank's overall average of 33 per cent. Nevertheless, SALs are good indicators of Bank priorities. Take, for example, the two trade adjustment loans in 1987 and 1988 (each for $300 million) and the two private sector development adjustment loans (1989 – $350 million and 1990 – $250 million), these had *no* conditionality at a time when the Bank was in the midst of its Washington Consensus-linked conditionality period (World Bank 1999a: 19). This indicates that Indonesia remained a special case for the Bank through the 1980s, despite the increasing levels of corruption and cronyism. Even the large-scale Policy Reform Support Loans (PRSLs) I and II (in 1998 and 1999 for respectively $1,000 million and $500 million) were not highly conditional for their size, containing respectively 12 and 18 conditions (World Bank 2003q).

The conditions on the PRSLs were core Washington Consensus ones – macroeconomic stability, banking reform, tariff reductions, eliminating trade restrictions, privatisation, liberalising markets and increasing competition (especially in crony conglomerates such as cloves, palm oil and forestry). In PRSL I, the only post-Washington Consensus (PWC) theme was governance, and in the second loan corruption and decentralisation appeared. The lack of strong conditionality was the subject of criticism in the Operations Evaluation Department's (World Bank 2003q: 27) review of these loans – this was a missed chance to 'move the reform program forward'. Given that the loans conditions were predominately Washington Consensus concerns, there is little doubt about the type of reform being referred to here.

The $600 million Social Safety Net Adjustment Loan (1999) ostensibly provided one-off assistance to those negatively impacted by the crisis but its underlying objective was to drive reform of government social expenditures. It sought to make social programmes more targeted and thus constrain expenditure in the medium term. The Bank largely designed the loan and saw it as a vehicle for 'reform', resulting in a high level of conditionality. This contradicts the PWC theme of country ownership. The loan contained 57 complex conditions covering everything from expenditure levels in specific safety net areas to public involvement in monitoring and evaluation and '[s]pecific corrective actions taken against an identified list of problems in implementation of safety net programs' (World Bank 1999b, Annex II). The Bank used the loan conditionality extensively, even in an unrelated (but core Washington Consensus) area – it held off disbursement of the first tranche as leverage for banking sector reform (Whitelum 2003: 303). The programme suffered from design and corruption problems and eventually, the second tranche of the loan ($300 million) was cancelled. The Bank (2003q: 25) stated the cancellation was 'because of lack of progress on governance issues' – and indeed, many conditions were not met even after extensions in timeframes. Undoubtedly the extensive conditionality proved administratively difficult for the Government of Indonesia (GoI), particularly in the midst of decentralisation and other reform. Conditionality also made the loan a political liability for the Wahid Government (Whitelum 2003: 311).

The Water Resources Sector Adjustment Loan (WATSAL) (1999, $300 million, $150 million disbursed) was the most controversial of the Bank's package of Crisis adjustment operations because of its introduction of tradeable water rights and facilitation of further privatisation of water resources management and operations (Hadad 2005). WATSAL was proposed *by the Bank* to progress reform in line with sectoral work carried out by itself and the Asian Development Bank (ADB) in 1997 (Hadad 2005: 67). Legislation, produced as part of the loan, was the subject of a challenge by non-governmental organisations (NGOs) and individuals to Indonesia's Constitutional Court in 2005. Its most interesting aspects were its conditionality and the level of country ownership in relation to the legislation. The legislation was drafted with little public consultation (Zaman 2002) and, because of the controversy surrounding it, was the subject of intense debate and amendments by the Indonesian House of People's Representatives (DPR). These amendments, and some interpretations by the responsible ministries, led to the Bank delaying the second and third loan tranches and eventually cancelling the third.

Nevertheless the Bank's report on the completed loan regarded it as quite successful in driving reform. The lessons learned includes a detailed discussion on the 'necessary and sufficient conditions for ambitious, major sector reforms'; which were 'an overriding trigger, such as a national or sector "crisis"', a local leader to champion reform, a clear strategy and a conducive political–economic environment (World Bank 2005f: 35). The report was also concerned to determine the most effective form of adjustment assistance to drive 'reform operations' in various circumstances – in other words, how to ensure the most leverage from loans. It also explored ways of implementing reforms that minimise political opposition and ensure full compliance. Issues discussed range from minimising legislation amendments to having broad participation in reform and regulation design. On technical assistance, it argued that 'reform "ownership" is crucial', thus 'preparation of reform deliverables by expatriate consultants should be decidedly avoided' (World Bank 2005f: 37). This is more than a classic piece of Bank-speak, the inverted commas around ownership indicates precisely how the Bank seeks to manage reform processes in such a way that they seem to be locally owned, while in reality establishing and managing the agenda itself.

With the view that adjustment lending does not provide enough leverage where regimes are not following the (Bank-determined) 'right' agenda, there was no adjustment lending to the governments of Wahid or Megawati. Whereas Habibie, who lacked a strong domestic power base and was thus particularly reliant on the support of international agencies, received three large, quick-disbursing programme loans within the six months prior to the election. Two months after Yudhoyono was sworn in, he was rewarded for strong talk on increasing economic growth, creating the right investment environment and fighting corruption with the First Development Policy Loan ($300 million) in December 2004. It was less conditional than those made in 1999, containing 10 'prior actions' (i.e. conditions) before release and 12 indicative conditions for a second loan. The conditions covered three areas, the first two of which are consistent with Washington Consensus concerns: reducing government debt and improving the investment climate (World Bank 2004i: 44–46). The third was a PWC one: governance and anti-corruption (expressed in a focus on accounting standards, accounting operations, corruption investigations). The loan was relatively tightly focused and it clearly demonstrates the PWC's role in extending and deepening financial discipline and transparency. Under the governance heading, one of the prior actions was development of a timetable for adoption of a Treasury single account. The completion report for the First Development Policy Loan (World Bank 2005i: 7) claimed there was country ownership of the reform programme, but it provided little evidence in support of the claim and it is difficult to gauge its accuracy.

Overall, in adjustment lending to Indonesia the Social Safety Net Adjustment Loan stood as indicative of the influence of a strong version of the PWC. Yet, the high level of conditionality and cancellation of the second tranche indicated the level of unease with the loan. The 2005 Implementation Completion Report on WATSAL signified the Bank's preference for driving reform regardless of country ownership. It was a clear indication of the Bank's hegemonic predisposition using coercion combined with little more, in this case, than a veil of consent.

Investment lending in Indonesia

The analysis of investment lending in Indonesia commences with the law, justice and public administration sector, which was by far the major sector of lending in the second case study period. This sector is divided into three subsectors: general law, justice and public administration projects; rural area development projects; and urban area development projects, which includes the series of Urban Development Projects that were classified by the Bank predominately as water, sanitation and flood protection but were multisectoral and the forerunners to the Urban Poverty Projects.

Given that the law, justice and public administration sector incorporates a large number of projects originally classified as water, sanitation and flood protection, this leaves only a small number of projects in this sector, which is the second sector analysed. Transportation is next, as it is a substantial sector during both periods, followed by energy and mining, health, agriculture and fishing and forestry and, lastly, education. There was one loan in both the finance and industry and trade sectors. The finance loan is included with law, justice and public administration and the industry and trade loan is included with education sector loans, as it was a human resource development project. The information and communications sector is not studied as there were only two loans and the one in the second case study period was a learning and innovation loan for $2.66 million, thus it would be impossible to undertake a meaningful analysis. The loans could not usefully be included in another sector.

Law, justice and public administration

General law, justice and public administration projects

This is quite a hodgepodge of loans; however, there are three reoccurring themes: land titling, private sector participation and public financial management. Land titling is a theme in three projects – Integrated Swamps Development, Land Administration and the Land Management and Policy

Table 9.2 Word Bank general law, justice and public administration sector lending to Indonesia: 1993–7 and 2000–4

Project Name	*Year approved*	*Approved amount (US$ millions)*
Loans 1993–7		
Flores Earthquake Reconstruction Project	1993	42.1
Integrated Swamps Development Project	1994	65.0
Land Administration Project	1994	80.0
Second Accountancy Development Project	1994	25.0
Industrial Technology Development Project	1995	47
Second Technical Assistance Project for the Public and Private Provision of Infrastructure	1995	28.0
Human Resources Capacity Building Project	1996	20.0
BEPEKA Audit Modernization Project	1997	16.4
Information Infrastructure Development Project	1997	34.5
Banking Reform Assistance Project*	1997	20.0
Loans 2000–4**		
Private Provision of Infrastructure Technical Assistance Loan	2003	17.1
Land Management and Policy Development Project	2003	65.6
Government Financial Management and Revenue Administration Project	2004	60.0

Notes:
* This loan's classification is finance, it is the only loan in the sector and thus included here.

Development Project. The Bank's interest in land titling derives partly from its lack of ease with the Indonesian Constitution's vesting of ultimate control of land, water and airspace with the state because of its social function (World Bank 1994d: 5). Combined with the *Pancasila* commitment to social justice, land in Indonesia is not a mere commercial commodity as in the West (Thorburn 2004: 35). This is a problem for the Bank because they see that private ownership facilitates land markets that underpin 'modern economic development' (World Bank 1994d: 2). As noted in the Vietnam case study, land markets as a way to create and reproduce private property are more than a core Washington Consensus condition, they are central to the liberal capitalist project that the Bank exemplifies.

The Integrated Swamps Development Project was a so-called second-stage transmigration project, that is one focused on rehabilitating original transmigration sites.[2] Rehabilitation was a necessity because transmigration loans were not only an environmental disaster, they often did little to improve the living standards of transmigrants, let alone those of local indigenous populations.[3] The project aimed to reduce poverty in 20 swamp transmigration locations in Sumatera and West Kalimantan. It included components on water control, rural infrastructure, and food and tree crop production as well as land titling. The land-titling component provided titles to original inhabitants – most of whom did not receive titles, whereas transmigrants did (World Bank 1994c: 15)! By the mid-1990s, it was well-known that transmigration projects had systematically violated the customary land rights of indigenous groups. Yet the Staff Appraisal Report (World Bank 1994c: 5) claimed that 'swamp lands are usually uninhabited before drainage, and therefore relatively free of land claims which often hinder large scale development elsewhere'. The project exhibited a surprising faith in the capacity to farm swamp lands and in transmigrant labour as the key to developing a large-scale tree cash-cropping industry. It utilised private sector participation in infrastructure development, but had virtually no discussion of community participation in design and implementation and equally no discussion of gender issues regarding land titling.

Limited community participation and gender analysis were also features of the Land Administration Project (World Bank 1994d: i), which had the rather lofty goals of fostering 'efficient and equitable land markets' and alleviating 'social conflicts over land'. Apart from the rather tricky notion of what 'equitable' land markets are, the idea that titling will resolve social conflict in the context of large-scale dispossession of indigenous peoples is rather problematic.[4] The Land Management and Policy Development Project (2003) in the second case study period, exhibited more sensitivity to such issues and, as a result, focused on the policy and regulatory framework rather than titling. It excluded areas with traditional land rights issues from pilot titling activities. The project also had a much more participatory approach – a lesson learned from the Land Administration Project (World Bank 2004k: 13).

The Land Management Project's gender analysis was slightly more developed than that of the Land Administration Project. The latter project argued that women's rights would be strengthened by titling of land because, under Indonesia law, land that either partner owns prior to marriage remains their property; thus titling would ensure that women retain their rights in cases of marriage dissolution (World Bank 1994d: 30–31). This ignores the reality that women do not generally own land prior to marriage. Further, it claimed that property acquired during marriage is, under marriage law, joint property and thus joint titling was not essential. The Land Management Project (World Bank 2004k: 21) acknowledged that titling in the husband's name only weakened the position of women. To remedy this, the project merely aimed to ensure that 90 per cent of participant women were *informed* of the right to have joint property titles. There was no discussion in either loan of women's rights in the case of property acquired jointly by unmarried couples – this is not an insignificant issue in Indonesia as marriage can be expensive (bride price and the costs of registering marriages) and thus out of reach of some.

Private sector participation was a key theme in four loans: the Industrial Technology Development, Information Infrastructure Development, Second Technical Assistance Project for Public and Private Provision of Infrastructure and Private Provision of Infrastructure Technical Assistance. The Industrial Technology Project (1995) aimed to improve the competitiveness of Indonesian industry, especially small to medium-sized enterprises (SMEs) via improvements in research and development (R&D), industrial measurement, standards, testing and quality and improvements in industrial technology policy. The Bank's 2005 evaluation of the loan noted three major issues with the loan, which they cannot, or do not wish to explain, yet which can be contextualised by anyone with a rudimentary knowledge of Indonesian politics.

First, the evaluation stated that it was 'not clear' why the project was approved given the context of significant budgetary restrictions on R&D institutions (World Bank 2005g: 5). One explanation is that Habibie was then Minister for Science and Technology and was an up and coming favourite in the administration. Second, the evaluation pointed to the inconsistency of having SMEs as the target of R&D and quality programmes that are normally the domain of big business. The unmentioned context here is the sensitivities of New Order support for Chinese big business versus indigenous business concentrated in the SME sector – when the indigenous SME sector felt too excluded, political and social disturbances often resulted. This project might be explained by the New Order's need to be seen supporting indigenous SMEs. Third, there were design defects in the technology transfer grant scheme targeted at SMEs. It was demand driven and operated on a first-come-first-served basis, which did not guarantee the best projects were supported. Indeed, it may have facilitated corruption, or at least nepotism, in scheme administration, although this later issue is not discussed (World Bank 2005g: 5–6).[5] Yet, nepotism was central to the New Order's distribution of wealth. This design 'fault' may have been deliberate. For a project evaluated in the PWC period, the lack of analysis of politics or corruption is quite striking but it does confirm that the Bank tends not to report on corruption where it would implicate them in support for corrupt regimes (Berkman 2008: 29).

The 1997 Information Infrastructure Development Project aimed to enhance private sector participation through providing information technology, post and tourism services. It had a strong focus on legal and regulatory 'reform', in particular the protection of intellectual property rights – a core Washington Consensus concern. The project also subsidised a science and technology network, a tourism information service and a programme to expand private sector access to technology. These are justified on the basis of the 'strong positive externalities' they generate (World Bank 1997b: 11). This is an interesting departure from the Bank's standard (Washington Consensus) position on the necessity for cost recovery in other infrastructure sectors (e.g. power or water supply). The Public and Private Provision of Infrastructure and Information Technology projects were clearly more the product of the New Order's agenda than the Bank's. Given the Bank acknowledgement that the New Order creamed substantial amounts from its loans, this indicates, albeit in a rather negative form, a fairly high level of regime 'ownership' of the Bank programme.

The 1995 Second Technical Assistance Project for Public and Private Provision of Infrastructure implicitly acknowledged corruption. Its solution was purely technical: the development of effective regulatory frameworks. This reflected the background analysis, which presented Indonesia as engaged in linear development from 'a primarily natural resource-based economy to a more human capital productivity-based economy; … from a largely rural economy to a more urban society', complemented by (liberal democratic) 'political transition featuring a more open debate of public policy issues and a rethinking of the role of Government, private sector and community organisations' (World Bank 1995e: 1). The project covered public and private sector provision of infrastructure because the GoI was 'still at an early stage' in the (supposedly) cost-effectiveness-driven transition of government from a supplier to a facilitator of services. Given the technical, problem-solving approach of the project, there was no discussion of political or community commitment to the regulatory frameworks or of private interest in participating in infrastructure provision (World Bank 1995e: 3).

Regulatory frameworks were also the focus of the Private Provision of Infrastructure Technical Assistance Loan (2003). It more explicitly acknowledged corruption (a PWC theme) and private provision of infrastructure moved from being an option to an 'imperative' about which no debate is required (World Bank 2003o: 9). Mistrust of public debate is quite evident in the loan documents, which claimed for example, that the public debate on the failings of private investments in infrastructure under the New Order regime was 'poorly-informed' and 'open to exploitation by those with vested interests in maintaining the status quo' (World Bank 2003o: 7). And while 'civil society' was to be involved in project oversight, public perceptions needed to be shaped to support private sector provision of infrastructure and privatisation (World Bank 2003o: 12–14). The project demonstrated that private infrastructure provision has become a Washington Consensus hegemonic principle.

PWC influences were visible in the allowance that tariff increases be accompanied by well-targeted subsidies and through the strong emphasis on transparency.

Public financial management was a theme in four loans – Second Accountancy Development, BEPEKA [state audit agency] Audit Modernization, Banking Reform Assistance and Government Financial Management and Revenue Administration. The Second Accountancy Project (1994) aimed not just to modernise the GoI accountancy system but to improve overall public and private sector accountancy standards via implementation of exams for public accountants and development and enforcement of internationally based accounting standards. The BEPEKA Project (1997) aimed to improve audit capacity. The focus here on GoI accountancy systems and auditing fits with the Washington Consensus focus on government failures but interestingly they can be seen as early examples of the PWC focus on governance 'reforms' that expand financial discipline over the state. Both projects implicitly acknowledged corruption though largely in the Washington Consensus sense as a problem of government. On local ownership, the Second Accountancy Project appraisal (World Bank 1994e: 23) noted only that while 'the Government is committed to improved enterprise reporting and disclosure, resistance to the changes which are introduced could come from some stakeholders'. The BEPEKA Project appraisal (World Bank 1997c: 9) listed a range of commitments by GoI to the project, yet the Bank's Implementation Completion Report (World Bank 2005b: 3) found that the required political will for project implementation was lacking.[6]

The Banking Reform Assistance Project (World Bank 1997a) was, as noted earlier, the Bank's first lending response to the Asian Financial Crisis. It is included under the public financial management theme because it had a strong focus on reforming government regulation and supervision of banking. It also assisted with the restructuring of private banks and preparation of state-owned banks for full or partial privatisation (World Bank 1997a: 4). The project clearly promoted core Washington Consensus concerns, it was also spectacularly unsuccessful even in the Bank's own terms. There was little GoI support for it as they failed to appoint counterparts or undertake other supposedly agreed actions (World Bank 2003q: 12–14).

In the second case study period, the Government Financial Management and Revenue Administration Project (World Bank 2004o) was underpinned by a Washington Consensus view of government failure, but its detail was shaped by the PWC governance agenda. Its overall objective was to facilitate 'poverty-reduction goals through higher resource mobilization and more effective public resource management' (World Bank 2004q: ii). The link to poverty reduction was a very indirect at best as there was no requirement that any savings generated through efficiencies or reduction in corruption be targeted to poverty reduction expenditures. Rather, the project relied on the generic PWC claim that better institutions and good governance assist in poverty reduction. The project sought to reduce possibilities for corruption and misuse of funds and had a strong focus on GoI ownership; sequencing of further reforms; safeguards in procurement; and risk analysis and minimisation. It is a further example of a PWC project to extend the fiscal discipline on the state through financial management systems.

Two projects do not fit any of the themes explored: the Flores Earthquake Reconstruction Project and the Human Resources Capacity Building Project. The Flores Project (1993) had no documentation, just a web entry. It seems to have focused on infrastructure reconstruction but was classified as law, justice and public administration, perhaps due to a focus on government planning and response to natural disasters. The Human Resources Project (1996) promoted human resource development in the health and education sectors via funding technical assistance for sectoral and feasibility studies, planning frameworks and training. It had a strong focus on decentralisation as, indeed, did four other loans in the first case study period (Integrated Swamps, Land Administration, Public and Private Provision of Infrastructure and the BEPEKA Project). This is because decentralised project administration was a Suharto-initiated reform from around 1992, albeit one with limited impacts. The Bank, however, systematically pursued the issue in its lending programme during the first case study period. In the second case study period, decentralisation was a reality and a problem for implementation not an agenda to be pursued by the Bank.

Projects in this sector overall demonstrated an increase in participatory rhetoric from the first to the second case study periods. The form of involvement was predominately NGOs undertaking monitoring and evaluation of projects. This form does not challenge the 'political insulation of technocrats' presiding over project design and implementation (Hadiz 2004: 698). The limited loans in the second case study period make it difficult to analyse ownership in this period, certainly all three loans are on issues that have been on the public agenda in Indonesia; however, the Bank approach clearly aimed to drive the reform agenda in particular directions.

Rural area development projects

The Village Infrastructure Projects (VIPs) provided block grants to target poor villages in Java and Sumatera to construct small-scale infrastructure. Villages that formed local community groups could select an infrastructure project to undertake from a 'menu'. The community managed construction using contractors or local paid labour. The project built on two existing GoI programmes providing funds to villages – the Program for Villages Left Behind (IDT), a grant programme that utilised government-paid community facilitators to assist community groups to decide and implement local projects; and the Presidential Instruction village grant programme. This programme funded inputs for infrastructure projects, with labour provided by the village as an in-kind contribution (World Bank 1995c: 2–4). Community facilitators from the IDT project were available to assist villages participating in VIPs plus they received Bank-funded engineering assistance.

Table 9.3 Word Bank rural development lending to Indonesia: 1993–7 and 2000–4

Project name	*Year approved*	*Approved amount (US$ millions)*
Loans 1993–1997		
Village Infrastructure Project	1995	72.5
Second Village Infrastructure Project	1996	140.1
Loans 2000–4		
Kecamatan Development Project (supplement)	2000	48.2
Second *Kecamatan* Development Project	2001	320.2
Third *Kecamatan* Development Project	2003	249.8

VIP pioneered a range of innovative approaches for the World Bank in Indonesia:

> [t]he project is innovative for the Bank in the extent of its decentralization/grassroot approach: the villages selected are to decide the works they want and that comply with a simple economic criteria; technical assistance is to be provided directly to village groups; financing will be provided directly through subdistrict bank units and be delinked from late budget releases. The focus is also on employment: villagers doing the work are to be paid cash in proportion to work progress and works are to be organized seasonally or as convenient for labour availability.
>
> (World Bank 1995c: 7)

So, VIP was innovative in three ways: first, it operationalised a scaled-up community development approach in a Bank-funded project; second, it adopted and promoted decentralised administration; and third, it departed from the Bank's standard project approach of only funding goods and services that are competitively procured by funding community labour at a subsistence pay rate as well as procuring goods and specialised labour competitively. Though, on this last point, *Kecamatan* Development Project (KDP) reports suggest that contractors, rather than directly engaged labour, undertook most of the work (World Bank 1998b: 6).

The first KDP (for $225 million) was approved in June 1998 and was the second project of any size or significance funded by the Bank after the onset of the Crisis. This was just four months after a trip by Wolfensohn to Jakarta. After being briefed on the Bank's current lending programme, which was focused on macroeconomic stabilisation, Wolfensohn reportedly responded: 'I can't tell the bloody press that these reforms are being financed by our money! I've got to tell them we're buying medicines, food for the poor, that's what I need to say!' (cited in Mallaby 2004: 196). KDP showed the Bank supporting the rural poor to earn a wage to purchase food.

KDP quickly became a flagship programme for the Bank – its sheer scale relative to lending in this period indicates its centrality to Bank strategy in Indonesia. KDP has been the face of the new Bank in Indonesia, it is 'under the radar' as Bank strategy required and also populist. It funds lots of small projects in poor communities, not big infrastructure or central government 'reform'. It was great for public relations as it showed money going to poor communities. In Mallaby's (2004: 205, 337) book, the programme received a very positive analysis. He presented it as innovative and even claimed that, in shifting the focus from human capital to social capital, the programme promoted 'revolutionary political and social change'.

In reality KDP is quite similar to VIP in both its stated operations and objectives and VIP, of course, built on existing GoI programmes. The key difference between them is that KDP operates a more extensive community-planning and training component (based on social capital analysis). It directly trains and funds thousands of community facilitators as well as engineers. The KDP community-planning component generally takes four to six months. Community participation is more self-selecting in KDP than under VIP, although both projects are targeted at poor villages.[7] Further, KDP's project menu is larger than VIPs; to infrastructure it added social expenditures (for example, for school scholarships and materials) and economic activities (essentially microfinance, which are referred to as 'revolving funds'). Until 2004, infrastructure was by far the largest activity (70 per cent of *kecamatan* grant funds) followed by microfinance (25 per cent), while social expenditures only accounted for around 5 per cent of grants. KDP also has a strengthened focus on information sharing, transparency and participatory monitoring and evaluation. It often engages local NGOs to undertake these activities.

The KDP appraisal documents were strongly informed by, and imbued with, the literature of social capital – yet, despite the prominence of social capital in PWC rhetoric, the case studies indicate that overall it has had limited influence on lending. The exception here is not surprising because a number of members of the social development team in Jakarta, who supervise KDP, researched and promoted social capital from Bank headquarters in Washington before their move.[8] Indeed, Indonesia was one of a small number of Bank sites selected for testing the impact of social capital on development. KDP was designed, or rather justified by, social capital studies, some of which were not completed until after the project was designed. According to Li (2005: 15), the key finding of the studies was that Indonesian villages 'already do – or could do, with appropriate facilitation and incentives – everything good governance and village development require'. Further, they characterised the state as largely a hindrance to village development, despite many examples of its positive impacts. It is difficult to know whether this hostility to the state was the result of neoliberal opposition to it or due to specific concerns about the Suharto regime – KDP's designers were undoubtedly part of the corruption fighter grouping in the Jakarta office.

The identified sources of poverty in the KDP analysis were lack of access to the state and the state's lack of responsiveness and inefficiency. There was no discussion of the impact of capitalist accumulation or of state economic and social policy on poverty. This confirms Fine's (2001a) finding that PWC social capital does not extend to social scientists engaging with 'economic' issues. The political–bureaucratic–business patronage system received only passing comment, via its impact on local-level governance, which was the proposed site for addressing poverty through 'improved planning and control of projects and resources close to home' (Li 2005: 16). Here is the Keynesian commitment to planning at the core of the establishment of the Bank itself, rewritten and reformulated for a New Institutional Economics (NIE)-influenced neoliberal age.

The Bank claims that KDP is different from its normal project because its focus is on process not outputs; it is the most developed expression of the Bank's version of participation in the case studies. Yet as Li (2005: 18) pointed out, every aspect of the process is delineated in a huge array of project manuals and other documents. Despite the Bank's (2003p: 29) rhetoric that the overarching design principle of the project is maximising end-user choice, there is no choice for communities in how participation is undertaken or how projects are planned and approved, the only choice is which activity communities undertake from the KDP menu. Once an activity is chosen, there are whole sets of manuals and rules instructing how activities are to be planned, implemented, administered and monitored. Even 'independent' local media monitoring of projects is organised and funded.

The four design principles of KDP are

(1) maximising 'contestation', which in practice means competitive procurement of goods and services;
(2) direct negotiation, which means making *kecamatan* responsible for adjudicating in a forced competition between the proposals of various villages;
(3) active sharing of project information – a principle derived from NGO community development projects and NIE theorising, which is rendered technical by the Bank's checklist approach;
(4) utilisation of existing village organisations – so long as they meet the Bank's checklist of what a participatory organisation looks like. This is another example of partial adoption of NGO community development principles rendered technical by the Bank.

KDP claims a strong gender focus – there must be women on the village community groups and the committee that competitively selects the projects to be supported across each *kecamatan.* Where a village wishes to submit two proposals, one must be from a local women's group (World Bank 1998b: 11). It does not require gender equity and it certainly does not challenge women's position in Indonesian society. KDP II contained additional measures to address gender sensitivity. Nevertheless, KDP III's appraisal found that gender (and inclusion) has been problematic. It seems that women's participation has not improved over the course of the project and, in some cases, it has worsened. This was explained as the result of decentralisation reviving traditional social institutions, not because of the gendered impact of the Crisis or because of the project's lack of engagement with gender (World Bank 2003 p: 39).

Li demonstrated that KDP does not challenge traditional power structures (despite them being mapped under the project). In one example, she deconstructed a project success story about the transformation of village culture. It celebrated a village protest regarding a delivery of lumber, which was less than specified in the contract. The village head and council of elders utilised traditional symbols in an orderly protest at the district parliament. The Bank saw the protest as one to celebrate because it was culturally authentic, 'quiet and orderly ... [and] directed at the appropriate authority ... They acted autonomously and responsibly *within* the limits experts prescribe' (Li 2005: 23–24). This example also indicates that village groups under KDP have been dominated by the village elite (village heads and elders). Further, corruption in relation to materials procurement has been a significant problem for the project and the Bank's own studies indicate that community participation is not effective in controlling it (Olken 2005). What Li's deconstruction also demonstrated was that KDP promotes an instrumental focus for people as project or contract managers in their community (see also Carroll 2006).

KDP largely bypasses local and district governments other than as a conduit for funds. Provincial bureaucracy plays a limited role in project management and supervision via a coordinating committee. Line ministries, such as the Department of Transport, etc., normally responsible for the provision and maintenance, of infrastructure are bypassed. Of course, managing and administering such a large project requires a whole range of structures and a programme of accountability that parallels the state. As Li (2005: 22) states, 'KDP is unabashedly governmental'. But this is neoliberal governmentalism – run by the community and lacking permanence because of separation from the state. The lack of permanence also creates a dilemma for the Bank in terms of sustaining project outcomes, a dilemma that is finally, if only partially, acknowledged in KDP III.

Bank staff recognise the frailty of the changes they promote but do not propose activities to achieve more fundamental transformations (Bebbington *et al.* 2004). Despite the undoubtedly progressive aspirations of the Bank team working on KDP, the more pertinent question is not how transformative KDP is, but how much it actually supports current state–society relations and networks of power. To return to Li (2005: 13): 'the KDP process (backed by its rule books, monitors and auditing devices) is designed to *shape* desires and act on actions, setting the conditions so that people will be disposed to behave as they should'. And, as we saw above, how people should behave is as 'critical customers' and as rational, competitive actors responsible for, and focused on their own development within the market (World Bank 2001e: 18). Equally, they are not supposed to focus on intangible national or international political or economic issues supposedly beyond their control.

The 'project telos' of KDP, indeed of all Bank community development projects, is the need for training and facilitation to enable communities to 'become'. Become what? – neoliberal communities that take 'responsibility for their own improvement by engaging with markets' and learn 'how to conduct themselves' in a competitive market (Li 2005: 5). Moreover, as Toby Carroll (2006: 16) pointed out, the market participation involves 'a system of surveillance and monitoring to instil a technically "idyllic" market – where returning to the two branches of new institutional economics – transaction costs are low and information flows freely'. Porter and Craig (2004: 393) conclude that the inclusion of communities in 'wider governance and market relations in subordinated, disaggregated ways … as regions coordinating their own service delivery' is a key purpose of the PWC. It is a project to embed neoliberal social, political and economic relations. The poor are included – but in a peripheral way so that their 'poverty can be "locally owned", and services imputed to them as "social income" while they work their way back step-wise into the global economy'.

Urban area development projects

The six Urban Development Projects (UDPs) were part of a series of Bank-funded projects supporting the GoI's Integrated Urban Development Program (originally the Integrated Urban Infrastructure Development Program). All of the projects operated with decentralised administration – central and provincial governments played key coordinating roles but implementation was undertaken by local government. However, not all GoI agencies supported this approach and thus some of the projects took a long time to prepare – six years in the case of the Kalimantan UDP (World Bank 2003d: 21). The projects all had as core objectives improved urban infrastructure provision and enhanced institutional capacity among local governments; some included a specific focus on urban poverty alleviation and others on environmental sustainability.

Table 9.4 Word Bank urban development lending to Indonesia: 1993–7 and 2000–4

Project name	*Year approved*	*Approved amount (US$ millions)*
Loans 1993–7		
Surabaya Urban Development Project	1994	175.0
Semarang Surakata Urban Development Project	1994	174.0
Kalimantan Urban Development Project	1995	136.0
Second East Java Urban Development Project	1996	117.0
Second Sulawesi Urban Development Project	1996	155.0
Bali Urban Infrastructure Project	1997	110.0
Loans 2000–4		
Second Urban Poverty Project	2002	100.0

All projects involved competitive tendering of activities in urban transport, water supply, solid waste management, sanitation and sewerage, drainage and technical assistance and training. Two other elements of UDP were the *Kampung* Improvement Program (KIP) and Market Improvement Program (MIP). The KIP was a government-assisted urban community self-help programme that had been operating in Indonesia since the 1960s. It had been partly funded through a number of Bank loans since the 1970s (World Bank 1994j: 9). After the Asian Financial Crisis hit, it was expanded in a number of the UDPs and most projects added a component to fund labour-intensive civil works. The KIP/MIP components were the main avenue for community participation in the UDPs; nevertheless, participation was a strong theme in the project documentation.

Equally, all the projects had a strong focus on private sector participation, mostly about tendering for infrastructure construction or rehabilitation. However, in at least four projects privatisation of services, particularly water supply and solid waste management, was proposed.[9] The three available implementation completion reports indicated that there was resistance from both the community and local administrations to water supply privatisation.[10] In general this is attributed to difficulties in raising water tariffs (a condition of *all* the UDP loans) in the wake of the Asian Financial Crisis. However, the Bali project also acknowledged that '[p]roblems encountered in the Jakarta water concessions likely contributed to the unwillingness of Bali local governments to complete restructuring as a prelude to initiating PSP [private sector participation] in water supply' (World Bank 2005c: 11).

The three implementation completion reports provide three very different stories about the outcomes of these projects from poor (Sulawesi), OK (Kalimantan) to good (Bali). The Sulawesi project was expanded from 18 to 32 small and medium-sized cities across Sulawesi at the behest of the GoI, thus the project was more complex than in Bali, which had a tight geographical focus, or in Kalimantan, which only incorporated five regional centres. Why the Bank, despite its misgivings, approved the expanded geographical focus, was not addressed by the completion report. A likely reason is GoI concern with 'regionally balanced development', a concern regarded as 'legitimate' by the Bank as indicated by the geographical spread of the urban and rural area development projects (World Bank 1994j: 10).

The Kalimantan and Sulawesi completion reports, written respectively in 2003 and 2004, provided some insight into the PWC view of corruption – or 'misprocurement' as it was called in a wonderful piece of 'Bank-speak'. In Sulawesi, 'irregularities' were found in 56 out of the 60 contracts reviewed by the Bank and there were 'weak fiduciary practices in procurement, implementation and financial management systems'(World Bank 2004e: 9). Here corruption is addressed in precisely the way that the analysis of PWC rhetoric suggests – a technical problem of market and government failure with the Bank blameless.

In the second case study period, the Urban Poverty Project (UPP) was an urban version of KDP and the PWC version of UDP-type interventions.[11] The project provided block grants to community units, which are neighbourhoods (*kelurahan*) rather than subdistricts (*kecamatan*) as is the case for KDP (Fang 2006: 74–76; World Bank 2002f). To be eligible for funding, neighbourhoods need to be constituted as democratically elected community committees, whereas in KDP the *kecamatan* group responsible for funding decisions is an informal group, although it includes the (government appointed) Council of Village Heads. UPP neighbourhood committees competitively allocate grant funding between proposals from members and resident groups. As in KDP, those submitting proposals need to undertake training.

In UPP I, over 90 per cent of grants were used for microfinance activities (World Bank 2002f: 10). The role of microfinance as a neoliberal replacement for social safety nets was discussed extensively in the Vietnam case study. However, it is worth noting here that KDP/UPP view microfinance through the Bank's commercial/financial paradigm, meaning it should operate profitably and not require donor support after establishment. However, repayments rates for both KDP and UPP microfinance funds have been poor. KDP III (World Bank 2003p: 24) included a project component to address the poor performance of KDP-funded microfinance projects and the broader legal and regulatory framework for microfinance.

The Second Urban Poverty Project posited that construction and management of urban infrastructure is often too big or complicated for community groups and requires involvement of local government. It also noted that bypassing local government may harm the relations between it and community organisations in the short and medium term and thus harm local development (World Bank 2002f: 6–8 and 20). It therefore included a component for projects to be undertaken through a partnership between local government and the local community. While this component is only around 17 per cent of Bank funds, it does indicate a shift in thinking on the role of the state.

Urban and rural area development projects were a significant component of Bank lending in both case study periods though their relative importance increased in 2000–4 as Bank overall lending declined. KDP accounted for 28 per cent of lending in the 2000–4 case study period and 33 per cent with UPP, whereas VIP and UDP projects only accounted for 20 per cent (but of a larger lending programme) in 1993–7. Cumulatively, to the end of 2005, KDP lending was $1,003.2 million. By 2005, the programme was expected to have reached 30,000 of Indonesia's 65,000 rural villages (World Bank 2003p: 27). Three UPPs have now been approved with lending totalling $474.2 million. These are large-scale projects in anybody's terms and they direct urban and rural lower classes towards becoming 'critical consumers' focused on local administration. Critical analysts of World Bank area development programmes in the 1970s and 1980s argued that such projects were about ensuring stability by 'defusing discontent' among the urban and rural poor (Bello *et al.* 1982: 15). Moreover, they divert the citizen's attention away from questions about national and international political economy.

These projects can also be seen as a modern version of McNamara's urban and rural lending activities that aimed to address poverty without trading-off growth. KPD goes further, aiming to make villagers efficient contributors and replicators of capitalism, via training in the 'habits of transparency, accountability, efficiency, and the rule of law' (Li 2005: 17). Li (2005: 1–9) described KDP in Foucauldian terms as a powerful example of a 'governance' or a 'conducting conduct' project. In Gramscian terms, governance is a method of organising consent to create the 'common sense' of neoliberal hegemony.

Water, sanitation and flood protection

The first Water Supply and Sanitation for Low Income Communities (WSSLIC) project aimed to provide infrastructure and hygiene/health education for underserved poor communities, whereas the second aimed to improving their 'health status, productivity, and quality of life' – a PWC reformulation focused more on poverty (World Bank 2000f: 2). Core Washington Consensus themes visible in both projects are private sector participation and treating water 'as an economic as well as social good' (World Bank 2000f: 4).

The WSSLIC projects evolved and operated in a similar way to VIP/KDP but funded only water supply and sanitation construction, and rehabilitation and related health interventions. Project administration was the same as KDP's with communities, after undertaking a planning phase, managing the construction of their own facilities. The projects cannot claim KDP's menu of choices in the use of funding; instead, much was made of the choice between 'a variety of appropriate technical options' in infrastructure and the choice to 'select and plan the construction of health infrastructure that the benefiting families want and *are willing to pay for*' (World Bank 2000f: 7, emphasis added). Participation was instrumentally focused – WSSLIC II (World Bank 2000f: 8, emphasis added) claimed that the main reform promoted by the project was 'strengthening the participatory planning process in order to foster increased beneficiary *demand responsiveness* in project outcomes'. These projects were essentially a variant on the area development projects analysed

Table 9.5 Word Bank water, sanitation and flood protection sector lending to Indonesia: 1993–7 and 2000–4

Project name	*Year approved*	*Approved amount (US$ millions)*
Loans 1993–1997		
Water Supply and Sanitation for Low Income Communities Project	1993	80.0
Loans 2000–4		
Second Water and Sanitation for Low Income Communities Project	2000	77.74
Western Java Environmental Management Project	2001	17.45

above, which promoted the 'common sense' of commodified social relations in all areas of human endeavour.

The West Java Environmental Management Project (World Bank 2001g: 10) was a small loan focused on improving solid waste management, increased cost recovery and 'privatisation of commercial services'. It included a grant component to assist with commercialisation of compost production, which was meant to assist the reduction of greenhouse gas emissions. There was a strong focus on participation, a PWC theme, but it was secondary to the focus on commercialisation and privatisation, Washington Consensus themes.

Transport

With the exception of a rail project, lending in this sector was focused on road transport. In the first case study period, loan objectives centred on reducing road transport costs, expanding the road networks and/or dealing with transport bottlenecks and building institutional strength in government agencies. The primary objective of the first project in the second case study period – the Eastern Indonesia Regional Transport Project (EIRTP 1, 2001) – was in contrast formulated in PWC language. It aimed to 'support efforts to stimulate economic growth and improve social welfare' in Eastern Indonesia (World Bank 2001f: 2). But this PWC formulation for transport projects disappeared by EIRTP 2 and the traditional focus on costs and institutional strengthening returned.

The appraisal document for the Fifth *Kabupaten* Roads Project (World Bank 1994b: i) claimed that reductions in vehicle operating costs result in reductions in input costs (particularly agricultural inputs) and increase rural incomes. EIRTP 1 (World Bank 2001f: 3) was slightly more cautious about the benefits of reduced costs claiming only an increase in the 'competitiveness of local products from the affected areas'. This demonstrates a neoliberal

Table 9.6 Word Bank transport sector lending to Indonesia: 1993–7 and 2000–4

Project name	*Year approved*	*Approved amount (US$ millions)*
Loans 1993–7		
Eastern Indonesia *Kabupaten* Roads Project	1993	155.0
Second Highway Sector Investment Project	1994	350.0
Fifth *Kabupaten* Roads Project	1994	101.5
Strategic Urban Roads Infrastructure Project	1996	86.9
Railway Efficiency Project	1996	105.0
Loans 2000–4		
Eastern Indonesia Regional Transport Project	2001	200.0
Second Eastern Indonesia Regional Transport Project	2004	200.0

faith in linear development, subject to existence of the appropriate enabling environment and increased local engagement with national and international markets. EIRTP 2 is also cautious but still claims that reduced vehicle operating costs and increased access to markets, etc., will assist in combating rural poverty.

All of the Bank loans in the sector expressed concerns about the lack of cost recovery in the transport sector. The road projects all had components to promote increases in vehicle taxes (in particular heavy vehicles, which they suggest are relatively undertaxed in relation to their contribution to road damage) and/or to reduce, or end, fuel subsidies (for example World Bank 1994f: 21; 2004r: 4). In other words, all the road transport loans actually aspired to *increase* overall vehicle operating costs but claimed their objective was reducing them. This is really an extraordinary contradiction and one only exacerbated by the feeble claims in the loans regarding access and poverty reduction. To be clear, my argument is not in favour of fuel subsidies – they can disproportionately benefit the non-poor and their impact needs to be studied on a case-by-case basis – rather, claims about the impact of transport projects on poverty require more substantial socioeconomic analysis and this argument indicates a purely rhetorical use of PWC language.

The Bank was not successful in increasing road user charges, which made tariff increases in railways impossible, particularly given the existing discrepancy in the relative levels of costs recovery and thus prices for the two services (World Bank 2005a: 11). This was a problem for the Railway Efficiency Project, which aimed to establish preconditions for the privatisation of railways and improve infrastructure. The project was not fully successful in its objectives; however, it did belatedly achieve a change in the structure of the railways from a public corporation to a limited liability company and formal separation of the rural and urban networks (unbundling) (World Bank 2005a: 2). The Bank claimed the project substantially increased knowledge of key stakeholders regarding reform and provided them with an understanding where resistance lay and how those who resisted could be 'socialized' (World Bank 2005a: 9–11). For an evaluation written in the PWC period, there is no indication here of a commitment to country ownership.

In the road projects, private sector participation was a strong theme in the first case study period. In the highway and urban roads projects, Bank documents indicated existing extensive participation in construction and maintenance of roads. With regards to rural roads, the Fifth *Kabupaten* Roads Project observed that the Bank had achieved a high level of private sector involvement in road construction but not in maintenance. Thus, increased private sector participation in rural road maintenance was its goal. A key mechanism for this was packaging of contracts in ways that made them attractive to medium-sized and larger contractors (World Bank 1994b: 14, 8–9).

In EIRTP 1 and 2 the focus was increasing the level of competition between private providers and the transparency and efficiency of government procurement and contract management in the new decentralised environment. In other words, the focus was reducing corruption – though in EIRTP 1 corruption was only explicitly referred to on one page of the appraisal document in relation to decentralisation. The discussion clarified that decentralisation could either make corruption better or worse (!) and that the overall 'risk of error' is high (World Bank 2001f: 25). EIRTP 2 (World Bank 2004r: 21–22) was a little more explicit and included a project anti-corruption plan. In both projects, anti-corruption measures were a matter of getting procurement and contracting arrangements, training, contract supervision, complaints handling, information provision and sanctions right. Thus corruption remained a technical issue requiring no analysis of the political environment.

One other interesting aspect of the road projects was their high level of conditionality. This is not so much in terms of the number of conditions, although both the railway project and EIRTP 2 have a high count with 22 and 27 conditions, respectively, rather it is the broad nature of conditions.[12] For example, the Second Highway Sector Investment Project (World Bank 1994f: 46) required that the Directorate General of Highways 'formulate its work programme and budgets on the basis of criteria, principles and procedures satisfactory to the Bank, and taking into account comments by the Bank'. This condition appears to refer to the Directorate's whole programme, not just Bank-funded sub-projects! The EIRTP 2 project supported development of a pilot road fund – a mechanism for expanding user charges in roads. A related condition was that a report on the road fund's implementation be furnished to the Bank and thereafter the GoI had to 'prepare and carry out an action plan for further expansion and continuation of the road fund activities taking into account the comments of the Bank on the report' (World Bank 2004r: 32). The road fund was only a pilot in the sense of getting the functioning of it right not to assess its applicability to the Indonesia context.

In the transport sector, the PWC appears to have had limited impact as was the case in Vietnam. This is not surprising given transport is a traditional 'technical' area of Bank lending and project staff still tend to be technical specialists. There was an increased focus on corruption but, as anticipated in the analysis of the Bank's approach to it, corruption was a technical issue to be dealt with by the right type and amount of procurement, supervision, etc. In the second case study period, there was increased focus on ensuring that Bank social and environmental safeguards were actually adhered to.

Energy and mining

The energy and mining sector has been a major area of activity since lending began. The sector is dominated by power projects, 21 of the 25 loans prior to 1993 were in power and all the loans in the case study periods are power projects, although the Java–Bali Power Restructuring and Strengthening Project did include a small component to restructure the State gas company. The power sector has been popular with other donors too, in particular the ADB, Japan Bank for International Cooperation (JBIC) and United States Agency for International Development (USAID).

Table 9.7 Word Bank energy and mining sector lending to Indonesia: 1993–7 and 2000–4

Project name	*Year approved*	*Approved amount (US$ millions)*
Loans 1993–7		
Cirata Hydroelectric Phase II Project	1993	104.0
Sumatera and Kalimantan Power Project	1994	260.5
Second Rural Electrification Project	1995	398.0
Second Power Transmission and Distribution Project	1996	373.0
Solar Home Systems Project	1997	20.0
Renewable Energy Small Power Project	1997	66.4
Loans 2000–4		
Java–Bali Power Sector Restructuring and Strengthening Project	2003	141.0

World Bank lending to the Indonesian power sector shifted around 1993, when they began pursuing privatisation of utilities. Its approach has been very similar to that outlined in the chapter on Vietnam. To briefly recap, the electricity privatisation model contains two core components: unbundling of profitable urban components of electrical utilities from unprofitable rural ones, effectively removing any capacity to cross-subsidise operations; and separation of electricity generation, transmission and distribution functions. Privatisation can be promoted gradually starting with the introduction of independent power producers (IPPs) in generation, or more radically through rapid restructuring and privatisation in both generation and distribution (Yi-chong 2005: 655–56; Amenga-Etego and Grusky 2005). Transmission functions are often left in state hands.

As the Cirata Phase II Project Appraisal Report (World Bank 1993b: 17) stated, in the early 1990s the Bank shifted its focus 'towards the restructuring of the sector's regulatory framework and PLN's [the State electricity utility] organization, and increased private sector participation'. Groundwork for restructuring was undertaken earlier with Bank studies and reports influencing the 1985 Electricity Act, which permitted private power production, and Presidential Decree 37/1992. This Decree authorised private sector participation in build-own-operate schemes in generation and permitted 'cooperatives and other legal entities to generate, transmit, and distribute power for public use' (World Bank 1995b: 3). Cirata Phase II's conditionality included an automatic adjustment mechanism for electricity tariffs, duly introduced in 1994. Conditions in the Suralaya Thermal Power Project (World Bank 1993b: 20) included compulsory reorganisation of PLN to give regional units autonomy (i.e. geographical unbundling), as well as progressive corporatisation and unbundling of the generation, transmission and distribution functions in the Java–Bali system (the urban, profitable side that is distinguished from the rest of the power system).

From the early 1990s, the GoI entered into contracts with a range of IPPs. Proposals were unsolicited and the subsequent contracts, backed by government guarantees, were at inflated prices. The process involved kickbacks to the Suharto regime and sweetheart deals for business cronies (Motoyama and Widagdo 1999). The Bank washed its hands of the arrangements, yet it was clearly initially supportive of getting private participation in the sector. For example, the Cirata Phase II appraisal (World Bank 1993b: 21, emphasis added) stated that:

> [t]he Bank is providing technical assistance to the 'Private Power Team' of the Ministry of Mines & Energy to negotiate the first [IPP] project at Paiton in East Java consisting of the construction of 2 x 600 MW coal-fired thermal units … Also, the Government is encouraging private sector participation by facilitating the sale of power to the grid from unsolicited power projects, as well as the wheeling of such power supplies through the grid to third parties. In order to *accelerate these developments*, the Bank is assisting in the reform of the regulatory framework in the sector.

The Sumatera and Kalimantan Power Project required conversion of PLN from a state utility to a limited liability corporation, which duly happened that year (World Bank 1994i, 2003g). It obliged the GoI to develop and implement regulations framing private sector participation for the sector. By the 1996 Second Power Transmission and Distribution Project, conditionality was clearly endeavouring to constrain the growth of unsolicited IPPs. All the reports and evaluations written subsequent to the Crisis – when the cost of IPP deals became public – emphasised that the Bank warned GoI of the drawbacks of unsolicited proposals and government guarantees (although in 2004 it happily provided a guarantee to get an IPP in Vietnam). One Bank report (2003g: 7) claimed that their capacity to influence the GoI had waned in the mid-1990s and it was, 'unlikely that a loan suspension on this issue would have had any impact on events either'. While the Bank cannot be held responsible for GoI actions, its complete washing of its hands is equally inappropriate given that it was actively involved in establishing the conditions for IPPs and privatisation in a country known for its increasing levels of corruption and cronyism. Equally, while suspending loans may not have ended corrupt practices, continuing them demonstrated public confidence in the regime's activities. The hand-washing strategy is not surprising though, as it is how the Bank has responded in other instances where the utility privatisation model has failed in practice – it's not anything wrong with the model, it's the imperfect world that needs to adapt (Yi-chong 2005: 652).

The functional unbundling of PLN began with the creation of two generation subsidiaries in Java–Bali in 1995. In the same year, the Bank funded its second Rural Electrification (RE II) Project. This built on an earlier project promoting greater private sector involvement in rural electrification through cooperatives and community organisations. The RE II project aimed to further expand private sector participation. The appraisal report (World Bank 1995b: 18) claimed that the major factor inhibiting PLN's RE operations was its mixing of them with its urban–industrial (i.e. the Java–Bali) system. Not surprisingly, it recommended separating 'the RE and non-RE missions, with appropriate transfer prices set for any inter-unit transactions' (World Bank 1995b: 19). This was to prevent cross-subsidisation of operations. Planning for and implementing unbundling were conditions of the loan.

The Solar Homes Systems Project and the Renewable Energy Small Power Project, both from 1997, focused on renewable energy but were squarely designed to advance RE privatisation. In the Solar Homes Project, it was expansion of private sector participation through subsidising acquisition of solar systems from private dealers. The dealers were made managers of a combination of grants (made from a related Bank Global Environment Fund grant) and hire-purchase loans. To fund the hire purchase, dealers were provided access to Indonesian bank loans, which were guaranteed by on-lent funds from the World Bank (World Bank 1996a). The Renewable Energy Project (World Bank 2004s) operated along similar lines, with a Global Environment Fund-funded grant component and access to credit from banks that were on-lent World Bank funds. But, in this project, the target was the creation of private sector renewable power generation. The grant component was to assist with feasibility studies and the credit to support construction. Owing to the Crisis, the Renewable Energy Project never became active and the Solar Homes Project only disbursed just over $80,000.

The 1996 Second Power Transmission Project sought 'functional decentralization (unbundling)' of PLN generation, transmission and distribution operations in Java–Bali. The Bank's completion report (World Bank 2004d: 5) noted that the plan to develop a regulatory framework for unbundling and a competitive electricity market was inconsistent with 'the prevailing electricity law, No. 15/1985, [which] was intended for a vertically integrated monopoly'. The absence of a new law was a problem for regulation implementation because: 'regulations are normally [sic] derived from laws'. In other words, the project attempted to bypass legal process in order to drive its agenda – which was also the case in Vietnam due to the Bank's haste to have IPPs operating in the country. However, the report regarded the project as a success because the restructuring agenda outlined in it, and in loans since 1993, was largely completed albeit at a much slower pace than envisaged (World Bank 2003n: 4). In 1998, the Habibie government, with much assistance from the Bank and the ADB, hastily finalised a Power Sector Restructuring Policy, providing the blueprint for radical geographical unbundling, functional unbundling and privatisation of the Java–Bali system. The plan focused privatisation initially on generation but, within a short period, it was meant to be applied to distribution too. Separate independent regulatory bodies were to govern the Java–Bali and rural systems. The new Electricity Law designed to frame this process was not passed until 2002, not late 1999 as originally envisaged because, low and behold, the new, more democratic parliament wanted to debate and amend the legislation. Sectoral 'reform' was also supported by large loans from the ADB and JBIC, while the Bank was relegated to supporting PLN's restructuring, which it did through grants for technical assistance until a new loan was agreed in 2003.

The 2003 Java–Bali Power Sector loan supported PLN investments in the transmission system, development of a resource planning system and implementation of a restructuring plan for PLN's Java–Bali operations into four or more generation companies, five distribution companies and one transmission company. Generation companies were to be spun-off first. The loan did not assist new generation activities, despite acknowledging that generation shortfalls in the near future are the 'most critical issue facing PLN' (World Bank 2003n: 9). This loan continued the Washington Consensus Bank model for utility privatisation and PWC rhetoric regarding local ownership and participation had little discernible impact. It also demonstrated little interest in NIE-influenced ideas regarding market failure and sequencing.

A final issue in the energy sector is the extent of local ownership of the 'reform' programme. During the first case study period, a World Bank loan report (1993b: 17) claimed a 'shared vision' between itself, GoI and PLN for the sector. Yet in a later, at times, frank assessment report (World Bank 2003g: 3) the Bank acknowledged that it's vision may not have been that of GoI. Actions during this time suggest that the Suharto regime was certainly interested in IPPs but not for the reasons the Bank supported them! Beyond that, the Suharto regime's position on radical privatisation is not clear.

In the post-Suharto period, the Habibie government took on unbundling and privatisation with gusto, but the programme may have been motivated by the need for donor approval (not just the Bank but also ADB, JBIC and USAID) and to secure funds. Privatisation may have been a way of separating the government from the sector in community perceptions. Governments since have been increasingly lukewarm about privatisation, they took time with reform and the final version of the Electricity Act contained quite a number of provisions about what constitutes a competitive market which must be met before the full competitive provision of the legislation come into force. After the Act was passed, the GoI was slow to establish the required regulatory agency. Thus, on country ownership of the electricity privatisation programme, it is reasonable to conclude that the evidence is shaky.

Health

The World Bank only began funding health projects in the 1980s, prior to that it would only fund population projects – in Indonesia it approved five of these between 1972 and 1991. The first actual health project was in 1980 and, while support for the sector remained small, there has been a steady flow of projects since. During the first case study period, World Bank-funded health projects conform to the Bank's two-pronged model outlined in the case study on Vietnam. This entails, 'the introduction of market forces into the health

Table 9.8 Word Bank health sector lending to Indonesia: 1993–7 and 2000–4

Project name	*Year approved*	*Approved amount (US$ millions)*
Loans 1993–7		
Fourth Health Project: Improving Equity and Quality of Care	1995	88.0
HIV/AIDS and STD Prevention and Management Project	1996	24.8
Iodine Deficiency Control Project	1996	28.5
Safe Motherhood Project	1997	42.5
Loans 2000–4		
Provincial Health Project I	2000	38.0
Provincial Health Project II	2001	103.2
Health Workforce and Services Project	2003	105.6

care sector, and the allocation of public resources according to criteria of technical and instrumental efficiency' (Laurell and Arellano 2002: 192).

In the Fourth Health Project (1995) the redirection and restriction of health services largely to preventative services for the poor was the main objective. The Bank (1995a: ii) clearly stated that services must 'conform to affordable, cost-effective standards of care'. On the introduction of market forces, the project promoted increased fees for '*nonessential* health service provided by public facilities' and 'expanding health insurance for the *better-off*' (World Bank 1995a: 11, emphasis added). Which health services are non-essential was not defined in this report. Other Bank reports do define non-essential services, but indirectly via the specification of essential services. The pertinent point is that the Bank considered it *their role* to define who shall get access to which health services on the basis of a particular approach to calculating costs in health care provision, rather than this being a role for the citizens involving complex questions of ethics. This approach continued throughout the second case study period. Project reports do not define who the 'better-off' or indeed the targeted 'poor' are. In the second case study period, Provincial Health II referred to the lowest quintiles and the Health Workforce and Services project (World Bank 2003i: 6) to only 30 per cent of GoI subsidies reaching the poorest 40 per cent of the population. Nevertheless, this is a crude analysis on which to justify major changes in spending and service provision.

The three subsequent projects in the first case study period were condition-specific interventions that all form part of the Bank's list of justifiable health interventions: HIV/AIDS prevention fits the Bank's narrow definition of a public health good. Both iodine deficiency control and safe motherhood are considered as justifiable interventions as they significantly reduce the 'global burden of disease' measured in 'disability-adjusted life years' at relatively low cost (Laurell and Arellano 2002: 195–96). The Safe Motherhood Project focused on increasing market mechanisms in the health sector through performance-based contracts for community midwives. Improved targeting of health care was pursued through vouchers for the poor. Both these mechanisms were dropped after the project, but the Bank lauded the fact that their use 'gained momentum and acceptability' (World Bank 2005d: 6).

The three Provincial Health Projects (the Health Workforce and Service Project was a renamed provincial project) in the second case study period all pursued the Bank's model for health in Indonesia's newly decentralised system. The model focuses on government health services only supplying a Bank-delineated package of predominately primary health care interventions. The push for introduction of market forces was more prominent in the second case study period than the first; projects aimed to blur the 'distinction between public and private health care delivery which are to operate under the same regulatory framework and thus be subject to the same criteria and standards in competing for service contracts on a level playing field' (World Bank 2003i: 23).

Each project had a component to assist the central Ministry of Health in areas that are part of the Bank's model of essential public health care. In Provincial Health I (World Bank 2000c: 5), it was the generic responsibility in 'health advocacy, information gathering and analysis, standard setting and some regulatory functions'. In Provincial Health II, it was communicable disease control and in the third project, its workforce health regulation. Overall the Bank's Washington Consensus model for health remains dominant in the PWC period in Indonesia. Even the PWC theme of participation had little penetration here. Equally, NIE analysis of market failures appears not to have an effect.

Agriculture, fishing and forestry

Water was the dominant issue in five of the 11 loans in the agriculture, fishing and forestry sector. From the first case study period, the World Bank's focus in water was not supporting investments in infrastructure, rather these were a platform for promoting sector 'reform'. That is, shifting the government's role from managing water and irrigation activities to regulating them and transferring responsibility for irrigation management to water user's groups (World Bank 2003m: 3). Water user's groups were designed to be independent entities responsible for implementing user-fees to recover the costs of their activities. This is Washington Consensus 'reform' intended to reduce government expenditure and responsibility and promote privatisation. Even the Dam Safety Project (1994) promoted the model through changing the government's role to monitoring and regulation (with the goal of establishing an independent regulatory agency) and separating regulation from activities connected to undertaking remedial works. Remedial work to improve dam safety was funded only as an interim step before full responsibility for dam maintenance was handed to dam managers (World Bank 1994a: 20).

The 1994 Java Irrigation Improvement Project pushed radical privatisation through decentralisation of river basin water resource management and dramatic

Table 9.9 Word Bank agriculture, fishing and forestry sector lending to Indonesia: 1993–7 and 2000–4

Project name	*Year approved*	*Approved amount (US$ millions)*
Loans 1993–7		
Integrated Pest Management Training Project	1993	32.0
Groundwater Development Project	1993	54.0
National Watershed Management and Conservation Project	1993	56.5
Dam Safety Project	1994	55.0
Java Irrigation Improvement and Water Resources Management Project	1994	165.7
Second Agricultural Research Management Project	1995	63.0
Kerinci-Seblat Integrated Conservation and Development Project*	1996	19.1
Nusa Tenggara Agricultural Area Development Project	1996	27.0
Sulawesi Agricultural Area Development Project	1996	26.8
Loans 2000–4		
Water Resources and Irrigation Sector Management Project	2003	70.0
Coral Reef Rehabilitation and Management Program II	2004	56.2

Note:
* World Bank classification was health and other social services but the project undertakes agricultural area development activities.

expansion of a programme to transfer small irrigation schemes to water user's groups.[13] The project ran into significant government opposition until Suharto's fall. Decentralisation, and Habibie's support for Bank-inspired water sector 'reform', changed the picture. After WATSAL was approved in May 1999 (see structural adjustment lending above), the project predominately assisted preparation of WATSAL reforms. It piloted collection of water users' fees and privatisation of small and large irrigation schemes (World Bank 2003e: 5–8).

The Water Resources and Irrigation Program (2003), in the second case study period, continued support for implementing WATSAL reforms. It was the first of a three-tranche, 11-year adaptable programme loan designed to provide the long-term '*hand-holding*' needed to implement reforms among local governments and water users who are 'ill prepared to assume their new responsibilities' (World Bank 2003m: 2–3, emphasis added). It continues a Washington Consensus-inspired Bank vision for the water sector in Indonesia. There is no sign here of PWC concerns with sequencing. The PWC was apparent but in decentralised project implementation (already a reality) and participation in project implementation only not planning. Water sector planning, in particular, involved minimal participation.

There were three agriculture area development projects (Kerinci-Seblat, Nusa Tenggara and Sulawesi) all of which operated under the traditional 'top-down' approach of providing selected farmers with agricultural inputs to improve productivity plus some funding for roads to improve markets access. The Bank regarded all three projects as unsuccessful, and the Nusa Tenggara and Sulawesi projects were restructured after the Crisis to focus predominately on microfinance for villages run along the standard Bank model. With Kerinci-Seblat much of the loan was cancelled after the onset of the Crisis.

The only other project in the second case study period was the Coral Reef Rehabilitation and Management Project, which had a strong participatory focus and also included a large ($10 million) village microfinance component (World Bank 2004p: 13). There were only two projects in the second case period and thus once again it is difficult to draw firm conclusions about World Bank directions in the sector, but relatively little appears to have changed and Washington Consensus themes still dominate.

Education

It is not possible to analyse shifts in World Bank policy on education in Indonesia given the dearth of projects in the second case study period. The Bank's approach to education visible in the first case study period can usefully be outlined. The loans in this period can be grouped by focus: vocational and skills, formal tertiary education and secondary, in particular, junior secondary education. All projects were underpinned by a particular understanding of Indonesia's

Table 9.10 Word Bank education sector lending to Indonesia: 1993–7 and 2000–4

Project name	*Year Approved*	*Approved amount (US$ millions)*
Loans 1993–7		
Professional Human Resources Development Project II*	1994	69.0
Skills Development Project	1994	27.7
University Research for Graduate Education Project	1994	58.9
Book and Reading Development Project	1995	132.5
Secondary School Teacher Development Project	1996	60.4
East Java and East Nusa Tenggara Junior Secondary Education Project	1996	99.0
Higher Education Support Project	1996	65.0
Central Indonesia Junior Secondary Education Project	1996	104.0
Sumatera Junior Secondary Education Project	1996	98.0
Quality of Undergraduate Education	1997	71.2
Loans 2000–4		
Library Development Project	2001	4.15

Note:

* The World Bank classifies this project as industry and trade – it is the only project in this sector and is similar to the skills development project classified as education, thus it is included here.

stage of economic development, namely the idea that Indonesia was, to use Rostow's language, in the 'take-off' stage, moving from early industrialisation to complexly transformed manufacturing. Indonesia had, as was appropriate, focused on universal primary education resulting in, 'high *payoffs* with regards to *economic* and social *development*' (World Bank 1994g: 1, emphasis added). Thus, Bank logic ran, in order to compete at higher levels, Indonesia needed to focus on middle- and higher-level skills. The Asian Financial Crisis demonstrated the frailty of even the achievements in primary education. It resulted in the redirection of a significant amount of funds from the Bank and other donors to scholarships for poor children and block grants for poor schools to sustain achievements.

Three interlinked themes were visible in all loans: decentralisation of educational decision-making, increasing the role of market forces in education and limiting government resources to those areas seen as having a significant economic payoff (Puiggrós 2002). In university sector projects, the focus on increasing the role of market forces was explicit in the 1994 Higher Education Project's support for expanding private universities and the use of incentive payments for staff to promote research. While the concern to limit central government expenditures remains prominent, the project justified GoI activity on the basis that it would improve quality in 'priority areas' for research and reform policy. The new policies would allow 'greater emphasis on private providers' and create a more efficient sector (World Bank 1994k: 9). By the time of the Higher Education Support project in 1996, the Bank extolled the GoI's 'New Paradigm' for higher education, which defined the state's role as shaping regulations and directing resources to high-priority areas (World Bank 2003c: 2). This role effectively limits government expenditures and facilitates private participation in the industry.

In the Junior Secondary Education Project, the focus was originally decentralisation to provinces; however, reform in 1999 achieved devolution to *kabupatens/kotas*. The project included a demonstration component of the school communities contract managing school construction, which succeeded in having this approach promoted nationally as a cost-effective development activity (World Bank 2005e: 11). The logical extension of this approach, which the Bank promoted, was to give control of schools to community boards, which should be private entities (Puiggrós 2002: 184). Given that encouraging private education was one of these project's original objectives, this was undoubtedly a back-door method of achieving that aim. The project also trialled the use of contracted teaching staff, which is also part of the Bank's focus on increasing market forces in education (World Bank 2005e: 13).

The implementation completion reports available on a number of the loans from the first case study period, produced during the PWC, provide no indications of a change in the World Bank's Washington Consensus policy for education. The policy involves limiting state expenditures via a focus on primary education; strategic investments in areas deemed to have notable economic payoffs; and increasing the market forces in the education sector. Indeed, as with the Vietnam case study, the limited Bank resources devoted to the sector in the PWC are perhaps the most powerful indicator of the Bank's overall view.

Conclusion: World Bank lending in Indonesia – more change but …

World Bank lending in Indonesia shifted more notably than was the case in Vietnam. The shifts were driven as much by the Bank's public disgrace over its relationship with the Suharto regime as its political judgements about the capacity of post-Suharto leaders. On post-Suharto or rather post-Habibie governments, the Bank considered they were not pursuing what the Bank (and IMF) saw as necessary economic reforms in Indonesia. When President Yudhoyono took office, there were some indications of renewed faith. To an extent, change was also driven by its mandate as a conservative lending institution – during and after the Crisis, the concern about Indonesia's lack of creditworthiness overrode the Bank's disbursement imperative. The reduction in lending also served to lower the Bank's profile in Indonesia, useful for a disgraced organisation. This disgrace drove most of the shift from formal, large-scale projects in the electricity and water supply and sanitation sectors and towards community development projects. Even with the electricity sector, the disgrace shaped what the Bank funded. So, while the Bank acknowledged that new generation capacity is the 'most critical issue facing PLN', they will not fund a large-scale utility sector that has been a domain for corruption.

In the second case study period, the sectoral priority became broadly defined 'governance' projects. Along with the Bank's deeply interventionist programme to shape the public sector, many governance activities focused on embedding civil society in market-based relations. It was really in the KDP and UPP projects that the impact and nature of the PWC was visible. Social capital analysis was at the forefront of the project justification; participation and community control and ownership were relatively strong themes and the Bank even stepped away for a moment from its standard procurement methods. But KDP and UPP aimed to restructure social relations and create neoliberal communities – communities that take 'responsibility for their own improvement by engaging with markets' and 'conduct themselves' appropriately in competitive markets (Li 2005: 5). The change in Bank procurement methods under the projects was possibly the most radical departure from the Washington Consensus. This change allows communities to pay community members to undertake components of small-scale infrastructure projects, but with the proviso that wages are below market rates for day labourers, which is below the cost of subsistence.

KDP and UPP also show a strong focus on poverty and there is a visible shift on Bank thinking on this issue between the two case study periods. In the first case study period, the Bank was of the view that Indonesia was in a second phase of industrialisation shifting from an initial 'take-off' based on low technology, labour-intensive manufactures towards higher technology manufacturing and less reliance on agriculture, forestry and fisheries. The Asian Financial Crisis showed that this analysis was premature at the very least and that poverty needed to be taken more seriously. This is not to say that during the New Order the Bank was not aware that rural and urban poverty represented a potential threat to stability – earlier funding for the VIPs and UDPs were essentially a way of 'defusing discontent' (Bello *et al.* 1982: 15). Rather, the Crisis discredited the idea that poverty was a peripheral issue that would be dealt with by economic growth. It now required specific measures. The Bank-supported measures start out as a strong version of the PWC with direct support for social expenditures under the Social Safety Net Adjustment Loan in 1999. However, after Habibie's presidency ended, the Bank reverted to a much weaker version of the PWC providing only indirect support via day wage employment under KDP and to a lesser extent UPP. Its main focus became promoting fiscal restraint by the state.

The PWC theme of decentralisation is systematically pursued throughout Bank loans in the first case study period. This was a formal policy of the GoI but more at the level of rhetoric than action. The Bank's insistence on decentralisation created implementation difficulties for projects approved early in the first case study period – the lack of country ownership led to slow disbursement and bureaucratic resistance. For projects approved later in the period, however, it meant they could be more easily adapted to the reality of decentralisation after 1999. In the second case study period, the Bank was concerned to make decentralisation work as they 'have invested a lot of resources into decentralization programmes around the world. Thus they have an ever-increasing institutional stake in their success' (Hadiz 2004: 706). Hadiz continues:

> [i]n ensuring the 'success' of these decentralization programmes, the Bank no doubt has to work with an array of entrenched elites, both national and local. This in itself restricts any serious consideration of factors of power, interest and conflict in the theoretical approach. The result is a theory of decentralization that tacitly endorses the non-disturbance of the existing social order to the greatest extent possible, while encouraging institutional tinkering in a supposed political vacuum.

This approach is clear in Bank lending in the second case study period. For example, the Provincial Health Projects did not analyse local power structures or indeed, in any detail local institutional arrangements and politics. They simply aimed to implement the same Bank-delineated package of interventions and increase the role of market forces in each location. It was a continuation of the one-size-fits-all model of Bank lending that the PWC was meant to address.

During the first case study period corruption (unsurprisingly) rarely rated a mention. In the second case study period, corruption became 'misprocurement' and was addressed by technical activities – an expanded programme of procurement and financial monitoring. A large number of Bank implementation completion reports on projects approved in the first case study period either did not mention corruption or claimed that there were only a couple of small instances affecting the particular project. It seems the Bank's earlier acknowledgement of the level of problems has itself been 'revised'.

In Indonesia, as in Vietnam, the Bank has been engaged in a long-term 'war of position'. In the first case study period, the Bank understood itself as engaged with a fundamentally market-oriented society that just needed the occasional push in the right direction. This was reinforced by its view of the New Order state as relatively strong and controlling. This view tempered its use of coercive techniques – consensus-based action was the norm. The Bank wanted to stay engaged and continue lending to Indonesia, thus it funded projects that nominally pursued the Washington Consensus agenda but were, in fact, strongly manipulated by the New Order to enrich its cronies. In the PWC period, the Bank has been more dogged in its pursuit of Washington Consensus hegemonic principles. It had some formal, legislative 'wins', in particular in water supply and electricity. However, it has not confronted New Order interests, which have reorganised themselves at the provincial and local level.

10 Conclusion

The first section of this book (re)interpreted the history of the World Bank utilising the Gramscian framework developed in Chapter 1. The framework centred on the key Gramscian concept of hegemony as a way of understanding how the US historic bloc organises consent both in the West and internationally. Following the work of Cox, the current hegemonic historic bloc was labelled *pax americana*. Chapter 2 overviewed changes in international power relations that accompanied *pax americana*. In keeping with the Gramscian framework, it explored changes in economic power and issues of leadership, alliances, networks and ideology. This last issue was central to the establishment of the Bank because it was the ideas unleashed by the Keynesian revolution in economic thought that provided the underlying rationale for international organisations in the economic, financial and trade spheres. While the 'Keynesian, modernisation, welfare model' provided the intellectual underpinnings of the Bretton Woods twin international financial institutions, US hegemony profoundly shaped the institutions too. Consequences for the International Bank for Reconstruction and Development (IBRD) include the weighted voting structure, conservative capitalisation and reliance on private capital markets, project lending, the Washington location and strong US executive influence.

Chapter 3 traced the trajectory of the Bank from a small organisation designed to assist with the postwar reconstruction needs of Europe to *the* most significant international development agency. This transition began with the 1947 Marshall Plan, which largely undermined the Bank's role in postwar reconstruction and led to the search for a new focus. The Bank found this in developing countries, though it initially only lent to 'creditworthy' developing countries and it continued to lend to high-income countries until 1979. Throughout the 1950s and for most of the 1960s, the Bank lent predominately for infrastructure projects. Decision-making was based on the Bank's assessment of a project's viability and its assessment of a country's overall creditworthiness. These assessments involved 'fly-in, fly-out' consultants armed with newly available economic data and new tools of econometric analysis. Projects were scrutinised in depth, judged on their estimated economic rate of return, subject to a range of conditions and implementation was monitored.

Lending was underpinned by a neoclassical view of development, which held that developing countries would 'catch up' with the West given the right technical and financial assistance. The Bank grew slowly in the 1950s but in 1961 the establishment of the International Development Association (IDA) provided a big boost to its profile, size and lending sectors, allowing it to expand slowly into what were previously regarded as 'soft' sectors such as agriculture, water supply, health and education. The IDA made the Bank a development agency.

The 1970s saw dramatic expansion and transformation of the Bank into the leading development institution – one no longer only coupled to *pax americana* but able to assist in its creation and reproduction. This change took place during the presidency of Robert McNamara but manifested the needs of the United States, in particular. As an upshot of the US strategy to centralise the role of its dollar in the world economy, which required increasing the flow of US private capital to the rest of the world – the Bank acted both as a conduit for this flow and as a ratings agency for other lenders. Moreover, throughout the Cold War, the Bank supported US geopolitical allies, and from the 1970s significant Bank resources were directed at 'defusing discontent' among the rural and urban poor in developing countries who might be 'vulnerable' to communism. Expanding resources for the Bank was also a political strategy to counter the calls for a new development agency more directly under UN control. The Bank was both the product, and an agent of, politico-economic change.

As McNamara's presidency came to a close, neoliberalism swept the globe. His introduction of structural adjustment lending in 1980 reflected this new politico-economic climate. Neoliberalism's rise in the Bank was as dramatic as it was across the West. The new President, A. W. Clausen, as a hardline advocate of supply-side economics, assisted its advance even using coercive tactics at times, including removing dissidents from the Bank. However, neoliberalism's rapid capture of the Bank equally indicated that the Bank was already a neoclassical, mainstream institution. Neoliberalism transformed into a set of hegemonic economic prescriptions shared between the Bank, the International Monetary Fund (IMF) and the US Treasury: this was the Washington Consensus. It prescribed a two-phased rewriting of countries' economic policy starting with large-scale changes to macroeconomic policy settings, which was largely the domain of the IMF, although the Bank increasingly intervened in this area as the organisations' missions meshed. Phase two was predominately the domain of the Bank; it covered microeconomic reform in everything from trade and tax to banking and governance.

The Washington Consensus was quite successful in facilitating the penetration of Western capital into all corners of the developing world. It also promoted more market-based forms of governance in many countries, which increased the access and security of Western capital. Yet there were many instances where 'agreed' reforms were never implemented or policy was reversed after a short period because it did not fit the needs of local elites and interest groups (i.e. national historic blocs). The Washington Consensus lacked an engagement with and an understanding of differing national politics. Further, its social costs were simply too high and the backlash it provoked was too politically costly and this limited if efficacy. Thus in 1986 the Reagan administration replaced Clausen with the more politically astute Barber Conable, who moderated some of the harsher Washington Consensus policies. Nevertheless, the United States continued its turbulent yet symbiotic relationship with the Bank by cutting an IDA replenishment and implementing an administrative overhaul that further reshaped the intellectual terrain of the Bank in neoliberal directions. The worsening debt crisis provided some relief for the Bank, as the US government response gave it a central role in managing debt rescheduling and relief.

That the Washington Consensus agenda did little to improve the quality of the Bank's project portfolio was powerfully demonstrated in the Wapenhans Report, which was commissioned in 1991 by the new President, Lewis Preston. It concluded that 37.5 per cent of Bank projects did not produce satisfactory outcomes according to Bank standards. Despite growing concerns regarding the social costs of adjustment and some pressure from the Japanese government to acknowledge the role of the state in development, in 1993 the Bank was still following the Washington Consensus agenda and declaring structural adjustment a success. A few issues were added to the Bank's agenda but its move beyond the Washington Consensus did not really occur until the Clinton administration appointee, James Wolfensohn, replaced Preston in 1995.

The gradual shift to the post-Washington Consensus (PWC), outlined in Chapter 4, did not substantially challenge the hegemonic principles of the Washington Consensus. Rather, it generally involved adding new issues to the policy 'reform' agenda, for example poverty reduction, local participation in development programmes and a concern with the sequencing of reform. At a fundamental level, this was an intellectual, political and social project to shore up Bank operations so that developing countries would continue to be able and willing to support *pax americana*: it was a passive revolution.

The second part of the book examined the impact of both the Washington Consensus and PWC on the lending practices of the World Bank via case studies of its lending practices in Vietnam and Indonesia. These detailed studies provide a framework on which to base some empirical conclusions about the extent to which the shift in rhetoric associated with the PWC has been incorporated into lending practices and thus providing insights into neoliberal development discourse more generally. As a way of concluding this study, this chapter returns to the ten features of the PWC as well as the issue of Bank as project manager that were outlined in Chapter 4 to see what light the case studies sheds on each topic.

Approach to monetary and fiscal policy

As suggested by the analysis of the PWC, the Bank still focuses on economic growth as the key determinant of development and poverty reduction, and its view of growth is centred on a neoliberal approach to monetary and fiscal policy. The PWC has seen changes at the margins of this approach; in particular, capital market liberalisation has been questioned both in the theoretical literature and by the international financial institutions (Broad 2004). The focus on money supply as the key economic policy tool has been discredited but 'getting the prices right' is still a hegemonic principle. An open current account remains 'law' as does the preference for consumption taxes over income taxes and the belief in full cost recovery for government provided services, especially utilities. The project to limit government expenditure has not been affected by the (rather limited) debate about the role of the state.

World Bank recommendations on monetary and fiscal policy in Vietnam and Indonesia did not display significant changes between 1993 and 2004. In Vietnam, across both case study periods, the Bank focused on price liberalisation to control the budget deficit and inflation and to 'get the prices right', currency devaluation, financial sector reforms and openness to foreign direct investment. There was an expansion of the Bank's structural adjustment programme between 2001 and 2003 – health, education, environmental sustainability, government planning and legal reform were added but they were framed in ways that supported the Bank's conservative fiscal policy agenda. For example, the Bank encouraged the GoV to limit education spending essentially to basic education and it encouraged the expansion of private education. Equally, health care in the PWC period was still regarded as primarily an individual rather than a community or state responsibility; the Bank promoted spending only on a limited package of primary health care interventions for the (generally ill-defined) poor.

In the first half of the 2000s, the Bank saw that Vietnam needed to progress more quickly towards a floating exchange regime but it accepted a role for controls on short-term capital flows. However, they promoted faster liberalisation in the foreign investment regime and interest rates policy following traditional Washington Consensus prescriptions (World Bank 2002a, annex D1: 4–7). A moderated view on regulation of short-term capital flows was the most significant impact of the PWC agenda on monetary and fiscal policy analysis.

In Indonesia, the Bank intensified its project to tighten the fiscal restraint on the state in the post-Suharto period. It demonstrated increased concern with the level of government debt, which did indeed jump after the Asian Financial Crisis, mostly due to the large devaluation of the *Rupiah*. The key outcome of this concern was a decrease in the scale of its own lending programme and an increase in the use of conditionality to remove price subsidies, in particular fuel subsidies. The Asian Financial Crisis resulted in the end of the quasi-fixed exchange rate system on which the Bank laid a part of the 'blame' for the Crisis (in combination with the liberalised current account and corruption). During the PWC case study period, the Bank was committed to floating exchange rates, a liberal current account and market interest rates; indeed, these Washington Consensus prescriptions were core criteria in determining the level of its 2002–4 lending programme (World Bank 2001a: 11–12). Surprisingly, in Indonesia, neither the PWC nor the Crisis seems to have altered Bank hostility to capital controls even on short-term capital flows.

Getting the macroeconomic fundamentals 'right' was still a 'given' in the PWC agenda. This is not something for public debate, as demonstrated in a Panos Institute study (2002: 18), which found that the Poverty Reduction Strategy Paper (PRSP) process did not provide an 'opportunity to debate the macroeconomic framework' in any of the 50 countries studied. This was also the case in Vietnam and Indonesia. Further, a review of 50 PRSPs found that only 14 per cent did *not* include a commitment to strict monetary policy and only 4 per cent did *not* include strict fiscal policy (Sumner 2006). It can be concluded that conservative monetary and fiscal policy are hegemonic principles of the PWC and that they effectively frame and constrain all other policy approaches.

Country specificity

The PWC claims to have left behind the 'one-size-fits-all' approach to development so negatively associated with the Washington Consensus. If this were the case, increased attention to, and analysis of, each country's specific social, political and economic realities would be apparent as would be an increased diversity of projects and approaches. At the level of the Bank's Country Assistance Strategy (CAS), this could present as better developed socio-economic analysis of local conditions as well as consideration of global and regional impacts. However, the social, economic and political analysis in the Vietnam CAS of 2002 was superficial. The economic analysis was brief and mainstream; it focused on the need for faster policy reform in order to build a market economy and achieve economic growth. The external environment was not analysed. The CAS claimed to promote the Government of Vietnam's (GoV) own agenda and be based on their planning documents, yet it simply did not accept the GoV objective of a '*socialist*-orientated market economy' and translated this to a neoliberal vision of '[h]igh growth through a transition to a market economy' (World Bank 2002a; Socialist Republic of Vietnam 2002: 6, emphasis added). Despite the constraints apparent in the CAS, the Bank is regarded the by GoV and others as having a quite open attitude in Vietnam and it has supported research and activities in a number of non-traditional areas.

In Indonesia, the 2001 CAS contained a more substantial social, political and economic background analysis than earlier CASs, or the 2002 CAS for Vietnam. The CAS (World Bank 2001a: 16) stated that country assessments should more fully evaluate 'political, institutional and social dimensions'. It had a strong focus on the PWC themes of participation, decentralisation, poverty and governance. Yet, at the end of the day, the level of the Bank's lending programme was determined chiefly by Washington Consensus concerns: 'prudent monetary, fiscal and debt management', bank restructuring privatisation, rice-trade liberalisation and reform of GoI procurement and financial management (World Bank 2001a: iii).[1]

The PWC lending programme in Indonesia did show country specificity in the large-scale *Kecamatan* Development Program (KDP) and Urban Poverty Project (UPP) projects (though the KDP has since been replicated in other countries). In utilities though, it was not visible; rather, the Bank's Washington Consensus model for privatisation of utilities prevailed. Indeed, the Bank used the political instability after the fall of the Suharto regime to pursue radical water and electricity privatisation. A 2003 loan in the electricity sector acknowledged that generation shortfalls in the near future were the 'most critical issue facing' the country (World Bank 2003n: 9). However, in an interesting reflection on commitment to country specificity the Bank would not fund new generation capacity and gave no explanation of why. Instead, it funded a project investing in the transmission system and implementing an action plan to unbundle the Indonesian electricity company's urban operations.

In Vietnam, the Bank was constrained by the GoV to pursuit of a gradual approach to privatisation. In water supply, the Bank pushed to expand corporatisation and private participation to district systems. In electricity, the Bank followed the model of introducing IPPs and separating urban and rural operations, funding separation of over 1000 rural electricity distributors from the national electricity corporation. On tariffs, in both water supply and electricity, the Bank's only policy view across both periods studied in Indonesia and Vietnam was that they must increase. This position was pursued in the wake of the Asian Financial Crisis and there was no analysis of the economic, social or political impacts of immediate increases: the formula dominated.

The average size of loans can also be considered an indicator of the Bank's trade-off between project quantity, country specificity and quality. This is because the Bank tends to aim for scale in its operations to meet its need to disburse loans but also because of the needs for cost-effective project development and management (Ranis 1997: 86). In Vietnam and Indonesia the average and median loan size remained, in both case study periods, close to the Bank's historically standard size of around $100 million.

Recipient government ownership

The Comprehensive Development Framework emphasised that recipient governments should own and control their development programme and projects. For the most part, the Bank main mechanism for ownership was a PRSP, developed as per the Bank's sourcebook. For Heavily Indebted Poor Countries (HIPC), a PRSP is a Bank condition for continued access to lending and it is meant to be a pre-condition for continued access to structural adjustment lending. The irony that countries are meant to 'own' their development programme through undertaking a Bank-specified and delineated process has been noted by a number of critics. The requirement that the Bank and IMF approve PRSPs was dropped in 2005; nevertheless, they still do not necessarily form the basis of the Bank's lending programme. This remains the role of the CAS.

The extent to which Vietnam and Indonesia took on board or 'owned' the process varied significantly. In Vietnam in 1999, the GoV requested involvement as a pilot Comprehensive Development Framework (CDF)/PRSP country. An interim PRSP was produced quickly to maintain access to structural adjustment lending and involved little public participation or country ownership (Wolff *et al.* 2002: iii). The full PRSP produced in 2002 had strong government ownership and was renamed the Comprehensive Poverty Reduction and Growth Strategy (CPRGS). Despite the high level of GoV ownership, the CPRGS had limited impact on GoV policy-making and provincial- and communal-level governments are unaware of it (Nørlund *et al.* 2003: 23). This obscurity is because the CPRGS process is separate from existing planning processes involving debate in party cells and mass organisations and approval by the National Assembly. The Bank originally wanted the CPRGS to become Vietnam's key planning document but (reluctantly) agreed to have it incorporated into the existing process. The irony regarding country ownership is obvious – the GoV had to persuade the Bank to allow the process to be country owned. But country ownership is high in Vietnam and the Bank's PWC agenda has at least allowed it to flourish.

In terms of the content of PRSPs, one analysis of 50 PRSPs showed that out of nine standard Washington Consensus policy prescriptions studied each PRSP included an average of six of them and there were 'very few instances of unorthodox policies being mentioned' (World Development Movement 2005: 10). It found that 72 per cent of PRSPs included policies on trade liberalisation; 90 per cent included policies on privatisation; 64 per cent included liberalising investment regimes; and 96 per cent had commitments to limiting state budgets. Vietnam was the one exception in policy on this last area; indeed, overall its PRSP only shows three out of the nine Washington Consensus policies – the second lowest count of the 50 countries studied.

Indonesia voluntarily prepared an interim PRSP in 2003 and a full PRSP in 2005. However, the process seems to be more obscure than in Vietnam, and it appears to have little impact on Government of Indonesia (GoI) policy (Tagaroa 2006). Country ownership of Bank projects has declined in Indonesia since the fall of Suharto, and the Bank utilised the Crisis situation to drive through major legislative and other changes (for example, in the water sector), although with the support of the Habibie Government. Despite a high degree of initial success in implementing its programme, some Bank plans have been delayed in the parliament, subject to legal challenges and protested against by large sections of civil society. It is also apparent that many of the Bank's projects in Indonesia were prepared by Bank staff not government officials. In Vietnam, the GoV appeared to have more control over the sectors and contents of projects than GoI bureaucrats do in Indonesia. It is still the case that documents submitted to the Bank's Board are fully prepared by Bank staff, whereas country ownership should mean that recipient countries at least prepare projects themselves – Bank staff could append an appraisal.

A reduction in conditionality could be considered an indication of the Bank handing over control to recipient governments. In Vietnam the median/average number of conditions did not change between the two case study periods (19/20.9) and in Indonesia there was a dramatic increase in the number of conditions from an average of 15.5 (median 13) in the first case study period to 25.5 (median 24) in the second. The Bank (2005h: 9) claimed that the average number of conditions on loans across its whole portfolio declined from over 35 in the early 1990s to 12 in 2005. Yet the number of 'benchmarks', which supposedly do not determine Bank funding in the way that conditions do, increased from 15 in the early 1990s to 23–34 in 2004–5 (World Bank 2005h: 10). The jump in conditions for Indonesia supports Griffin's (2006: 578) finding that while the Bank's overall average number of conditions decreased, in countries regarded as higher risks, the number of conditions and benchmarks increased significantly.[2]

Analysed by sector, the only area that saw a substantial *increase* in the number of conditions was public sector governance (World Bank 2005h: 11). Not only has there been an increase in the number of conditions on governance issues but the form of conditions has also become more invasive (Griffin 2006: 579; Harrison 2004: 71). This 'post-conditionality' increases the Bank's level of engagement into everyday governance of developing countries, including more systematic involvement with political and civil society. The case studies showed a significant increase in projects in the law, justice and public administration sector – in Vietnam, projects went from 9 per cent of the value of new commitments in 1993–7 to 18 per cent in 2000–4; in Indonesia they skyrocketed from 7 to 47 per cent. Further, while every condition did not become more invasive, conditionality remained very broad. For example, the Bank often required recipient governments to discuss with them their plans for a whole sector and for sector studies, plans or legislative reviews to be undertaken in line with terms of reference it approved. Conditionality clearly does not always result in the Bank getting its way; nevertheless, the case studies provided limited indications that the Bank is reducing its tools of influence in the name of country ownership. Equally, conditionality aimed to mould countries' structures in particular ways; in particular, it was increasingly aimed at transforming not just economic but also political and civil society.

The role of the state

The PWC theoretically allows space for an expanded view of the role of the state in contrast to the Washington Consensus hostility to it. The state can complement rather than compete with markets. In a weak form, the PWC state only provides a good policy environment for business, in other words an active, pro-capitalist state (Cammack 2003: 5; Crawford 2006). A further step provides more space for state institutions to engage with market imperfections (information and transaction costs). In a strong version, the PWC genuinely engages with the state as an actor; it promotes critical analysis of actors and interests in society and the distribution of power and resources between them (Wodsak 2002: 44). The case studies indicated that the Bank utilised a weak version of the PWC role of the state framed by the Washington Consensus project of limiting the size of the state and by New Institutional Economics' (NIE) lack of interest in power and class (Carroll 2005). The project to privatise utilities, contract out activities and limit expenditures in health, education and social safety nets prevailed. The PWC state is a technocratic and managerial one, where the 'policy aims are implicit and not part of an open political negotiation' (Masina 2006: 26). This is not surprising given that this is the role of the state that best fits post-1970s *pax americana*, wherein globalisation is 'being consolidated via the nation-state system' (Berger 2004: 208).

The tensions and contradictions produced by the Washington Consensus hostility to the state competing with the PWC acknowledgement of its necessity are visible in Bank lending. For example, in Vietnam, the 2004 Poverty Reduction Support Credit (PRSC) III included as a condition the number of enterprises registered each month, which the Bank (2004h: 17) justified on the basis that '[e]ssentially private sector development is the combined outcome of policy actions in many areas, from financial sector reform to better governance and public administration' – a PWC view of the state as a facilitator of business. In the same series of loans, the redundancy package for workers from equitised state-owned enterprises (SOEs) offered workers little more than a single lump-sum payment. It aimed to limit social safety nets expenditure to one-off payments – this is *adjustment welfare*. These approaches assisted in minimising expenditure and role of the state in welfare, while at the same time Bank logic made the state responsible for business development.

In Indonesia, World Bank lending in the PWC focused on community development projects and decentralised governance projects. The largest community development activities were the series of KDP loans. KDP largely bypassed local and district governments while creating governance structures that effectively parallel the state but lack its permanence. This is another example of the PWC tension around the state, resolved in this case through a form of neoliberal governmentalism (Li 2005). In the Bank's decentralised governance projects (sector specific projects in health, transport and water supply), the tension was resolved by directing provincial and district governments toward neoliberal 'solutions'. That is, configuring them as far as possible as technocratic contract managers and, where they do provide services, limiting the scope of those services.

Market failure and the pace and sequencing of reforms

The PWC gives attention to market failure in addition to the Washington Consensus focus on government failure and sees the sequencing of reform programmes as critical to outcomes. In the study, examples were sought of analysis of market failure, increased attention to the development of regulatory frameworks relevant to local conditions prior to liberalisation and analysis of local conditions prior to privatisation. There were virtually no examples to be found but there were a number of prominent examples where projects simply ignored these issues in order to implement Washington Consensus hegemonic principles.

A key difference between the Bank and the GoV since at least 1998 has been the pace of reform: the Bank has consistently urged faster and more dramatic reform while the GoV preferred a more cautious approach. The issue that most concerned the Bank was the pace and extent of SOE equitisation; it was pursued through conditions in the Bank's three PRSCs. Privatisation is also administratively and managerially complex and has stretched the regulatory capacity of the government. Valuation of land and assets has been particularly difficult, yet the Bank pushed to have audit requirements prior to privatisation dropped because it was slowing the equitisation process. This has facilitated corrupt practices such as the undervaluation of assets. The Bank's continuing silence on this issue indicates PWC 'lessons' about market failure and pace and sequencing of reform are second to the Washington Consensus push for market structures and privatisation.

In the power sector, in 2004 the Bank backed the introduction of an IPP in Vietnam two years prior to the introduction of a new National Electricity Law that made IPPs legal; concern with sequencing was not visible here. The IPP was built with the support of a Bank guarantee, Asian Development Bank (ADB) and Japan Bank for International Cooperation (JBIC) funds and a 20-year, US dollar-denominated, set price power purchase agreement with the state-owned electricity company. At the end of the day, the GoV assumed virtually all the risk. This is a strong indication that the Bank still regards government failure as more problematic than market failure. In Indonesia, the Bank claimed after 1998 to have consistently warned against guaranteed (inflated) price IPP arrangements. However, public documents do not fully support their claim; rather, they indicate that the Bank was more concerned with increasing private sector involvement than with market or government failure. The studies of Vietnam and Indonesia indicate that PWC theorising on market failure and the pace and sequencing of reform has had little practical impact on Bank lending.

A focus on poverty reduction and the social costs of adjustment

In Vietnam, the Bank assisted the GoV focus on poverty at a statistical and analytical level and has devoted significant resources to assisting in mapping and understanding poverty. The Bank has played a role in sharpening the focus on, and understanding of, poverty in GoV policy-making. Loans in the PWC period utilised poverty more frequently in their project justification. For the most part, however, these justifications were highly generalised and often problematic, for example correlations between poverty reduction and all weather roads or between rural microfinance and direct 'poverty alleviation and equitable growth' (World Bank 2002c: 3). Microfinance was a key area of

Bank project activity to directly address poverty, and microfinance loans were among the first organised by the World Bank when it re-engaged with Vietnam. This was at a time when, following a period of restructuring broadly along neoliberal lines, poverty was declining; however, the social welfare system, which had been neglected since the mid-1980s, was in a state of disrepair. This resulted in increasing levels of unrest, especially in the countryside. The Bank's support for microfinance in Vietnam can thus be seen as part of a neoliberal policy response to problems arising from structural adjustment, as Weber (2004: 362) so clearly puts it, microfinance is 'a neoliberal safety net *for* neoliberal political restructuring'. Moreover, the Bank publicly supports it as an approach to poverty reduction – but it is an approach that eschews the need for social safety nets as 'a welfare-based approach to poverty alleviation that disenfranchises the poor and establishes new dependency relations' (Gibbons *et al.* 2000: 266).

As a consequence of the Asian Financial Crisis, the Bank increased analytical work on poverty in Indonesia; it remained, however, significantly underdeveloped. The Bank did fund a Social Safety Net Adjustment Loan (in 1999 for $600 million) that aimed to provide one-off assistance to those negatively impacted by the Crisis. It also sought to make social expenditures more targeted, which had the added benefit of assisting the constraint of social expenditure in the medium term. The Bank largely designed the loan and saw it as a vehicle for reform resulting in a high level of conditionality. But its uncomfortableness with the loan resulted in only part of the loan being disbursed. This loan was a strong indication of the PWC social agenda, yet the neoliberal hegemonic principle of constraining state expenditure dominated.

The Bank's PWC approach to poverty reduction in practice involved support for basic education; health care expenditure on preventative measures and a limited number of curative services that it considers have a large impact on people's disability-adjusted life years; some adjustment welfare – that is, one off assistance after redundancy or an economic shock; and some funding for projects that employ day labour at below the minimum wage. Looking at this package, Porter and Craig's (2004) argument that the Bank approach to poverty reduction is to get the poor above one dollar a day but little more than that, seems very accurate.

Social capital and civil society participation

The PWC regarded civil society as a distinct realm for analysis and intervention and, in the second half of the 1990s, the Bank sometimes employed social capital analysis to understand it. Its social capital theory saw civil society as the glue that holds society together and a missing link in development. The PWC claimed a genuine appreciation for local knowledge and practices tempered by concerns about coherence and coordination (Wodsak 2002: 91). It also focused on expanded local participation in the planning, design and implementation of activities. The case studies demonstrated that the PWC dichotomises between civil society and the state/market and between civil society and non-governmental organisations (NGOs) or civil society organisations. Civil society was constructed as a positive and natural arena in which individuals spontaneously collaborate. However, the Bank's social capital approach considered that the 'civil' component of society needs assistance or facilitation to achieve their full potential as neoliberal communities responsible for their own development and engaged with markets (Li 2005: 5). NGOs, in contrast, do not always share the Bank's vision of development and are often regarded by the Bank with suspicion (Whitelum 2003).

Social capital was not utilised as an analytical tool in Vietnam. Bank engagement with civil society was, surprisingly, at one level both more extensive and more cooperative in Vietnam than in Indonesia, which has a much more developed and active NGO sector despite New Order repression. In Vietnam, the Bank reasonably successfully promoted itself as a 'white knight' supporting the rights of civil society organisations that are, in the Bank's story, suppressed by the communist regime. The Bank even claimed a shared development 'vision' with Vietnamese NGOs. However, the NGO community is quite small in Vietnam and, outside the party-based mass organisations, it is strongly linked to and dependent on Western development NGOs. Further, the Bank's reputation for participative practices was largely based on poverty studies and surveys rather than on the operation of projects, where its practices were less developed in the PWC case study period than in Indonesia. This was, in part, because the Bank operates with and through the GoV, which has largely been uninterested in accepting funds for community development-type activities from the Bank. It was also because the Bank's vision of participation in project activities was narrow and instrumental. For example, in rural electrification projects, communities were consulted to determine the potential economic rates of return from electrification and their willingness to pay for it. Even the Bank's Operations Evaluation Department (2002: 1) have questioned the real extent of participation and concluded that in general, 'the language of NGO/CBO involvement in Bank-supported projects outstripped the reality'.

In Indonesia, the Bank only seriously started to engage with NGOs after the fall of Suharto, and as a result of this and its closeness to the previous regime many NGOs remain suspicious of the Bank. Bank officials did not understand the suspicion and remained tied to a sub-set of NGOs that are willing to engage with them and that share their 'development vision for Indonesia and values the Bank's development agenda as a way forward' (Whitelum 2003: 197). As is to be expected, they do not engage with more radical, transformative NGOs (Whitelum 2003: 210).

The Washington office of the Bank selected Indonesia as a trial country for social capital studies and projects. Yet its use was limited to the project in which it was trialled – KDP. It was not visible in other social sector projects and certainly not in economic or infrastructure analysis. KDP is the Bank's most sophisticated version of community development-type activities, yet every aspect of its operations are specified in Bank approved manuals – from how the participatory process is undertaken to how the projects are planned, implemented, administered and monitored (Li 2005). KDP demonstrates that the Bank's version of participation is instrumental not transformative and aimed at producing critical consumers – rational, competitive actors responsible for and focused on their own development, not critical citizens who may question domestic and international power structures or demand rights.[3]

KDP is still running, but social capital was going out of fashion in the Bank by 2004. Participation remains a key tool and it has impacted on the way the Bank does business. Yet it seems increasingly necessary to look critically at its purpose, form and outcomes. Kapoor (2005: 1212) convincingly deconstructed participatory development, concluding that its role is to 'protect and advance institutional authority'. Indeed, he noted how:

> in one fell swoop: participation becomes a disciplinary mechanism for the World Bank/IMF to hold the poorest Third World states 'to account' … and, in turn for these states to keep civil society organisations in check; and participation helps advance neoliberalism, promoting 'partnerships' to co-opt Third World states *and* (elite) NGOs into the structural adjustment programme.
>
> (Kapoor 2005: 1214)

In Gramscian terms, participation has become a tool to pursue the PWC passive revolution – it is a moral, intellectual and educative engagement to construct civil society in the neoliberal image.

Decentralisation

Decentralisation is directly connected to participation, because the Bank claims that it equals local participation in decision-making. As Hadiz (2004: 701) notes, decentralisation has been an attractive policy for international development agencies because it appears to respond to the criticism of their past technocratic and one-size-fits-all policies. However, this claim is shallow because the PWC approach to decentralisation, derived from NIE, is strongly technocratic, i.e. just chooses the form and amount of decentralisation in various policy areas. Further, it tends to place responsibility for policy-making on sectoral issues in the hands of (now locally situated) technocrats rather than political society.

In Vietnam, the Bank's support for decentralisation was political as well as technical. The Bank is not comfortable with Vietnam's consensus-based system combining mass organisations, the Communist Party and a formally elected government. It promoted the creation of legislative frameworks for formal liberal democratic institutions such as (Western-style) NGOs and trade unions (Turk 2005). This reflected the Bank's PWC project of transforming the economy and the state. However, in terms of Bank projects, decentralisation was largely technical, it manifested itself in issues such as whether planning for rural roads should have been done by bureaucrats at the district or commune level or which institutional framework was best for communities to manage electricity distribution.

In Indonesia, decentralisation was pursued through Bank loans in the first case study period, when it was a formal policy of the GoI but not actively pursued by it. The Bank's activity may have been because, despite its closeness to the Suharto regime, it felt a need to promote transformation of political and social relations along liberal democratic lines. After Indonesia's radical decentralisation in 1999, Bank projects focused on ensuring decentralisation worked. Indeed, the Bank has invested a lot of resources into decentralisation programmes around the world and it has been the biggest donor to these projects in Indonesia (Turner *et al.* 2003: 130). It has 'an ever-increasing institutional stake' in decentralisation's success (Hadiz 2004: 706). This is difficult in Indonesia because there is a clear tension between any project to reorder society through democratic decentralisation and the reality that projects have bound it to 'entrenched elites, both national and local … [which] in itself restricts any serious consideration of factors of power, interest and conflict' (Hadiz 2004: 706).

The Indonesian Provincial Health Projects are a good example of the technocratic form of Bank projects. They did not analyse local power structures or indeed, local institutional arrangements and politics in any detail. They funded implementation of the same Bank-delineated package of health interventions and activities to increase the role of market forces in each location. There was little genuine local political or civil society input to the form and structure of local health services and they directed provincial governments along a neoliberal path, where the state funded only limited interventions for the poorest and the role of the market was central.

Health and education

The PWC appears to have only marginally broadened the Bank's approach to health and education. Overall, focus remained on increasing the role of market forces but the PWC approach was visible in the encouragement for governments to direct resources to areas seen as having significant economic payoffs. In education, this meant basic education and in health it was a package of primary health care interventions plus limited curative treatments available only to the 'poor'. The Bank's Washington Consensus model for these sectors predominated over concerns about country ownership.

A striking thing about the Bank's role in health and education in Vietnam and Indonesia was that, while Bank resources devoted to research and policy development in health and education seem to have increased, project lending remained negligible. In Vietnam, education accounted for only six per cent of Bank approvals in 2000–4 and health and other social services for one per cent. In Indonesia, education declined from 13 per cent of new loan approvals in 1993–7 to five per cent in 2000–4. Health expenditure did increase from four to 14 per cent thanks to the series of Provincial Health projects.

Corruption

The PWC continues the Washington Consensus concern with corruption but supposedly on the basis of government *and* market failures. The focus on property rights and institutions is equally rejuvenated as these are essential to minimising transaction and information costs and thus to economic growth; they are a prerequisite to 'getting the prices right' (North 1998: 23–25). The PWC promotes incorporation of conventions and norms in institutions and suggests that transferring Western systems to the developing world is unlikely, on its own, to improve performance. However, the case studies provided no examples of Bank concern about corruption caused by market failure. Further, the tendency to apply Western legal, political and financial solutions to developing countries appears to be fundamentally intact.

The Bank as a project manager

By 2003–5, adjustment lending declined to 30 per cent of new approvals, meaning that investment lending was again the dominant mode of Bank activity. The PWC had limited impact on the project model for investment lending and their procurement requirements. Yet these two structures profoundly shape the outcomes of Bank projects but they seem to have received less critical attention in the past decade than previously. Investment lending generally operates with a three- to five-year project cycle and given this and the Bank's need to disburse money, its main focus is generally negotiating the next project. Bank staff still prepare most projects and the Bank funds pre-appraisal work through trust funds and grants or existing bank loans. Even where recipient governments control funds, the Bank's view on the appropriate consultants and contractors for jobs tends to predominate. The Bank also prepares the appraisal of each project that is submitted to its Board.

A raft of Bank requirements directs the operation of a project once approved. Bank investment loans can only be utilised for work that is tendered out. Tendering methods and types are specified for every dollar of a project. Project accounting must be done to Bank standards, generally with separate accounts, software and Bank-approved staff. Project manuals, yearly work programmes, project staff, sector restructuring plans and a whole range of other items must be undertaken 'to the satisfaction of the Bank'. As Mason and Asher (1973: 479) note in their moderate history of the Bank:

> [i]nternational competitive bidding, reluctance to accord preference to local suppliers, emphasis on financing foreign exchange costs, insistence on a predominant use of foreign consultants, attitudes towards public sector industries, assertion of the right to approve project managers – all proclaim the Bank to be a Western capitalist institution.

Procurement procedures for non-consultancy work must be undertaken in line with one of the Bank's three standards: international competitive bidding

(ICB), national competitive bidding (NCB) and local shopping. According to Caufield (1998: 242), in 1995 the amount of Bank procurement specified for ICB was 56 per cent. For 2004, for non-consultant contracts subject to prior review, over 74 per cent were subject to ICB (World Bank Group Website). The overall figure for Bank investment loans may be lower as contracts subject to prior review would tend to be larger value loans that are mostly subject to ICB. Nevertheless, this figure is surprisingly high – Indonesia and Vietnam showed a move towards an increased use of NCB procedures in the second case study period, particularly in regional and rural infrastructure projects. But the suggestion of change was generally superficial; procurement reflected the reality that international firms were very unlikely to bid for such projects. Even local contractors were difficult to find as much of the work had previously been done by the state (e.g. road construction). So, loans were accompanied by training for the private sector in bidding for projects. The use of NCB may well indicate a new level of penetration in the Bank's project to create markets in developing countries. The only project that deviated from standard Bank procurement arrangements was KDP. Here communities were able to pay workers for day labour at below minimum wages as well as use competitive procurement for goods and civil works.

Use of Bank consultants also influences recipient governments. In 2004, there were 3,581 consultant contracts worth $1.33 billion under Bank investment loans subject to prior review (World Bank Group Website). Add to this, consultants under investment loans not subject to prior review, those hired from the Bank's operating budget and those hired from trust funds or the associated operating budgets and the Bank's budget for consultants is likely over $2 billion. Of the $1.3 billion in prior review consultant contracts, just over 44 per cent were awarded to organisations or individuals from Organization for Economic Cooperation and Development (OECD) countries. But this figure is deceptive because it hides the number of contracts now won by local subsidiaries of Western companies.

There are only a few academic studies of the impact of consultants (foreign or otherwise) but one recent effort by Natasha Hamilton Hart is illuminating. She argued that the common impact of the use of consultants derives from the 'commercially mediated' nature of the relationship (Hamilton-Hart 2006: 260). Consultants produce and reproduce international standards that are used to measure the performance of governments. Further, and perhaps more importantly, 'consultant use configures government organisations in ways that ensure their structural openness' (Hamilton-Hart 2006: 266). This openness has a physical dimension in the presence of consultants in government agencies and an ideological dimension in that this presence has been 'strongly associated with government receptivity' to managerial 'reforms'. Using donor-funded consultants trains and 'configures government organisations as contract managers'. And it demands increasing compliance with the financial transparency schemes of the PWC era. Hamilton-Hart (2006: 266) concludes that donor funds for consultancies spreads 'a particular model of government, one that is not generically western or modern but specifically American'.

Conclusion

The case studies showed only a few indications that the Bank has moved beyond its traditional concern with economic growth within a market capitalist framework. It was clear that the concern with social issues rested, to a large extent, on their impact on social stability as well as on the operation of markets and economic development more generally (Wodsak 2002: 98). The changes that did occur were influenced by the East Asian 'developmental state' model, NIE, NGOs and the American political climate. So, the *post*-Washington Consensus in a hyphenated form is appropriate as it indicates the fundamental link to the hegemonic principles of the Washington Consensus. It also gives a sense that the PWC is not a new and stable form of hegemony; rather, while it has confronted some of the tensions and instability of the Washington Consensus both theoretically and as a modus operandi for the Bank, it has created new ones.

A number of critical International Political Economy (IPE) scholars have come to a similar view about the PWC, though from different perspectives and using different terminology. The PWC has been seen as a project to reinvent liberalism (Berger and Beeson 1998), embed liberalism (Harrison 2004: 64–66; Weber 2006) or to legitimate and thus secure it (Porter and Craig 2004). Porter and Craig, whose focus was on the way recent shifts aimed at 'embedding, legitimating and securing liberal reform', analysed the shift using the Polanyian notion of a double movement:

> [t]he first movement, economic liberalization and integration, involves the breaking up or disembedding of traditional and local social regulation by market relations, enabling increased, unfettered penetration of market forces ... This is followed by the second, embedding movement, where acting almost intuitively a range of what Polanyi called 'enlightened reactionaries' rally to mitigate the social disruptions of market-led liberalization.
>
> (Porter and Craig 2004: 390)

Li's (2005: 2) study on the KDP draws on the Foucauldian idea of government as a means to 'conduct conduct', which is quite similar to Gramsci's idea about the role of political society in governing through, and organising, consent. My study finds the Gramscian notion of passive revolution most illuminating in describing the nature of the shift to the PWC. In these terms, the PWC has been a project of *pax americana* to manage change in order to ensure its dominant position is maintained and the possibility of progressive change is contained. It has been a global project and its implementation required (among other things) a global organisation that can appear to have broader interests and that can at the same time adapt to local social forces. Up until the appointment of Paul Wolfowitz at least, the World Bank was very successful in its ideological campaign, selling its focus on poverty reduction and country-specific and -owned development strategies, but this detailed examination of its lending exposed examples where this was little more than rhetoric, while other components such as decentralisation or participation served the expansion of capitalism more than would appear from a surface examination.

What this analysis also demonstrates is the scale of the challenge to those wanting to champion and implement non-neoliberal reform through international agencies in the wake of the current global financial crisis's demonstrations of its failings and inadequacies. The hegemonic principles of the Washington Consensus have so deeply permeated the Bank that a decade of reform did little to change the attitude on things like constraining the size and role of the state, privatisation and allowing countries to own their development programmes.

It would be remiss (and indeed, inadequate in terms of the Gramscian framework) to conclude without making a few comments about how Vietnam and Indonesia moderated the impact of Bank policies, that is to say without acknowledging the undoubted ongoing relevance and capacity of states themselves. While the study did not aim to provide a comprehensive analysis of the autonomy or capacity of the Vietnamese or Indonesian states, it has provided some insights into both the shape of their historic blocs and the way in which these blocs have interacted with the Bank. In Vietnam, the state was committed to gaining public support from the Bank, although for a period in the late 1990s this was less the case. Despite the disinclination to publicly disagree with the Bank, Vietnam's policy implementation displayed a strong degree of autonomy. In some instances, the GoV utilised Bank assistance to follow quite a different path than that suggested by the Bank. More often though, it used the assistance to develop its own policy-making capacity, to improve the centre's financial relationship with the provinces or to undertake reform in a way that reasserted the influence of the party and state (Painter 2005). The Bank has been part of the changing ideological terrain in Vietnam regarding the role of states and markets but neither the level of change nor the influence of the World Bank or other donors should be exaggerated.

In Indonesia, the Bank had a strong degree of influence on policy-making during the Suharto regime, yet at the same time it suffered from quite a degree of 'capture'. The GoI convinced the Bank that it was a developing Asian 'tiger' and that the authoritarian Suharto provided the required structure and stability. Yet the Asian Financial Crisis and the Bank's embarrassment regarding its support for the corrupt regime led the Bank to rewrite its view of Indonesia's economic status and to attempt to utilise the political crisis to pursue dramatic economic and political 'reform'. At the same time, the Bank programme was not simply imposed – President Habibie utilised support from the international financial institutions as part of his political strategy. When Habibie departed, Indonesia's relations with the Bank shifted again as subsequent administrations did not need its public support to the same extent. In this context, the Bank significantly cut the size of its lending programme and focused on governance at both a central government and civil society level. Despite this reduction in influence, the post-Habibie governments do not appear to have had the same capacity as the GoV to direct the Bank's activities.

Notes

1 Introduction

1 The IFC invests in private enterprises via loans and guarantees and provides risk management and advisory services. MIGA was established to guarantee foreign investors against losses from non-commercial risks such as expropriation, currency inconvertibility and transfer restrictions or war and civil disturbances. ICSID's role is conciliation and arbitration of investment disputes.

2 All currency references are to US dollars unless specified otherwise.

3 There are around 95 researchers in the Development Research Group but the Bank's formal definition of its research activities is very narrow and excludes most of its analytical and advisory services (Banerjee *et al* 2006: 24–27).

4 Notably, the UK's Department for International Development (DFID) has substantially increased its research programme over the past few years; however, it is still substantially smaller in size and influence than the Bank.

5 The World Bank is an international bureaucracy and Gramsci (1971: 175) noted that bureaucracies are subject to the will of competing states but also have their own dynamics that results in the development of their own interests and logics. International institutions also operate differently in different locations, they utilise what Gramsci (1971: 188) called democratic centralism to allow adaptation to different local social, political and economic realities. This adaptive capacity is central to the survival of the organisation and the social forces they represent. Studying what can be modified and, more pertinently, what can never be challenged regardless of location sheds much light on the nature of neoliberal ideology. A Gramscian framework also directs attention to how World Bank policies and programmes are best understood in the coercion/consent dialectic and whether the post-Washington Consensus has seen a significant shift in this balance. The framework points to questions about whether the post-Washington Consensus represents structural and fundamental transformation or whether it involves utilising the state to shape the current historic bloc.

2 Creating a World Bank

1 Keynesianism here is used as per John Davis' definition – a tradition arising from reformulation and translation (Keynes's *General Theory* is notoriously difficult to read) of Keynes' key ideas and concepts in the domains of economic theory and government policy (Davis 1995: 1). This definition acknowledges the vital contribution of both economists (e.g. Alvin H. Hansen in the United States) and policy-makers in developing the Keynesian tradition. It also helps to separate the renewed proliferation of interest from the mid-1980s in Keynes's life and writings

and the interpretation of his thought per se. For examples of these later trends see Moggridge (1992) and Skidelsky (1983; 1992).

2 The point here is that White is both influenced by the Keynesian 'revolution' and part of it, in particular, in the revolution in government policy, as opposed to the revolution in economic theory. In 1935 when White travelled to England, he was in his second year in Treasury and already concerned about restoration of international monetary stability. He met with Keynes and other contemporaries with similar concerns (Boughton 1998). On the recruitment of Keynesians in the US administration more generally see Ikenberry (1992: 300–301).

3 The statement on adjustment implies a commitment to adjustment for surplus as well as deficit countries, which was a dispute that Keynes lost with the United States in relation to the IMF.

4 Australia, for example, formed a group in 1953 with the Union of South Africa that Vietnam joined in 1957 and New Zealand joined in 1965. In 1971, the group was (not surprisingly) without Vietnam. In 2003, Australia has an Executive Director on the Bank via voting with New Zealand, Cambodia, Republic of Korea, Mongolia, Palau and seven Pacific Island nations. The Australian Director and Korean alternate have a voting power of 3.45 per cent.

3 From Savannah to structural adjustment

1 In his doctoral dissertation utilising recently opened US and Soviet archival sources, Bruce Craig concluded that White was not a formal spy but did 'hold some special status within the hierarchy of Soviet intelligence'. His clear commitments to US hegemony in the decision-making of the Bretton Woods institutions confirms the view of Craig that White did 'not seek to harm U.S. interests but sought only to advance Soviet/American cooperation … and thereby bolster the cause of world peace'. This contrasts to the frequent simplistic presentations of White as a communist traitor (Craig 1999: iii).

2 For a general discussion of Keynes's view of the Savannah meeting see Harrod (1966: 629–40).

3 Further, national accounts do not include illegal activities or leisure as productive activities yet they do include the military, the police and private security services. The dominance of neoclassical economics led to the 'classical distinction between production and non-production activities [being] displaced by the notion that all socially necessary activities, other than personal consumption, resulted in a product' (Shaikh and Tonak 1994: 2–3).

4 The negative pledge is a commitment by borrowers that prohibits the establishment of a priority for other debts over debts due to IBRD. It ensures the IBRD proportionally shares in security created in favour of other creditors.

5 The Articles of Agreement refer to balance of payments constraints on overseas borrowing as the condition for access to IDA funds but relative poverty, as measured by per capita income, has been the main criteria (Kapur *et al.* 1997: 194).

6 Notably, 60 per cent of IDA commitments from its formation until June 1971 went to India and Pakistan, and overall one-third of Bank Group lending in 1960s went to them (Mason and Asher 1973: 401).

7 1970 was the first year of net negative transfers overall for the Bank, although some countries had net negative years earlier (Rich 1994: 80). Woods was personally concerned about issues of debt and development outcomes; he called for a review of these issues, which led to the creation of the influential Pearson Commission. The Commission, reporting in 1969, called the then debt situation 'explosive' (Caufield 1998: 89).

8 McNamara said in 1962 that 'running the Department of Defense is not different from running Ford Motor Company or the Catholic Church, for that matter, Once you get to a certain scale, it's all the same' (Shapley 1993: 515).

9 Both the Bank and its staff are renowned for their beliefs in their own capacity, often seen as verging on arrogance. The actual and presumed 'superiority' over borrowing country capacity is clearly demonstrated by a comment in 1989 from one of the then Vice Presidents, William Cosgrove, that 'borrowers may now be more skilled than Bank staff' (cited in Caufield 1998: 214).
10 On the links between Hayekian thought at the World Bank's post-Washington Consensus development discourse see Crawford (2006: 127–35).
11 On the role of US think-tank see George (1997). On the role of the press see Toye (1993: 93–94).

4 From Washington to post-Washington Consensus

1 On the dominance of economists in regional departments see Berkman (2008: 26–27). On the dominance of US academia, Ritzen (2005: 111) notes that in the Bank's 2001 promotions round to the level just below senior management 'virtually all persons who were promoted had a PhD from an American university'.
2 See also (Kapur *et al.* 1997: 513–18; Toussaint 1999: 141–50). For good evaluations of the Washington Consensus policies see *inter alia* (Rapley 2002: 66–93; Toye 1993).
3 This is in contrast to how the oil shocks, via the recycling of petrodollars and the creation of new donor countries, undermined the Bank's influence, especially over middle-income countries (Kapur *et al.* 1997: 475).
4 The Bank had, virtually since its inception, included macroeconomic policy concerns in its project loans to countries. However, its real influence was often limited and its interests in policy conditionality actually declined in the 1950s in favour of a focus on projects before increasing again from the mid-1960s and substantially from the mid-1970s (Kapur *et al.* 1997, Chapters 9 and 10; Mason and Asher 1973, Chapter 6).
5 For a good overview and analysis of the successes and failures of Washington Consensus policies see Rapley (2002: 73–110).
6 The discussion here of NIE is limited to those aspects that appear to have most impacted the World Bank. It has a broader research agenda including interest in property rights, public choice, quantitative economic history and cognition. On the early impact of NGOs on the Bank see Nelson (1995).
7 While Wolfensohn's views were broadly in line with those of the Administration, his appointment was the result of a large and intensive personal campaign detailed in Mallaby (2004: 70–83).
8 1998 and 1999 were very big years for Bank lending ($28.5 and $26.2 billion) and adjustment lending accounted for over 52 per cent of lending commitments. In 2000, lending declined to $15.3 billion and then steadily grew to $22.3 billion in 2005. Adjustment lending has generally been in the $5–6 billion range, accounting for around 30 per cent of lending. 2002 was an exception as adjustment lending jumped back up to just over 50 per cent of new commitments (World Bank 2003r: 36, 2006b: i).
9 Stiglitz involved the Bank in SAPRI. For information on the network see Structural Adjustment Participatory Review Initiative Network. For a review of its final report and an analysis of the Bank's late withdrawal see IDEAs (2004).
10 The original site was www.worldbank.org/poverty/scapital, access date July 2004. It has since been downgraded to a topic under the Bank's PovertyNet site.
11 Even the social scientist who promoted social capital in the Bank acknowledge its 'severe limitations in practice' (Harriss 2007: 163).
12 Note that most the comparisons in the press release are on the basis of percentage of average income per capita required to meet the costs of, for example, establishing a business. While absolute comparisons would also be misleading, it is bizarre to

suggest that basic legal, environmental and other arrangements required for establishing other than the simplest of businesses (while protecting the public good) can be achieved in a developing country for the equivalent of 8 per cent of average national income, where that income is often less than US$1,000 per annum.

5 Introduction to Part II

1 The OECD Development Assistance Committee defines ODA as 'Grants or Loans to … (developing countries) which are: (a) undertaken by the official sector; (b) with promotion of economic development and welfare as the main objective; (c) at concessional financial terms [if a loan, having a Grant Element of at least 25 per cent]. In addition to financial flows, Technical Co-operation is included in aid. Grants, Loans and credits for military purposes are excluded. Developing countries (Part I) are defined by the DAC every three years, countries in transition (Part II) are classified as receiving Official Aid (OA) not ODA. Credits from the IDA are generally concessional enough to be regarded as ODA. Other funds from donor countries or multilateral agencies that do not meet this definition are classified as: Other Official Flows (OOF). IBRD loans and IMF loans are generally included in this category as their grant element is less than 25 per cent. Funds for commercial purposes or designed to facilitate exports are also regarded as OOF (OECD Development Assistance Committee 2005).

2 From author's survey of active portfolios in July 2004, undertaking using the World Bank's projects database, available online.

6 Vietnam: an overview

1 For an account of how provincial government operates see the interesting study of Ho Chi Minh City by Gainsborough (2003)

2 Kolko noted that the IMF remained engaged with Vietnam after the war and made loans from its Trust Fund (later the Structural Adjustment Facility) in 1976 and 1978. The conditions on these loans (which Vietnam needed for debt repayments) were, he argued, a significant influence on *Doi Moi* as was the IMF's refusal to provide further loans in 1985. He concluded that *Doi Moi* indicates a full acceptance of IMF structural adjustment (Kolko 1997: 32–33).

3 While I do not engage directly with these debates, it is important to acknowledge that this work is informed more by the critical position than the neoliberal one.

4 Kolko (1997: 34) is one of the few analysts who give adequate weight to the economic impact of the American war and the engagement with Cambodia in understanding the crisis in 1986.

5 The term 'post-conditionality' is from Griffin (2006).

6 The OED report blames this on lack of interest from the facilitators and 'the absence of systematic effort on the part of the IMF to encourage public discussion'. Given that it was the Bank who organised the participatory processes, this is an odd claim in an otherwise very frank assessment of the PRSP process.

7 World Bank lending in Vietnam

1 Vietnam received a small number of grants of under $10 million, mainly under the auspices of the Global Environment Fund. Given the focus is on loans these were excluded from the case study.

2 Between 1990 and 1999, analytical work accounted for 26 per cent of Bank work in Vietnam on lending, supervision and analysis. This compares to a Bank-wide average of 18 per cent (World Bank 2001i: 11–12).

3 Examples of trust fund activity include $810,000 from the Policy and Human Resources Development Fund for the Rural Energy project in 2002 and two grants

from the Global Environment Fund for the System Efficiency Improvement, Equitization and Renewables Project, one in 2001 for $350,000 and in 2002 for $4.97 million.

4 This is standard Bank policy and, in Asia, has already resulted in a number of electricity boards facing 'financial ruin as a result of unpredicted falls in the value of their currencies in the 1990s, after signing up to a number of private power generation projects' (Bayliss and Hall 2002: 4). In Vietnam, current currency controls reduce, but do not eliminate, such exchange rate risks.

5 Note the Japanese presence here – not surprising since the Japan Bank for International Cooperation also provided considerable funds for the construction of power plants to EVN, which were constructed by Japanese companies.

6 Moreover, Bank reports acknowledged that there is a lack of evidence to demonstrate a strong link between RE and economic growth or poverty reduction amongst the rural poor, indeed a number of studies have show a negative or neutral impacts. Various Bank evaluations are summarised in Songco (2002: 1–9).

7 Component C of the project to improve hazardous road sections was cancelled by the Bank as the GoV wanted to undertake the work itself rather than contract it out. Bank loans are simply not flexible enough to allow a $1.1 million (of a $195.6 million programme) safety component to be other than out-sourced regardless of safety and efficiency gains.

8 The summary of donor activity in Vietnam highlighted that transport, especially roads, has been a major area of activity for the big three providers of ODA: Japan, the World Bank and the ADB. Australia and other bilateral providers of ODA have also funded roads and bridges. Taylor noted that donors possess 'resounding unanimity as to the beneficial impacts of roads' and this has resulted in 'swift and spectacular' action (Taylor 2004: 242).

9 Total project costs were $74.63 million of which $9.0 million was a Global Environment Fund grant and $39.5 million a Bank investment loan. Of the loan funds, $38.02 million was allocated to component two of the project that covers plantation establishment, extension, land-use certification and microfinance. Figures on the relative allocation to each component of Bank loan funds were not available; however, total planned expenditure for microfinance was $38.55 million (World Bank 2004j).

10 This includes the 51 per cent of the Agriculture Rehabilitation Credit that was microfinance in the Finance sector; if the whole amount of this credit is included then microfinance only accounted for 80 per cent of lending.

11 These figures exclude three loans from early in the first case study period for which the documentation containing conditions is not available. Calculations of the number of conditions counted the various sub-conditions as separate conditions, for example condition (b) sub-conditions i–v were counted as five conditions.

12 This low rate is surprising because most microfinance schemes target women and their key (if questionable) argument is that microfinance empowers women. One academic study found that some of the strongest evidence supporting the pro-poor argument for microfinance comes from projects that target women in Asia (Weiss *et al.* 2005: 259). For a critical perspective on women's control of microfinance and microfinance organisations see Fernando (1997: 155–56).

13 One report stated that the project needed restructuring as it obliged the Ministry of Education and Training 'to spread itself thin and imposed a significant burden on its institutional capacity to implement the project' (World Bank 2003b: 3). Despite many different problems outlined in the report, the Bank rated the project outcome and its own performance as satisfactory! The Staff Appraisal Report for the Regional Blood Transfusion Centres Project noted that Bank projects in the health and education sectors 'had long implementation difficulties' though it was less direct about the reasons stating merely that the difficulties were broadly due to problems with institutional readiness (World Bank 2002b: 14).

14 The number of pages devoted to procurement in Staff Appraisal Reports increases from two to three pages on average in the first case study period to 12–16 pages in the second case study period.

8 Indonesia: an overview

1 A key exception was Indonesia's oil industry, where through Ibnu Soetowo, Director of the state-owned Pertamina, Suharto had access to high levels of off-budget funding.
2 For a good description of the impact of the development programme across parts of the archipelago see (Vickers 2005: 188–96).
3 Data sources: GDP growth from United Nations Common Database, Gini ratio 1971–93 from Hill (2000: 197) and Gini ratio 1993–2002 from (BPS-Statistics Indonesia *et al.* 2004).
4 A key exception being the Bre-X gold mine scam (Vickers 2005: 202–3).
5 ODA excludes IMF loans. If these are added in the aid to GDP ratio increases to around 10 per cent of GDP in 1998. ODA was also the major source of development expenditure, accounting for over 80 per cent during 1998 – up from just over 30 per cent in the previous year (Chowdhury and Sugema 2005: 189–91).
6 Kapur *et al.*'s two-volume official history of the Bank only devoted around 12 pages to Indonesia, plus a few other short references, and said nothing of the relationship through the 1980s and 1990s. The volumes were published in 1997, thus it is difficult to tell whether the quietness on Indonesia is because they presumed the relationship to be rather unproblematic or whether the problems were already clear and perhaps too sensitive to deal with.
7 Indonesia took over as chair of the CGI in 2005 after the International NGO Forum on Indonesian Development pointed out that the Bank being chair was an anachronism in the supposed age of country ownership of its development programme. They argued that only with Indonesia itself as chair would the country 'be able to make their own choices about the type and model of development that would be adopted. And this would mean that Indonesia could be fully responsible for its implementation and for the loans it borrows' (International NGO Forum on Indonesia Development 2004: 10).
8 The chart utilises World Bank sectoral classifications except for transmigration, which is included as a separate category. Older projects were classified under a different system, which was quite similar so most projects could be easily shifted to current classifications. For example, the old system separated electricity from oil and gas and mining, whereas now there is an energy and mining classification. Some projects required more analysis; for example, there was an urban development category but of these most projects from this were transferred to water, sanitation and flood protection as this was the major activity.
9 On the way the Bank largely withdrew from the finance and banking sector after some critical reports on projects see World Bank (1999a: 20). On the 'Bank's tendency to understate its own leverage over the Indonesian government' particularly regarding problematic projects see Whitelum (2003: 282).

9 World Bank lending in Indonesia

1 The total amount cancelled between 1998 and 2000 was over $1.6 billion (World Bank 2001a: 14).
2 Between 1976 and 1989, the World Bank approved $630 million (disbursed = $500 million) to support transmigration. This part-financed the official resettlement of over 2.3 million people, which then prompted the spontaneous resettlement of a further 2 million people. The Bank's loans were a catalyst for funding from other bilateral and multilateral donors. In 1987, the Bank decided against new funding

for projects but in 1992, it began support for second-stage transmigration projects (Rich 1994: 34–38).

3 The average cost of moving a family under the programme was $7,000 (Adhiati and Bobsien 2001: 2). Yet a World Bank review found that 50 per cent of transmigrants were living below the poverty line and 20 per cent below subsistence (Rich 1994: 36–37).

4 Having said that, the project evaluation was indicated the project was well received and largely free of conflict (Thorburn 2004: 35). The good outcomes were undoubtedly assisted by the geographical focus on Java, where there are relatively few conflicts regarding indigenous land.

5 The matching grant component was run by a subcontractor at a cost of $826,007, in order to hand out $516,450 in subsidies to SME! Despite all the problems the Bank evaluated its own performance as satisfactory (World Bank 2005g: 10–15).

6 Interestingly this report also claims that the Asian Financial Crisis and the associated upheaval in Indonesia did not impact project implementation (World Bank 2005b: 10) However, only $14.63 million of the planned $16.4 million was disbursed and there were two partial loan cancellations.

7 KDP claims a better targeting system than VIP but it maintains the requirement to fund clusters of poor villages to reduce costs for facilitation and support, see World Bank (1998b: 4–6). On VIP targeting see World Bank (1996c: 3).

8 For an insider's account see Bebbington *et al.* (2004) and the recent edited book including a number of insider's accounts, which was reviewed by Harriss (2007).

9 These are Semarang-Surakarta, Kalimantan, East Java and Bali (World Bank 1994h).

10 Reports are available for Kalimantan, Sulawesi and Bali. The report on the Kalimantan UDP referred to an implementation completion report for the Semarang-Surakarta UDP but it is not available on the Bank website (World Bank 2003d)

11 A third UPP was approved by the Bank in May 2005 and additional funding of $135.5 million for UPP 2 was approved in May 2007.

12 Further, most of the railway project conditions are multipart (World Bank 1996b: 52–54).

13 The Java project was very complex with multiple components, each with a number of sub-components. It operated in multiple provinces and *kabupatens*. It did not heed the Bank's own warnings about the problems of complex loans (World Bank 2004f: 18). The multiple components seem to be the product of the Bank's need for scale in lending. Use of an adaptable programme loan provided 11 years for implementation. Most projects in the second case study period again had standard Bank four or five year project cycles; nevertheless, they maintained complex, multicomponent programme designs.

10 Conclusion

1 Rice trade liberalisation is sold as pro-poor because it is assumed that trade barriers increase the price of rice and that this hurts the poor (World Bank 2001a: 21). Once again neoliberal economic theory is presented as fact – there is no reference to analytical work to actually demonstrate this in practice. Given the number of times such broad Bank claims regarding the impact of protectionism on prices have not be empirically the case, this is a good demonstration of how neoliberalism has become 'common sense' in the Bank.

2 Interestingly, there is little information available in either the academic or Bank literature with regards to trends in the Bank's use of informal conditionality such as supplementary letters and oral agreements, which was a key avenue of conditionality in the 1980s (Woods 2006: 70).

3 It is interesting too that despite being derived from an analysis of conditions in Indonesia, KDP has become a model for projects in Afghanistan, East Timor and Iraq.

Bibliography

Adhiati, M.A.S. and Bobsien, A. (2001) 'Indonesia's Transmigration Programme – an Update', Down to Earth, International Campaign for Ecological Justice in Indonesia. http//dte.gn.apc.org/ctrans.htm (accessed November 2005).

Akram-Lodhi, A.H. (2005) 'Vietnam's Agriculture: Processes of Rich Peasant Accumulation and Mechanisms of Social Differentiation', *Journal of Agrarian Change*, 5 (1): 73–116.

Amenga-Etego, R.N. and Grusky, S. (2005) 'The New Face of Conditionalities: The World Bank and Water Privatization in Ghana', in D.A. Mcdonald and G. Ruiters (eds) *The Age of Commodity: Water Privatization in Southern Africa*, London: Earthscan.

Anderson, P. (1976) 'The Antinomies of Antonio Gramsci', *New Left Review*, 100: 5–78.

Anon. (2004a) 'IMF Ceases Loans to Vietnam', *Vietnam News Brief Service*, 13 April.

—— (2004b) 'A Very Big French Turn-Off – Electricite De France', *The Economist*, 3 July, 372: 77.

—— (2008) 'Saying Sorry; That Greenspan put – finally in its place', *Financial Times*, 25 October.

Arrighi, G. (1993) 'The Three Hegemonies of Historical Capitalism', in S. Gill (ed.) *Gramsci, Historical Materialism and International Relations*, Cambridge: Cambridge University Press.

—— (1994) *The Long Twentieth Century: Money, Power, and the Origins of Our Times*, London: Verso.

Ascher, W. (1990) 'The World Bank and U.S. Control', in M.P. Karns and K.A. Mingst (eds) *The United States and Multilateral Institutions*, Boston: Unwin Hyman.

Asian Development Bank (2005) www.adb.org (accessed August 2005).

Aspinall, E., Feith, H. and Van Klinken, G. (eds) (1999) *The Last Days of President Suharto*, Clayton, Monash Asian Institute.

Augelli, E. and Murphy, C.N. (1993) 'Gramsci and International Relations: A General Perspective and Example from Recent US Policy Towards the Third World', in S. Gill (ed.) *Gramsci, Historical Materialism and International Relations*, Cambridge: Cambridge University Press.

Banerjee, A., Deaton, A., Lustig, N., Rogoff, K. and Hsu, E. (2006) 'An Evaluation of World Bank Research, 1998–2005', World Bank. http://econ.worldbank.org/WBSITE/EXTERNAL/EXTDEC/0,contentMDK:21165468~pagePK:64165401~piPK:64165026~theSitePK:469372,00.html (accessed May 2007).

Bates, R.H. (1981) *Markets and States in Tropical Africa*, Berkeley: University of California Press.

Bayliss, K. and Hall, D. (2002) 'Unsustainable Conditions – the World Bank, Privatisation, Water and Energy', Public Services International. www.psiru.org (accessed April 2005).

Bebbington, A., Guggenheim, S., Olson, E. and Woolcock, M. (2004) 'Exploring Social Capital Debates at the World Bank', *The Journal of Development Studies,* 40 (5): 33–64.

Beder, S. (2003) *Power Play: The Fight for Control of the World's Electricity*, Melbourne: Sage Publications.

Bello, W. (1994) *Dark Victory: The United States, Structural Adjustment, and Global Poverty*, London: Pluto.

Bello, W., Kinley, D. and Elinson, E. (1982) *Development Debacle: The World Bank in the Philippines*, San Francisco: Institute for Food and Development Policy and Philippine Solidarity Network.

Berger, M.T. (2004) *The Battle for Asia: From Decolonization to Globalization*, London and New York: RoutledgeCurzon.

Berger, M.T. and Beeson, M. (1998) 'Lineages of Liberalism and Miracles of Modernisation: The World Bank, the East Asian Trajectory and the International Development Debate', *Third World Quarterly,* 19 (3): 487–504.

Berkman, S. (2008) *The World Bank and the Gods of Lending*, Sterling VA: Kumarian Press.

Bhagwati, J.N. (1982) 'Directly Unproductive Profit-Seeking (DUP) Activities', *Journal of Political Economy,* 90 (5): 988–1002.

Bieler, A. and Morton, A.D. (2004) 'A Critical Theory Route to Hegemony, World Order and Historical Change: Neo-Gramscian Perspectives in International Relations', *Capital & Class,* 82: 85–113.

Block, F.L. (1977) *The Origins of International Economic Disorder: A Study of United States International Monetary Policy from World War II to the Present*, Berkeley: University of California Press.

Bogdanowicz-Bindert, C.A. (1986) 'The Debt Crisis: The Baker Plan Revisited', *Journal of Interamerican Studies and World Affairs,* 28 (3): 33–45.

Boughton, J.M. (1998) 'Harry Dexter White and the International Monetary Fund', *Finance & Development,* 35 (3): 39 – 41.

Boumans, M. (2005) *How Economists Model the World into Numbers*, London and New York: Routledge.

Bourchier, D. (2001) 'Conservative Political Ideology in Indonesia: A Fourth Wave?' in G. Lloyd and S. Smith (eds) *Indonesia Today: Challenges of History,* Lanham: Rowman &Littlefield Publishers Inc.

BPS-Statistics Indonesia, Bappenas and UNDP Indonesia (2004) 'National Human Development Report 2004, the Economics of Democracy: Financing Human Development in Indonesia', Indonesia: BPS-Statistics Indonesia, Bappenas and UNDP Indonesia.

Broad, R. (2004) 'The Washington Consensus Meets the Global Backlash: Shifting Debates and Policies', *Globalizations,* 1 (2): 129–54.

—— (2006) 'Research, Knowledge, and the Art of "Paradigm Maintenance": The World Bank's Development Economics Vice-Presidency (DEC)', *Review of International Political Economy,* 13 (3): 387–419.

Brunet-Jailly, J. (1999) 'Has the World Bank a Strategy on Health?' *International Social Science Journal,* 51 (161): 347–61.

Burgess, M. (1995) 'The World Bank – the East Asian Miracle', *Asian Studies Review,* 18 (3): 147–53.

Cairncross, A. (1988) 'The Development of Economic Statistics as an Influence on Theory and Policy', in D. Ironmonger, J.O.N. Perkins and T.V. Hoa (eds) *National Income and Economic Progress: Essays in Honour of Colin Clark,* London: Macmillan Press.

Cammack, P. (2002) 'Attacking the Poor', *New Left Review,* 13: 125–34.

—— (2003) *What the World Bank Means by Poverty Reduction. Staying Poor: Chronic Poverty and Development Policy.* Manchester: IDPM, University of Manchester.

Carroll, T. (2005) 'Efficiency of What and for Whom? The Theoretical Underpinnings of the Post-Washington Consensus' Socio-Institutional Neoliberalism', Working Paper No. 122, Perth: Asia Research Centre, Murdoch University, July.

—— (2006) 'The World Bank's Socio-Institutional Neoliberalism: A Case Study from Indonesia', Workshop on the World Bank, Lee Kwan Yew School of Public Policy, National University of Singapore, 18 September.

Caufield, C. (1998) *Masters of Illusion: The World Bank and the Poverty of Nations,* London: Macmillan.

Chang, H.-J. (2002) *Kicking Away the Ladder: Development Strategy in Historical Perspective,* London: Anthem Press.

Chang, H.-J., Palma, G. and Whittaker, D.H. (1998) 'The Asian Crisis: Introduction', *Cambridge Journal of Economics,* 22 (6): 649–52.

Chossudovsky, M. (1997) *The Globalisation of Poverty: Impacts of IMF and World Bank Reforms,* London: Zed Books.

Chowdhury, A. and Sugema, I. (2005) 'How Significant and Effective Has Foreign Aid to Indonesia Been?' *ASEAN Economic Bulletin,* 22 (2): 186–216.

Consultative Group Meeting for Vietnam (2004) *Moving Towards 2010: Vietnam Partnership Report,* Hanoi: Vietnam Development Information Center.

Cox, R.W. (1986) 'Social Forces, States and World Orders: Beyond International Relations Theory', in R. Keohane (ed.) *Neorealism and Its Critics,* New York: Columbia University Press.

—— (1996) 'Gramsci, Hegemony, and International Relations: An Essay in Method', in R.W. Cox and J.W. Sinclair (eds) *Approaches to World Order,* Cambridge: Cambridge University Press.

Craig, B. (1999) 'Treasonable Doubt: The Harry Dexter White Case, 1948–53', PhD thesis Washington DC: History, American University.

Crawford, G. (2006) 'The World Bank and Good Governance: Rethinking the State or Consolidating Neo-Liberalism?' in A. Paloni and M. Zanardi (eds) *The IMF, World Bank and Policy Reform,* Oxon: Routledge.

Crouzet, F. (2001) *A History of the European Economy, 1000–2000,* Charlottesville: University Press of Virginia.

Davis, J.B. (1995) 'Introduction: The Interpretation of Keynes's Work', in J.B. Davis (ed.) *The State of Interpretation of Keynes,* Boston: Kluwer Academic Publishers.

De Vylder, S. (1995) 'State and Market in Vietnam: Some Issues for an Economy in Transition', in I. Nørlund, C.L. Gates and V.C. Dam (eds) *Vietnam in a Changing World,* Surrey: Curzon Press Ltd, Nordic Institute of Asian Studies.

Duc, T. (2004) 'Repayment of ODA', *Thoi bao Kinh te Viet Nam,* 27 June: 46–48.

Duong, P.B. and Izumida, Y. (2002) 'Rural Development Finance in Vietnam: A Microeconometric Analysis of Household Surveys', *World Development,* 30 (2): 319–35.

Easterly, W. (2001) *The Lost Decades: Developing Countries' Stagnation in Spite of Policy Reform 1980–1998*, Washington: The World Bank.

Eklof, S. (1999) *Indonesian Politics in Crisis: The Long Fall of Suharto, 1996–98*, Copenhagen: Nordic Institute of Asian Studies.

Evans, M. (2004) Embedding Market Reform through Statecraft – the Case of Equitization in Vietnam. Workshop on Equitisation in Vietnam. Institute of Social Science, Ho Chi Minh City.

Fang, K. (2006) 'Designing and Implementing a Community-Driven Development Programme in Indonesia', *Development in Practice,* 16 (1): 74–79.

Fealy, G. (2001) 'Parties and Parliaments: Serving Whose Interests?' in G. Lloyd and S. Smith (eds) *Indonesia Today: Challenges of History,* Lanham: Rowman & Littlefield Publishers.

Fernando, J.L. (1997) 'Nongovernmental Organizations, Micro-Credit, and Empowerment of Women', *The Annals of the American Academy of Political and Social Science,* 554: 150–73.

Fforde, A. (2004) 'Vietnam in 2003: The Road to Ungovernability?' *Asian Survey,* 44 (1): 121–29.

Fine, B. (2001a) 'The Social Capital of the World Bank', in B. Fine, C. Lapavitsas and J. Pincus (eds) *Development Policy in the Twenty-First Century: Beyond the Post-Washington Consensus,* London: Routledge.

—— (2001b) *Social Capital Versus Social Theory: Political Economy and Social Science at the Turn of the Millennium*, London: Routledge.

—— (2005) 'The New Development Economics', in K.S. Jomo and B. Fine (eds) *The New Development Economics: After the Washington Consensus,* New Delhi: Tulika Books.

Freeman, N. (1993) 'Vietnam: The Siege Ends', *New Statesman & Society*, 16 July, 6: 10–11.

Gainsborough, M. (2003) *Changing Political Economy of Vietnam: The Case of Ho Chi Minh City*, London: Routledge.

Galbraith, J.K. (1975) 'How Keynes Came to America', in M. Keynes (ed.) *Essays on John Maynard Keynes,* Cambridge: Cambridge University Press.

—— (1977) *The Age of Uncertainty*, London: British Broadcasting Company.

Gardner, R.N. (1980) *Sterling-Dollar Diplomacy in Current Perspective: The Origins and the Prospects of Our International Economic Order*, 3rd edn, New York: Columbia University Press.

Gee, J.M.A. (1991) 'The Neoclassical School', in D. Mair and A.G. Miller (eds) *A Modern Guide to Economic Thought: An Introduction to Comparative Schools of Thought in Economics,* Aldershot: Edward Elgar.

George, S. (1997) 'How to Win the War of Ideas: Lessons from the Gramscian Right', *Dissent,* 44 (3): 47–53.

George, S. and Sabelli, F. (1994) *Faith and Credit: The World Bank's Secular Empire*, London: Penguin Books.

Germain, R.D. and Kenny, M. (1998) 'Engaging Gramsci: International Relations Theory and the New Gramscians', *Review of International Studies,* 24 (1): 3–21.

Gibbons, D., Quiñones, B., Remenyi, J. and Seibel, D.H. (2000) 'Microfinance for and by the Poor: Lessons from Experience', in J. Remenyi and B. Quiñones (eds) *Microfinance and Poverty Alleviation: Case Studies from Asia and the Pacific,* London: Pinter.

Gill, S. and Law, D. (1993) 'Global Hegemony and the Structural Power of Capital', in S. Gill (ed.) *Gramsci, Historical Materialism and International Relations,* Cambridge: Cambridge University Press.

Gosovic, B. (2000) 'Global Intellectual Hegemony and the International Development Agenda', *International Social Science Journal,* 52 (166): 447–56.

Gowan, P. (1999) *The Global Gamble: Washington's Faustian Bid for World Dominance,* London: Verso.

—— (2003) 'US: UN', *New Left Review,* 24: 5–28.

Gramsci, A. (1971) *Selections from the Prison Notebooks of Antonio Gramsci,* London: Lawrence and Wishart.

—— (1995) *Further Selections from the Prison Notebooks,* London: Lawrence and Wishart.

—— (1996) *Prison Notebooks,* New York: Columbia University Press.

Gray, P.D. (2005) 'Interview', Senior Energy Economist, World Bank, Hanoi, Vietnam, 12 April.

Griffin, P. (2006) 'The World Bank', *New Political Economy,* 11 (4): 571–81.

Groom, A.J.R. (2000) 'Getting to "Go": The Birth of the United Nations System', in P. Taylor and A.J.R. Groom (eds) *The United Nations at the Millennium: The Principal Organs,* London and New York: Continuum.

Gwin, C. (1997) 'U.S. Relations with the World Bank, 1945–92', in D. Kapur, J.P. Lewis and R. Webb (eds) *The World Bank Its First Half Century, Volume 2: Perspectives,* Washington DC: Brookings Institution Press.

Hadad, O.N. (2005) 'Indonesia's Water Resources Policy: Effects of Globalization and World Bank Policy', *Jurnal Konstitusi,* 2 (2): 45–85.

Hadiz, V.R. (2004) 'Decentralization and Democracy in Indonesia: A Critique of Neo-Institutionalist Perspectives', *Development and Change,* 35 (4): 697–718.

Haggard, S. (2000) *The Political Economy of the Asian Financial Crisis,* Washington DC: Institute for International Economics.

Hai, B.D. (2003) *New Focus on Redundant Workers,* Ho Chi Minh City: Institute of Social Sciences.

Hamilton-Hart, N. (2006) 'Consultants in the Indonesian State: Modes of Influence and Institutional Implications', *New Political Economy,* 11 (2): 251–70.

Harrison, G. (2004) *The World Bank and Africa: The Construction of Governance States,* London: Routledge.

Harriss, J. (2007) 'Book Review: Anthony Bebbington, Michael Woolcock, Scott E. Guggenheim and Elizabeth A. Olson (eds) *The Search for Empowerment: Social Capital as Idea and Practice at the World Bank*', *Development in Practice,* 17 (1): 162–64.

Harrod, R.F. (1966) *The Life of John Maynard Keynes,* 1st edn, London: Macmillan.

Harvie, C. (2000) 'The Financial Crisis in Indonesia: The Role of Good Governance', in T.V. Hoa and C. Harvie (eds) *The Causes and Impact of the Asian Financial Crisis,* Houndmills: Macmillan Press Ltd.

Hassan, M.K. (2002) 'The Microfinance Revolution and the Grameen Bank Experience in Bangladesh', *Financial Markets Institutions and Instruments,* 11 (3): 205–65.

Hermes, N. and Lensink, R. (2001) 'Changing the Conditions for Development Aid: A New Paradigm?' *Journal of Development Studies,* 37 (6): 1–9.

Hettne, B. (1982) *Development Theory and the Third World,* Helsingborg: Schmidts Boktryckeri AB.

Hill, H. (2000) *The Indonesian Economy,* 2nd edn, Cambridge: Cambridge University Press.

Hobsbawm, E. (1999) *Age of Extremes: The Short Twentieth Century 1914–1991,* London: Abacus.

Höông B, N.L. (2004) Labour's Mastery through Owning of Shares. Workshop on Equitisation in Vietnam. Institute of Social Science, Ho Chi Minh City.

Howson, R. (2006) *Challenging Hegemonic Masculinity*, London, New York: Routledge.

Hung, H.X. (2005) 'Equitization of State-Owned Enterprises in Vietnam: Results, Obstacles, and Solutions', *Vietnam Economic Review,* 1: 30–35.

Hunt, E.K. (2002) *History of Economic Thought: A Critical Perspective*, 2nd edn, New York: M.E. Sharpe.

Ikenberry, G.J. (1992) 'A World Economy Restored: Expert Consensus and the Anglo-American Postwar Settlement', *International Organization,* 46 (1): 289–321.

International Monetary Fund (IMF) (2005) 'Website', www.imf.org (accessed November 2005).

International Development Economics Associates (IDEAs) (2004) 'The World Bank Engages Its Critics, and Backs Off, Book Review: SAPRIN (2004). Structural Adjustment: The SAPRIN Report, the Policy Roots of Economic Crisis, Poverty and Inequality. Zed Books London', www.networkideas.org (accessed June 2004).

International NGO Forum on Indonesia Development (2004) 'Overview of the Process and Substance of Indonesia's PRSP', www.infid.de (accessed November 2005).

Ironmonger, D. (1988) 'Statistical Perspectives and Economic Stability', in D. Ironmonger, J.O.N. Perkins and T.V. Hoa (eds) *National Income and Economic Progress: Essays in Honour of Colin Clark,* London: Macmillan Press.

Islam, I. and Chowdhury, A. (2000) *The Political Economy of East Asia: Post Crisis Debates*, Oxford: Oxford University Press.

James, H. and James, M. (1994) 'The Origins of the Cold War: Some New Documents', *The Historical Journal,* 37 (3): 615–22.

Joint Donor Report to the Vietnam Consultative Group Meeting (2003) 'Vietnam Development Report 2004: Poverty', www.vdic.org.vn (accessed June 2004).

Kapoor, I. (2005) 'Participatory Development, Complicity and Desire', *Third World Quarterly,* 26 (8): 1203–20.

Kapur, D., Lewis, J.P. and Webb, R. (1997) *The World Bank Its First Half Century, Volume 1: History*, Washington DC: Brookings Institution Press.

Kaufman, B.E. (2007) 'The Institutional Economics of John R. Commons: Complement and Substitute for Neoclassical Economic Theory', *Socio-Economic Review,* 2: 3–45.

Kennedy, P. (1989) *The Rise and Fall of the Great Powers: Economic Change and Military Conflict from 1500 to 2000*, New York: Vintage Books.

Kerkvliet, B.J.T. (1998) 'Land Regimes and State Strengths and Weaknesses in the Philippines and Vietnam', in P. Dauvergne (ed.) *Weak and Strong States in Asia-Pacific Societies,* St Leonards: Allen &Unwin.

Keynes, J.M (1936/1973) *The General Theory of Employment, Interest and Money*, London: Macmillan for the Royal Economic Society.

Kingsbury, D. (2005) *The Politics of Indonesia*, 3rd edn, Oxford: Oxford University Press.

Kolko, G. (1997) *Vietnam: Anatomy of a Peace*, London: Routledge.

Krueger, A.O. (1974) 'The Political Economy of the Rent-Seeking Society', *American Economic Review,* 64: 291–303.

Laurell, A.C. and Arellano, O.L. (2002) 'Market Commodities and Poor Relief: The World Bank Proposal for Health', in V. Navarro (ed.) *The Political Economy of Social Inequities: Consequences for Health and Quality of Life,* Amityville: Baywood Publishing Company Inc.

Lears, T.J.J. (1985) 'The Concept of Cultural Hegemony: Problems and Possibilities', *The American Historical Review,* 90 (3): 567–93.

Lee, K., Lin, J.Y. and Chang, H.-J. (2005) 'Late Marketisation Versus Late Industrialisation in East Asia', *Asian-Pacific Economic Literature,* 19 (1): 42–59.

Leech, D. and Leech, R. (2006) 'Voting Power in the Bretton Woods Institutions', in A. Paloni and M. Zanardi (eds) *The IMF, World Bank and Policy Reform,* London: Routledge.

Li, T. (2005) 'Government through Community: The World Bank in Indonesia', Invited Paper for the Hauser Colloquium: Globalization and Its Discontents, New York University School of Law, October 18.

Little, I., Scitovsky, T. and Scott, M. (1970) *Industry and Trade in Some Developing Countries: A Comparative Study*, London: Oxford University Press for the Development Centre of the OECD.

Love, J. (1991) 'The Orthodox Keynesian School', in D. Mair and A.G. Miller (eds) *A Modern Guide to Economic Thought: An Introduction to Comparative Schools of Thought in Economics,* Aldershot: Edward Elgar.

Macintyre, A. (1990) *Business and Politics in Indonesia*, North Sydney: Asian Studies Association of Australia in association with Allen &Unwin.

Mallaby, S. (2004) *The World's Banker: A Story of Failed States, Financial Crises, and the Wealth and Poverty of Nations*, New York: The Penguin Press.

Masina, P.P. (2006) *Vietnam's Development Strategies*, London: Routledge.

Mason, E.S. and Asher, R.E. (1973) *The World Bank since Bretton Woods*, Washington, DC: The Brookings Institution.

McCarty, A. (2001) Governance Institutions and Incentive Structures in Vietnam. *Building Institutional Capacity in Asia.* Jakarta.

McIntosh, A.C. (2003) *Asian Water Supplies: Reaching the Urban Poor,* London: Asian Development Bank and International Water Association.

Meade, J. (1975) 'The Keynesian Revolution', in M. Keynes (ed.) *Essays on John Maynard Keynes,* Cambridge: Cambridge University Press.

Moggridge, D.E. (1992) *Maynard Keynes, an Economist's Biography*, London: Routledge.

Morton, A.D. (2003) 'Historicizing Gramsci: Situating Ideas in and Beyond Their Context', *Review of International Political Economy,* 10 (1): 118–46.

Morton, D.A. (1999) 'On Gramsci', *Politics,* 19 (1): 1–8.

Motoyama, H. and Widagdo, N. (1999) 'Power Sector Restructuring in Indonesia: A Preliminary Study for Advocacy Purposes', Bank Information Centre USA. http://bicusa.org (accessed May 2006).

Nelson, P.J. (1995) *The World Bank and Non-Governmental Organizations: The Limits of Apolitical Development*, Houndmills: Macmillan.

Nguyen, D.T. (2001) 'Social Welfare Aspects of Development in a Transition Economy: Application to Vietnam', Doctor of Philosophy Wollongong: Department of Economics, University of Wollongong.

Nielson, D.L., Tierney, M.J. and Weaver, C. (2006) 'Bridging the Rationalist-Constructivist Divide: Re-Engineering the Culture of the World Bank', *Journal of International Relations and Development,* 9: 107–39.

Nørlund, I. (2001) 'Vietnam – a Country View of the Partnership Process', Paper supplied to the author, July.

Nørlund, I., Ca, T.N. and Tuyen, N.D. (2003) 'Dealing with the Donors: The Politics of Vietnam's Comprehensive Poverty Reduction and Growth Strategy', Policy Papers 4/2003, Helsinki: Institute of Development Studies, University of Helsinki.

North, D.C. (1998) 'The New Institutional Economics and Third World Development', in J. Harriss, J. Hunter and C.M. Lewis (eds) *The New Institutional Economics and Third World Development,* London: Routledge.

OECD Development Assistance Committee (2005) 'International Development Statistics Online', www.oecd.org/dac (accessed August 2005).

Oliver, R.W. (1971) *Early Plans for a World Bank*, Princeton: Department of Economics, Princeton University.

Olken, B.A. (2005) 'Monitoring Corruption: Evidence from a Field Experiment in Indonesia', National Bureau of Economic Research Working Paper No. 11753. http://papers.nber.org/papers/w11753 (accessed April 2006).

Painter, M. (2003) 'The Politics of Economic Restructuring in Vietnam: The Case of State-Owned Enterprise "Reform"', *Contemporary Southeast Asia,* 25 (1): 20–43.

—— (2005) 'The Politics of State Sector Reforms in Vietnam: Contested Agendas and Uncertain Trajectories', *The Journal of Development Studies,* 41 (2): 261–83.

Panos Institute (2002) 'Reducing Poverty: Is the World Bank's Strategy Working?' www.panos.org.uk (accessed March 2005).

Patnaik, P. (1999) 'The Political Economy of Structural Adjustment: A Note', in M. Rao (ed.) *Disinvesting in Health: The World Bank's Prescriptions for Health,* New Delhi: Sage.

Payne, D. (2005) 'Interview', Co-Director, VUFO-NGO Resource Centre, Hanoi, Vietnam, 12 April 2005.

Pearce, K.A. and Hoover, K., D. (1995) 'After the Revolution: Paul Samuelson and the Textbook Keynesian Revolution', in A.F. Cottrell and M.S. Lawlor (eds) *History of Political Economy: Annual Supplement to Volume 27,* Durham: Duke University Press.

Peet, R. (2003) *Unholy Trinity: The IMF, World Bank and WTO*, London: Zed Books.

Pincus, J. (2001) 'The Post-Washington Consensus and Lending Operations in Agriculture: New Rhetoric and Old Operational Realities', in B. Fine, C. Lapavitsas and J. Pincus (eds) *Development Policy in the Twenty-First Century: Beyond the Post-Washington Consensus,* London: Routledge.

Pincus, J. and Ramli, R. (1988) 'Indonesia: From Showcase to Basket Case', *Cambridge Journal of Economics,* 22 (6): 723–34.

Porter, D. and Craig, D. (2004) 'The Third Way and the Third World: Poverty Reduction and Social Inclusion in the Rise of "Inclusive" Liberalism', *Review of International Political Economy,* 11 (2): 387–423.

Poverty Working Group/World Bank (1999), *Vietnam Development Report 2000: Attacking Poverty.* Report. No. 19914 November 15.

Puiggrós, A. (2002) 'World Bank Education Policy: Market Liberalism Meets Ideological Conservatism', in V. Navarro (ed.) *The Political Economy of Social Inequities: Consequences for Health and Quality of Life,* Amityville: Baywood Publishing Company Inc.

Ranis, G. (1997) 'The World Bank near the Turn of the Century', in R. Culpeper, A. Berry and F. Stewart (eds) *Global Development Fifty Years after Bretton Woods: Essays in Honour of Gerald K. Helleiner,* London: North South Institute/Macmillan Press.

Rapley, J. (2002) *Understanding Development: Theory and Practice in the Third World,* Boulder: Lynne Reinner Publishers Inc.

Rich, B. (1994) *Mortgaging the Earth: The World Bank, Environmental Impoverishment, and the Crisis of Development*, Boston: Beacon Press.

Rieffel, L. (2004) 'Indonesia's Quiet Revolution', *Foreign Affairs,* 83 (5): 98–103.

Rist, G. (1997) *The History of Development: From Western Origins to Global Faith*, London: Zed Books.

Ritzen, J. (2005) *A Chance for the World Bank*, London: Anthem Press.

Robinson, J. (1978) *Contributions to Modern Economics*, Oxford: Blackwell.

Robinson, M.S. (2001) *The Microfinance Revolution: Sustainable Finance for the Poor*, Washington DC: World Bank and the Open Society Institute.

Robison, R. (1993) 'Indonesia: Tensions in State and Regime', in K. Hewison, R. Robison and G. Rodan (eds) *Southeast Asia in the 1990s: Authoritarianism, Democracy and Capitalism*, St Leonards: Allen &Unwin.

Robison, R. and Hadiz, V.R. (2004) *Reorganising Power in Indonesia: The Politics of Oligarchy in an Age of Markets*, New York: RoutledgeCurzon.

Rohland, K. (2004) 'Recurring Themes', *Vietnam Economic Times*, November: 12–13.

Roll, E. (1973) *A History of Economic Thought*, 4th edn, London: Faber and Faber Ltd.

Rupert, M. (1998) '(Re-)Engaging Gramsci: A Response to Germain and Kenny', *Review of International Studies*, 24: 427–34.

Sam, T.T.M. and Hai, B.D. (2004) An Overview of the Most Crucial Period of Equitization in Vietnam. Workshop on Equitisation in Vietnam. Ho Chi Minh City, Institute of Social Sciences.

Sassoon, A.S. (2001) 'Globalisation, Hegemony and Passive Revolution', *New Political Economy*, 6 (1): 2001.

Scammell, W.M. (1983) *The International Economy since 1945*, 2nd edn, London: Macmillan Education Ltd.

Segall, M., Tipping, G., Lucas, H., et al. (2002) 'Economic Transition Should Come with a Health Warning: The Case of Vietnam', *Journal of Epidemiological Community Health*, 56: 497–505.

Shaikh, A.M. and Tonak, E.A. (1994) *Measuring the Wealth of Nations: The Political Economy of National Accounts*, Cambridge: Cambridge University Press.

Shapley, D. (1993) *Promise and Power: The Life and Times of Robert McNamara*, Boston: Little, Brown and Company.

Simon, R. (1991) *Gramsci's Political Thought: An Introduction*, London: Lawrence & Wishart Ltd.

Skidelsky, R. (1983) *John Maynard Keynes, Volume I Hopes Betrayed 1883–1920*, London: Macmillan.

—— (1992) *John Maynard Keynes, Volume II the Economist as Saviour*, London: Macmillan.

Socialist Republic of Vietnam (2002) 'The Comprehensive Poverty Reduction and Growth Strategy', Hanoi, May.

Sommers, D. (1984) 'An Institution Emerges', *Finance & Development*, 21 (2): 30–32.

Songco, J.A. (2002) 'Do Rural Infrastructure Investments Benefit the Poor? Evaluating Linkages: A Global View, a Focus on Vietnam', Policy Research Working Paper No. 2796, Washington DC: The World Bank, East Asia and Pacific Region, Poverty Reduction and Economic Management Sector Unit, February.

St. Clair, A.L. (2006) 'The World Bank as a Transnational Expertised Institution', *Global Governance*, 12 (1): 77–95.

Stern, N. and Ferreira, F. (1997) 'The World Bank As "Intellectual Actor"', in D. Kapur, J.P. Lewis and R. Webb (eds) *The World Bank Its First Half Century*, Volume 2: *Perspectives*, Washington DC: Brookings Institution Press.

Stiglitz, J. (2002) *Globalization and Its Discontents*, London: Penguin Books.

Structural Adjustment Participatory Review Initiative Network www.saprin.org/ (accessed July 2004).

Sumner, A. (2006) 'In Search of the Post-Washington (Dis)Consensus: The "Missing" Content of PRSPS', *Third World Quarterly,* 27 (8): 1401–12.

Suryahadi, A. and Sumarto, S. (2003) 'Poverty and Vulnerability in Indonesia before and after the Economic Crisis', *Asian Economic Journal,* 17 (1): 45–64.

Tagaroa, R. (2006) 'Indonesian PRSP', Jakarta, GAPRI (Anti Impoverishment Movement In Indonesia) 14 February.

Taylor, P. (2000) 'Managing the Economic and Social Activities of the United Nations System: Developing the Role of ECOSOC', in P. Taylor and A.J.R. Groom (eds) *The United Nations at the Millennium: The Principal Organs,* London: Continuum.

Taylor, P. (2004) 'Redressing Disadvantage or Re-Arranging Inequality? Development Interventions and Local Responses in the Mekong Delta', in P. Taylor (ed.) *Social Inequality in Vietnam and the Challenges to Reform,* Singapore: Institute of Southeast Asian Studies.

Thee, K.W. (2001) 'Brief Reflections on Indonesian Economic History', in G. Lloyd and S. Smith (eds) *Indonesia Today: Challenges of History,* Lanham: Rowman &Littlefield Publishers Inc.

Thee, K.W. (2003) 'The Indonesian Economic Crisis and the Long Road to Recovery', *Australian Economic History Review,* 43 (2): 183–96.

Thorburn, C.C. (2004) 'The Plot Thickens: Land Administration and Policy in Post-New Order Indonesia', *Asia Pacific Viewpoint,* 45 (1): 33–49.

Todaro, M.P. (1977) *Economic Development in the Third World: An Introduction to Problems and Policies in a Global Perspective*, London: Longman.

Tønnesson, S. (2000) 'The Layered State of Vietnam', in K.E. Brødsgaard and S. Young (eds) *State Capacity in East Asia,* Oxford: Oxford University Press.

Toussaint, E. (1999) *Your Money or Your Life! The Tyranny of Global Finance*, London: Pluto Press.

Toye, J. (1993) *Dilemmas of Development*, 2nd edn, Oxford: Blackwell Publishers.

Turk, C. (2005) 'Interview', Senior Poverty Specialist, Poverty Reduction and Economic Management, World Bank, Hanoi, Vietnam, 7 April.

Turley, W. (1999) 'Viet Nam: Ordeals of Transition', in K.D. Jackson (ed.) *Asian Contagion: The Causes and Consequences of a Financial Crisis,* Boulder: Westview Press.

Turner, M., Podger, O., Sumardjono, M. and Tirthayasa, W.K. (2003) *Decentralisation in Indonesia: Redesigning the State*, Canberra: Asia Pacific Press.

United Nations Conference on Trade and Development (2006) *World Investment Report 2006: FDI from Developing and Transition Economies: Implications for Development*, Geneva: United Nations.

United Nations Human Development Report 2006 'Statistics', http://hdr.undp.org/hdr2006/statistics/ (accessed April 2007).

Urquidi, V.L. (1996) 'Reconstruction Vs. Development: The IMF and the World Bank', in O. Kirshner (ed.) *The Bretton Woods – GATT System: Retrospect and Prospect after Fifty Years,* Armonk: M.E. Sharp.

USA Commodity Futures Trading Commission www.cftc.gov/ogc (accessed November 2004).

Van Arkadie, B. and Mallon, R. (2003) *Viet Nam: A Transition Tiger?*, Canberra: Asia Pacific Press at The Australian National University.

Van der Eng, P. (2001) 'Indonesia's Economy and Standard of Living in the 20th Century', in G. Lloyd and S. Smith (eds) *Indonesia Today: Challenges of History*, Lanham: Rowman &Littlefield Publishers Inc.

Van Dormael, A. (1978) *Bretton Woods: Birth of a Monetary System*, London: Macmillan Press Ltd.

Vickers, A. (2005) *A History of Modern Indonesia*, Cambridge: Cambridge University Press.

Wade, R. (1996) 'Japan, the World Bank, and the Art of Paradigm Maintenance: *The East Asian Miracle* in Political Perspective', *New Left Review*, 217: 3–36.

Wade, R. (2001a) 'Making the World Development Report 2000: Attacking Poverty', *World Development*, 29 (8): 1435–41.

Wade, R. (2001b) 'Showdown at the World Bank', *New Left Review*, 7: 124–37.

Wade, R. (2002) 'US Hegemony and the World Bank: The Fight over People and Ideas', *Review of International Political Economy*, 9 (2): 215–43.

Weaver, C. and Leiteritz, R.J. (2005) '"Our Poverty Is a World Full of Dreams:" Reforming the World Bank', *Global Governance*, 11 (3): 369–88.

Weber, H. (2004) 'The "New Economy" and Social Risk: Banking on the Poor?' *Review of International Political Economy*, 11 (2): 356–86.

Weber, H. (2006) 'A Political Analysis of the PRSP Initiative: Social Struggles and the Organization of Persistent Relations of Inequality', *Globalizations*, 3 (2): 187–206.

Weiss, J., Montgomery, H. and Kurmanalieva, E. (2005) 'Micro-Finance and Poverty Reduction in Asia', in J. Weiss (ed.) *Poverty Targeting in Asia*, Cheltenham: Edward Elgar.

Whitelum, B. (2003) 'Rhetoric and Reality in the World Bank's Relations with NGOs: An Indonesian Case Study', PhD thesis, Canberra: Australian National University.

Wilson, J.S. (2001) 'Why Foreign Aid Fails: Lessons from Indonesia's Economic Collapse', *Law and Policy in International Business*, 33 (1): 145–77.

Winters, J.A. (1996) *Power in Motion: Capital Mobility and the Indonesian State*, Ithaca: Cornell University Press.

Wodsak, V. (2002) 'World Bank Reform – a Critical Investigation: Change and Continuity in the World Bank's Approach to Development in the 1990s', MA thesis, Kingston, Ontario, Canada: Political Studies, Queen's University.

Wolff, P., Auracher, T., Beckers, C., *et al.* (2002) 'The Comprehensive Poverty Reduction and Growth Strategy in Vietnam: Process, Donor Contribution, and Prospects for Its Implementation', Report No. 9/2002, Bonn: German Development Institute, November.

Woods, N. (2006) *The Globalizers: The IMF, the World Bank, and Their Borrowers*, Ithaca and London: Cornell University Press.

World Bank (1993a) *The East Asian Miracle: Economic Growth and Public Policy*, Oxford: Oxford University Press.

World Bank (1993b) 'Staff Appraisal Report: Indonesia Cirata Hydroelectric Phase II Project', Report No. 11544-IND, April 14.

World Bank (1994a) 'Staff Appraisal Report: Indonesia Dam Safety Project', Report No. 12815-IND, May 6.

World Bank (1994b) 'Staff Appraisal Report: Indonesia Fifth Kabupaten Roads Project', Report No. 12671-IND, April 19.

World Bank (1994c) 'Staff Appraisal Report: Indonesia Integrated Swamps Development Project', Report No. 12166-IND, May 17.

World Bank (1994d) 'Staff Appraisal Report: Indonesia Land Administration Project', Report No. 12820-IND, August 16.

World Bank (1994e) 'Staff Appraisal Report: Indonesia Second Accountancy Development Project', Report No. 12883-IND, July 29.
World Bank (1994f) 'Staff Appraisal Report: Indonesia Second Highway Sector Investment Project', Report No. 12161-IND, February 7.
World Bank (1994g) 'Staff Appraisal Report: Indonesia Second Professional Human Resource Development Project', Report No. 13537-IND, November 8.
World Bank (1994h) 'Staff Appraisal Report: Indonesia Semarang-Surakarta Urban Development Project', Report No. 12656-IND, May 16.
World Bank (1994i) 'Staff Appraisal Report: Indonesia Sumatera and Kalimantan Power Project', Report No. 12662-IND, May 27.
World Bank (1994j) 'Staff Appraisal Report: Indonesia Surabaya Urban Development Project', Report No. 12516-IND, March 15.
World Bank (1994k) 'Staff Appraisal Report: Indonesia University Research for Graduate Education Project', Report No. 12841-IND, May 16.
World Bank (1994l) 'Viet Nam – Structural Adjustment Credit I Program Information Document', Report No. PIC1073, 5 September.
World Bank (1995a) 'Staff Appraisal Report: Indonesia Fourth Health Project', Report No. 13991-IND, May 22.
World Bank (1995b) 'Staff Appraisal Report: Indonesia Second Rural Electrification Project', Report No. 12920-IND, February 3.
World Bank (1995c) 'Staff Appraisal Report: Indonesia Village Infrastructure Project for Java', Report No. 13776-IND, April 26.
World Bank (1995d) 'Staff Appraisal Report: Viet Nam Power Sector Rehabilitation and Expansion Project', Report No. 13586-VN, April 14.
World Bank (1995e) 'Technical Annex on the Republic of Indonesia Second Technical Assistance Project for the Public and Private Provision of Infrastructure', Report No. T-6606-IND, June 2.
World Bank (1996a) 'Staff Appraisal Report: Indonesia Solar Home Systems Project', Report No. 15983-IND, December 17.
World Bank (1996b) 'Staff Appraisal Report: Republic of Indonesia Railway Efficiency Project', Report No. 15646-IND, October 17.
World Bank (1996c) 'Staff Appraisal Report: Republic of Indonesia Second Village Infrastructure Project', Report No. 15467-IND, September 13.
World Bank (1996d) 'Staff Appraisal Report: Socialist Republic of Viet Nam Rural Finance Project', Report No. 15088-VN, April 2.
World Bank (1996e) 'Staff Appraisal Report: The Socialist Republic of Vietnam Rural Transport Project', Report No. 15537-VN, September 24.
World Bank (1996f) 'Staff Appraisal Report: Viet Nam Power Development Project', Report No. 14893-VN, January 2.
World Bank (1997a) 'Project Appraisal Document on a Proposed Loan to the Republic of Indonesia for a Banking Reform Assistance Project', Report No. 17165-IND, November 20.
World Bank (1997b) 'Project Appraisal Document on a Proposed Loan to the Republic of Indonesia for an Information Infrastructure Development Project (IIDP)', Report No. 17106-IND, October 16.
World Bank (1997c) 'Project Appraisal Document on a Proposed Loan to the Republic of Indonesia for the Bepeka Audit Modernization Project', Report No. 16602-IND, May 21.
World Bank (1997d) 'Staff Appraisal Report: Socialist Republic of Vietnam Water Supply Project', Report No. 16299-VN, May 20.

World Bank (1997e) 'Staff Appraisal Report: The Socialist Republic of Vietnam Forest Protection and Rural Development Project', Report No. 16569-VN, September 23.

World Bank (1998a) 'Country Assistance Strategy of the World Bank Group for the Socialist Republic of Vietnam', Report No. 18375, August 20.

World Bank (1998b) 'Project Appraisal Document on a Proposed Loan to the Republic of Indonesia for a Kecamatan Development Project', Report No. 17397 IND, April 21.

World Bank (1998c) *Assessing Aid: What Works, What Doesn't, and Why*, New York: Oxford University Press.

World Bank (1999a) 'Indonesia Country Assistance Note', Report No. 19100: Operations Evaluation Department, March 29.

World Bank (1999b) 'Report and Recommendations of the President of the IBRD on a Proposed Social Safety Net Adjustment Loan to the Republic of Indonesia', Report No. P7307-IND, April 27.

World Bank (1999c) *The World Bank Annual Report 1999*, Washington: World Bank.

World Bank (2000a) *Attacking Poverty: World Development Report 2000/20001*, New York: Oxford University Press for The World Bank.

World Bank (2000b) *Entering the 21st Century: World Development Report 1999/2000*, Oxford: Oxford University Press for The World Bank.

World Bank (2000c) 'Project Appraisal Document on a Proposed Credit to the Republic of Indonesia for Provincial Health I', Report No. 20423-IND, May 10.

World Bank (2000d) 'Project Appraisal Document on a Proposed Credit to the Socialist Republic of Vietnam for a Rural Energy Project', Report No. 20351-VN, May 1.

World Bank (2000e) 'Project Appraisal Document on a Proposed Credit to the Socialist Republic of Vietnam for the Mekong Transport and Flood Protection Project', Report No. 20405-VN, November 20.

World Bank (2000f) 'Project Appraisal Document on a Proposed IDA Credit to the Republic of Indonesia for a Second Water &Sanitation for Low Income Communities Project', Report No. 20132-IND, May 16.

World Bank (2001a) 'Country Assistance Strategy of the World Bank Group for Indonesia', Report No. 21580-IND, January 4.

World Bank (2001b) 'Project Appraisal Document on a Proposed Credit to the Socialist Republic of Vietnam for a Community Based Rural Infrastructure Project', Report No. 21215-VN, June 4.

World Bank (2001c) 'Project Appraisal Document on a Proposed Credit to the Socialist Republic of Vietnam for a Northern Mountains Poverty Reduction Project', Report No. 21233-VN, September 5.

World Bank (2001d) 'Project Appraisal Document on a Proposed Credit to the Socialist Republic of Vietnam for the Ho Chi Minh City Environmental Sanitation Project', Report No. 21030-VN, February 20.

World Bank (2001e) 'Project Appraisal Document on a Proposed Loan to the Republic of Indonesia for a Second Kecamatan Development Project', Report No. 22279-IND, May 23.

World Bank (2001f) 'Project Appraisal Document on a Proposed Loan to the Republic of Indonesia for the Eastern Indonesia Region Transport Project', Report No. 22273-IND, November 12.

World Bank (2001g) 'Project Appraisal Document on a Proposed Loan to the Republic of Indonesia for the Western Java Environmental Management Project', Report No. 21029-IND, May 15.

World Bank (2001h) 'Report and Recommendation on a Proposed Poverty Reduction Support Credit to the Socialist Republic of Vietnam', Report No. P-7446-VN, April 23.

World Bank (2001i) 'Vietnam – Country Assistance Evaluation', Report No. 23288: Operations Evaluation Department, November 21.

World Bank (2002a) 'Country Assistance Strategy of the World Bank Group for the Socialist Republic of Vietnam', Report No. 24621-VN, September 16.

World Bank (2002b) 'Project Appraisal Document on a Proposed Credit to the Socialist Republic of Vietnam for a Regional Blood Transfusion Centres Project', Report No. 22128-VN, March 18.

World Bank (2002c) 'Project Appraisal Document on a Proposed Credit to the Socialist Republic of Vietnam for a Second Rural Finance Project', Report No. 23817-VN, May 2.

World Bank (2002d) 'Project Appraisal Document on a Proposed Credit to the Socialist Republic of Vietnam for a System Efficiency Improvement, Equitization and Renewables Project', Report No. 24192-VN, June 4.

World Bank (2002e) 'Project Appraisal Document on a Proposed International Development Association Partial Risk Guarantee to Mekong Energy Company Ltd in the Social Republic of Vietnam', Report No. 24692, August.

World Bank (2002f) 'Project Appraisal Document on a Proposed Loan to the Republic of Indonesia for the Second Urban Poverty Project (UPP 2)', Report No. 23810-IND, May 15.

World Bank (2002g) 'Project Performance Assessment Report Agriculture Rehabilitation Project (Credit 2561-Vn)', Report No. 24291, June 11.

World Bank (2002h) *Vietnam: Transforming Public Procurement*, Hanoi: World Bank.

World Bank (2003a) *A Guide to the World Bank*, Washington DC: World Bank.

World Bank (2003b) 'Implementation Completion Report on a Credit to the Socialist Republic of Vietnam for a VN-Primary Education Project', Report No. 25967-VN, April 21.

World Bank (2003c) 'Implementation Completion Report on a Loan to the Government of Indonesia for a Higher Education Support Project: Development of Undergraduate Education', Report No. 26039, June 27.

World Bank (2003d) 'Implementation Completion Report on a Loan to the Republic of Indonesia for a Kalimantan Urban Development Project', Report No. 25720-IND, June 24.

World Bank (2003e) 'Implementation Completion Report on a Loan to the Republic of Indonesia for the Java Irrigation Improvement and Water Resources Management Project', Report No. 26199, June 30.

World Bank (2003f) 'Indonesia Country Assistance Strategy FY 2004–7', Report No. P080082, Washington: World Bank, December.

World Bank (2003g) 'Indonesia Power Sector Thematic Overview and Project Performance Assessment Report Suralaya Thermal Power Project and Sumatera and Kalimantan Power Project', Report No. 25960: Operations Evaluation Department, May 21.

World Bank (2003h) 'Program Document for a Proposed Credit to the Socialist Republic of Vietnam for a Second Poverty Reduction Support Credit', Report No. P-7584, May 30.

World Bank (2003i) 'Project Appraisal Document on a Proposed Credit and Loan to the Republic of Indonesia for a Heath Workforce and Service Project', Report No. 25294-IND, May 19.

World Bank (2003j) 'Project Appraisal Document on a Proposed Credit to the Socialist Republic of Vietnam for a Primary Education for Disadvantaged Children Project', Report No. 23846-VN, April 3.
World Bank (2003k) 'Project Appraisal Document on a Proposed Credit to the Socialist Republic of Vietnam for a Public Financial Management Project', Report No. 25480-VN, April 24.
World Bank (2003l) 'Project Appraisal Document on a Proposed Credit to the Socialist Republic of Vietnam for a Road Network Improvement Project', Report No. 27368-VN, November 24.
World Bank (2003m) 'Project Appraisal Document on a Proposed Loan and Credit to the Republic of Indonesia for the Water Resources and Irrigation Sector Management Program in Support of the First Phase of the Water Resources and Irrigation Sector Program', Report No. 25941-IND, May 23.
World Bank (2003n) 'Project Appraisal Document on a Proposed Loan to the Republic of Indonesia for a Java-Bali Power Sector Restructuring and Strengthening Project', Report No. 25414-IND, June 4.
World Bank (2003o) 'Project Appraisal Document on a Proposed Loan to the Republic of Indonesia for a Private Provision of Infrastructure Technical Assistance Loan', Report No. 25820, April 25.
World Bank (2003p) 'Project Appraisal Document on a Proposed Loan to the Republic of Indonesia for a Third Kecamatan Development Project', Report No. 25538-IND, June 2.
World Bank (2003q) 'Project Performance Assessment Report Indonesia Banking Reform Assistance (Loan No. 4255-IND), Policy Reform Support Loan I (Loan No. 4368-IND), Policy Reform Support Loan II (Loan No. 4470-Ind)', Report No. 27177: Operations Evaluation Department, November 4.
World Bank (2003r) *The World Bank Annual Report 2003,* Washington DC: World Bank.
World Bank (2004a) 'From Adjustment Lending to Development Policy Lending: Update of World Bank Policy', Operations Policy and Country Services. www.worldbank.org (accessed July 2004).
World Bank (2004b) 'Implementation Completion Report on a Credit to the Socialist Republic of Vietnam for a Payment System and Banking Modernization Project', Report No. 27635, June 15.
World Bank (2004c) 'Implementation Completion Report on a Credit to the Socialist Republic of Vietnam for a Second Highway Rehabilitation Project', Report No. 29375-VN, June 30.
World Bank (2004d) 'Implementation Completion Report on a Loan to the Republic of Indonesia for a Second Power Transmission and Distribution Project', Report No. 27426, March 31.
World Bank (2004e) 'Implementation Completion Report on a Loan to the Republic of Indonesia for a Second Sulawesi Urban Development Project', Report No. 25719, March 31.
World Bank (2004f) 'Implementation Completion Report on a Loan to the Republic of Indonesia for the Nusa Tenggara Agriculture Area Development Project', Report No. 28036, March 31.
World Bank (2004g) 'Press Release: Doing Business 2005: Poor Nations Struggle to Reduce Red Tape for Business, Miss Large Growth Opportunities', www.worldbank.org (accessed September 2004).

World Bank (2004h) 'Program Document for a Proposed Credit to the Socialist Republic of Vietnam for a Third Poverty Reduction Support Credit', Report No. 28916-VN, May 25.

World Bank (2004i) 'Program Document for a Proposed First Development Policy Loan to the Republic of Indonesia', Report No. 30418-IND, November 23.

World Bank (2004j) 'Project Appraisal Document on a Proposed Credit and Grant from the Global Environment Facility Trust Fund to the Socialist Republic of Vietnam for a Forest Sector Development Project', Report No. 26767-VN, May 19.

World Bank (2004k) 'Project Appraisal Document on a Proposed Credit to the Government of the Republic of Indonesia for a Land Management and Policy Development Project', Report No. 28178-IND, March 31.

World Bank (2004l) 'Project Appraisal Document on a Proposed Credit to the Socialist Republic of Vietnam for a Second Rural Energy Project', Report No. 29860-VN, October 21.

World Bank (2004m) 'Project Appraisal Document on a Proposed Credit to the Socialist Republic of Vietnam for the Urban Upgrading Project', Report No. 27526-VN, March 31.

World Bank (2004n) 'Project Appraisal Document on a Proposed Credit to the Socialist Republic of Vietnam for the Urban Water Supply Development Project', Report No. 29128-VN, November 22.

World Bank (2004o) 'Project Appraisal Document on a Proposed Credit to the Socialist Republic of Vietnam for the Vietnam Water Resources Assistance Project', Report No. 27395-VN, March 3.

World Bank (2004p) 'Project Appraisal Document on a Proposed Loan and Credit and a GEF Grant to the Republic of Indonesia for the Coral Reef Rehabilitation and Management Project (Phase II)', Report No. 28836-IND, May 3.

World Bank (2004q) 'Project Appraisal Document on a Proposed Loan to the Republic of Indonesia for a Government Financial Management and Revenue Administration Project in Support of the First Phase of the GFRMAP Program', Report No. 29910-IND, November 22.

World Bank (2004r) 'Project Appraisal Document on a Proposed Loan to the Republic of Indonesia for the Second Eastern Indonesia Region Transport Project', Report No. 28071-IND, May 18.

World Bank (2004s) 'Project Completion Note on a Loan/GEF Grant to the Republic of Indonesia for the Renewable Energy Small Power Project', Report No. 30244, October 12.

World Bank (2004t) 'Project Performance Assessment Report Vietnam Highway Rehabilitation Project 1 (Credit 2549-VN), Rural Transport Project 1 (Credit 2929-VN)', Report No. 28168, March 9.

World Bank (2004u) *The World Bank Annual Report 2004, Volume 1 Year in Review*, Washington: World Bank.

World Bank (2005a) 'Implementation Completion Report on a Loan to Indonesia for a Railway Efficiency Project', Report No. 31719, June 29.

World Bank (2005b) 'Implementation Completion Report on a Loan to Indonesia for the Bepeka Audit Modernization Project', Report No. 31858, March 28.

World Bank (2005c) 'Implementation Completion Report on a Loan to the Republic of Indonesia for a Bali Urban Infrastructure Project', Report No. 31464-IND, June 28.

World Bank (2005d) 'Implementation Completion Report on a Loan to the Republic of Indonesia for a Safe Motherhood Project', Report No. 32667, June 30.

World Bank (2005e) 'Implementation Completion Report on a Loan to the Republic of Indonesia for East Java and East Nusa Tenggara Junior Secondary Education Project', Report No. 32507, June 30.

World Bank (2005f) 'Implementation Completion Report on a Loan to the Republic of Indonesia for the Water Resources Sector Adjustment', Report No. 32665, June 29.

World Bank (2005g) 'Project Performance Assessment Report Indonesia Industrial Technology Development Project (Loan No. 3972)', Report No. 32733, July 5.

World Bank (2005h) 'Review of World Bank Conditionality': Operations Policy and Country Services, September.

World Bank (2005i) 'Simplified Implementation Completion Report: Republic of Indonesia First Development Policy Loan (Loan No. 4761-IND)', Report No. 33213-ID, August 2.

World Bank (2006a) 'Indonesia: Key Indicators', www.worldbank.org (accessed February 2006).

World Bank (2006b) *The World Bank Annual Report 2006,* Washington: World Bank.

World Bank and International Finance Corporation (2004) 'Doing Business: Benchmarking Business Regulation', www.doingbusiness.org/ (accessed September 2004).

World Bank Group Website *www.worldbank.org* (accessed March 2003).

World Bank Group Website *www.worldbank.org* (accessed March 2007).

World Bank Group Website (2009) 'PRSP Sourcebook', http://web.worldbank.org/WBSITE/EXTERNAL/TOPICS/EXTPOVERTY/EXTPRS/0,contentMDK:20175778~pagePK:148956~piPK:216618~theSitePK:384201,00.html (accessed January 2009).

World Bank Operations Evaluation Department (2002) 'Non-Government Organizations and Civil Society Engagement in World Bank Supported Projects: Lessons from OED Evaluations', Lessons and Practices No. 18, Washington August 28.

World Bank Operations Evaluation Department and IMF Independent Evaluation Office (2005) 'The Poverty Reduction Strategy Initiative: Finding from 10 Country Case Studies of World Bank and IMF Support', www.worldbank.org/oed (accessed June 2006).

World Development Movement (2005) 'One Size for All: A Study of IMF and World Bank Poverty Reduction Strategies', www.wdm.org.uk/news/presrel/current/onesize.htm (accessed March 2007).

Yi-chong, X. (2005) 'Models, Templates and Currents: The World Bank and Electricity Reform', *Review of International Political Economy,* 12 (4): 647–73.

Zaman, M. (2002) 'Restructuring of the Water Sector in Indonesia: An Institutional and Legislative Challenge', Bank Information Centre. www.bicusa.org (accessed July 2005).

Index